END-OF-LIFE DECISION-MAKING IN EAST ASIA

LEGAL CHALLENGES, CULTURAL NORMS, AND ADVANCE PLANNING

END-OF-LIFE DECISION-MAKING IN EAST ASIA

LEGAL CHALLENGES, CULTURAL NORMS, AND ADVANCE PLANNING

YUKIO SAKURAI

2025

COMMON GROUND

First published in 2025 as part of the
Aging and Social Change

Common Ground Research Networks
University of Illinois Research Park
2001 South First St, Suite 201L, Champaign, IL, 61820, USA

Library of Congress Cataloging-in-Publication Data

Names: Sakurai, Yukio, author.
Title: End-of-life decision-making in East Asia : legal challenges,
    cultural norms, and advance planning / Yukio Sakurai.
Description: Champaign : Common Ground Research Networks, 2025.
Identifiers: LCCN 2025027208 (print) | LCCN 2025027209 (ebook) | ISBN
    9781966214694 (hardback) | ISBN 9781966214762 (paperback) | ISBN
    9781966214779 (adobe pdf)
Subjects: LCSH: Terminal care--Law and legislation--East Asia. | Terminal
    care--Law and legislation--Japan. | Terminal care--East Asia--Decision
    making. | Terminal care--Japan--Decision making. | Euthanasia--Law and
    legislation--East Asia. | Euthanasia--Law and legislation--Japan. |
    Assisted suicide--Law and legislation--East Asia. | Assisted
    suicide--Law and legislation--Japan. | Death--Social aspects.
Classification: LCC KNC700.T47 S25 2025 (print) | LCC KNC700.T47 (ebook)
    | DDC 344.504/197--dc23/eng/20250606
LC record available at https://lccn.loc.gov/2025027208
LC ebook record available at https://lccn.loc.gov/2025027209

ISBN (HBK): 978-1-966214-62-5
ISBN (PBK): 978-1-966214-63-2
ISBN (PDF): 978-1-966214-64-9

TABLE OF CONTENTS

Acknowledgments/Acronyms/Note/Tables & Figures   *vii-xi*

1 Introduction   1-16

    1-1 Family Involvement or Proactive Preparations   1-5

    1-2 Importance of the East Asian Project   5-10

    1-3 Objective and Prior Research of the Study   10-13

    1-4 Methodology   13-16

2 Theoretical Foundation   17-37

    2-1 Vulnerability Approach and Safeguarding Law   17-20

    2-2 Individual Autonomy and Relational Autonomy   20-29

    2-3 Value Model for the East Asian Project   29-34

    2-4 Notes on Law and Bioethics in Health care   34-37

3 ADs and ACP in the International Context   39-52

    3-1 Origins and Types of Advance Directives   39-42

    3-2 Limitations and Criticisms of ADs and ACP   43-45

    3-3 Comparison and Evaluation of ADs across Asia   46-48

    3-4 International Response to Voluntary Assisted Dying   48-52

4 ADs and ACP in the Japanese Context   53-85

    4-1 Laws Concerning Human Life and Death in Japan   53-55

    4-2 Issues of Healthcare Policy in Japan   55-61

    4-3 Legal and Ethical Framework for ADs and ACP   61-69

    4-4 Relational Autonomy-Based Approach to ADs   70-78

    4-5 ACP Studies in Japan   78-85

5 ADs and ACP in the East Asian Context   87–128

    5-1 Responses of South Korea, Taiwan, and Singapore

    to ADs and ACP   87–105

    5-2 A Comparative Analysis of ADs and ACP between

    East Asian Countries and Area   106–119

    5-3 Discussion on ADs and ACP in the East Asian Model   119–128

6 Advance Decision-Making for Future Disability in East Asia   129–162

    6-1 A Comparative Analysis of Models between

    the U.S., Europe, and East Asia   129–140

    6-2 Legal Relationship between Doctors, Patients,

    and Family Members   140–149

    6-3 Proposals for Advance Decision-Making

    for Future Disability in East Asia   149–162

7 Conclusion   163–165

Bibliography/Legislation/Court Case   *167–210*

Appendix 1-2   *211–222*

Index   *223–228*

Exchange Rate

As per the prevailing exchange rates on December 6, 2024 US$1 was equivalent to ¥150.

ACKNOWLEDGMENTS

The book has been enriched by the contributions of numerous international researchers who provided data and expert insights from their respective regions. The author extends special gratitude to the Six East Asian Researchers who kindly responded to questionnaires and offered valuable advice: Park In-Hwan (South Korea); Sieh-Chuen Huang, Chao-Tien Chang, and Daniel Fu-Chang Tsai (Taiwan); and Sumytra Menon and Tracey Chan (Singapore).

The author also wishes to thank researchers from Australia, Italy, Japan, and Scotland for their invaluable comments and feedback, including Christopher Gyngell, Shih-Ning Then, Piers Gooding, and Terry Carney (Australia); Gianluca Montanari Vergallo (Italy); Asao Ogawa, Satoshi Kodama, and Tetsu Isobe (Japan); and Adrian D. Ward (Scotland, member of the European Law Institute, Vienna).

An Amemiya, Age 9

Gratitude is also extended to the many researchers who contributed through discussions at fieldwork sites, online meetings, international conferences, and other forums between April 2023 and March 2025. These engagements, including publications and presentations, have significantly shaped this research.

Finally, the author acknowledges that this work has been made possible by a foundation of good health and the unwavering support of family members, for which they are deeply grateful.

Izumi Amemiya, Age 7

ACRONYMS

ACP advance care planning

AD advance directive

AI artificial intelligence

ALRC Australian Law Reform Commission

AMD advance medical directive

AMDA Advance Medical Directive Act of 1996 (Singapore)

ASLI Asian Law Institute

CPA continuing power of attorney

CRPD Convention on the Rights of Persons with Disabilities

DNAR Do Not Attempt Resuscitate

ELDA Act on Decisions on Life-Sustaining Treatment for Patients in Hospice and Palliative Care at the End of Life of 2016 (South Korea)

ELI European Law Institute

EPA enduring power of attorney

EU European Union

HPCA Hospice Palliative Care Act of 2000 (Taiwan)

LPA lasting power of attorney

MCA Mental Capacity Act

MCI mild cognitive impairment

MHLW Ministry of Health, Labour, and Welfare

NGO Non-Governmental Organization

NPO Non-Profit Organization or Not-for-Profit Organization

NSW New South Wales

POLST physician orders for life-sustaining treatment

PRAA Patient Right to Autonomy Act of 2016 (Taiwan)

ULC Uniform Law Commission

VAD voluntary assisted dying

WHO World Health Organization

2007 Guidelines Guidelines for Process of Medical Decision-Making in the End-of-Life of 2007 (Japan)

2018 Guidelines Guidelines for Process of Medical and Care Decision-Making in the End-of-Life of 2018 (Japan)

LIST OF FIGURES AND TABLES

Figure 1.1: Trends in the Rate of Aging in the World   6

Figure 2.1: The Modified Multidimensional Model of Elder Law   30

Table 3.1: Types of Advance Directives in Greater Asia   46

Table 3.2: Countries' Responses to Voluntary Assisted Dying   49

Table 4.1: Overview of the Euthanasia Cases in Japan   62

Table 4.2: Advance Directives in Japan   69

Table 4.3: A List of Comments Organized by End-of-Life Topic   82

Table 5.1: Overview of Criteria for Discontinuation of Life-Sustaining
        Treatment for Patients in the Dying Process
        (Article 17 to Article 18)   90

Table 5.2: Comparison of Advance Directives between South Korea,
        Taiwan, and Singapore   108

Table 6.1: Comparison between England, State of Victoria, and the U.S.   133

CHAPTER 1

Introduction

This chapter examines the current demographic situation in East Asia, highlighting key aging-related trends and their implications for end-of-life care. It then introduces the research question that guides this study, situating it within broader discussions on advance decision-making. Additionally, the chapter outlines the study's objectives and reviews previous research to establish a foundation for analysis. Finally, it explains the methodology employed, detailing the approach used to investigate legal frameworks, cultural factors, and policy developments in the region.

1.1 Family Involvement or Proactive Preparations

1.1.1 Family Involvement versus Proactive Preparation

A Japanese proverb states, "When you get old, be guided by your children." This old saying reflects a traditional Japanese belief that older adults should hand over control and authority to their children and adhere to their guidance. This traditional saying continues to exert its influence in contemporary Japan. The traditional beliefs, held by a significant proportion of the population, are not easily amenable to change, given the long-standing history and cultural significance. In Japan, it is not uncommon for older adults to depend on their family members for support with end-of-life care.

Consequently, a large proportion of Japanese people engage in social activities show a certain level of interest in health care, yet rarely take their own initiative to prepare for the future. This is indicative of a family involvement system, which may in part be related to the fact that the majority of older adults die in hospitals.[1] It is commonly believed that older adults should be hospitalized at the end of life and receive care from healthcare professionals under the public health insurance system.[2] Gastrostomy tubes are frequently inserted in older adults with impaired swallowing function, and life-sustaining treatments have been administered, resulting in prolonged bed rest. Many older adults have accepted such treatments without question.

However, the 2011 survey findings indicated that there were only a limited number of cases in which the patient themselves had elected to undergo a gastrostomy procedure. In most cases, the decision was made by the patient's family members.[3] Of the patients with gastrostomies, over 90% were confined to bed rest. Mere life-sustaining treatments, which leave older adults bedridden for prolonged periods, are no longer a priority for this demographic.

Instead, they are focusing on maintaining a high quality of life until their final moment. This phenomenon is not limited to the older demographic; it is also increasingly observed among healthcare professionals. The 2014 Science Council of Japan report highlights a shift in the purpose of medical treatment: "from saving and prolonging life to quality of life/quality of death."[4] This implies that traditional beliefs may be subject to revision if a significant proportion of the population, including experts, supports the proposed amendment, based on their current values.[5]

In other developed countries, a decision-making approach different from that observed in Japan is followed. In these countries, individuals are encouraged to

---

[1] In Japan, most older adults died predominantly in hospitals (65.9%), followed by clinics (1.5%), nursing care clinics (4.4%), and at home (17.2%). Nursing homes accounted for 10%, and other locations 1%. Nursing homes accounted for 10% of deaths, while other locations constituted 1%. Japan, Ministry of Health, Labour, and Welfare (MHLW) (2021) "Part 1 Population and Households Chapter 2 Population Dynamics: Table 1–25 Death Composition and Ratio" [in Japanese] https://www.mhlw.go.jp/toukei/youran/indexyk_1_2.html.

[2] In Japan, the health insurance system limits monthly patient medical payments to reduce their financial burden. For those aged 70 and older, the cap is 57,600 yen (US$384) for inpatient care and 18,000 yen (US$120) for outpatient care, assuming a 10% co-payment rate. The cap varies by income but generally stays below tens of thousands of yen (under US$667) per month.

[3] All Japan Hospital Association (2011) "Assessment of the Actual Situation of Older Adults with Gastrostomy and Survey Research on Management in Nursing Homes and Residential Homes" [in Japanese] 11. https://www.ajha.or.jp/voice/pdf/other/110416_1.pdf.

[4] Arai, Hidenori, Ouchi, Y., Toba, K., Endo, T., Shimokado, K., Tsubota, K., Matsuo, S., Mori, H., Yumura, W., Yokode, M., Rakugi, H. and Ohshima, S. (2015) "Front-runner of Super-aged Societies." *Geriatrics & Gerontology International* Volume 15, Issue 6: 673-687. https://doi.org/10.1111/ggi.12450.

[5] In recent years, hospital deaths among older adults have declined, while deaths at home and in nursing homes have risen. A Yamagata University survey shows 61.1% of respondents prefer dying at home, yet only 14.4% do so, highlighting a gap between preferences and reality. Saito, Tomoko, Tsuneo Konta, Sachiko Kudo, et al. (2024) "Factors Associated with Community Residents' Preference for Living at Home at the End of Life: The Yamagata Cohort Survey" *Global Health & Medicine* Volume 6 Issue 1, 70–76. https://doi.org/10.35772/ghm.2023.01072.

assume responsibility for their own decisions and to engage in proactive planning regarding their significant matters. To facilitate this, legal instruments are in place that allow individuals to formalize their intentions as legal documents, provided they have sufficient mental capacity. Such documents include lasting powers of attorney ("LPA") for asset management, advance directives ("ADs") for healthcare, and advance care planning ("ACP") for the end of life of older adults.

An AD is defined as "a patient's or healthy person's declaration of intention in advance for medical treatment to be performed when he/she loses the capacity to make decisions in the future."[6] ACP is defined as "a process that supports adults at any age or stage of health in understanding and sharing their personal values, life goals, and preferences regarding future medical care. The goal of ACP is to help ensure that people receive medical care that aligns with their values, goals, and preferences during serious and chronic illness."[7]

1.1.2 Social Factors to Require Proactive Measures in Japan

In the contemporary era, various social factors prevalent in Japan necessitate that older adults adopt proactive planning regarding end-of-life medical care, rather than relying on family involvement. First, Japan is experiencing a surge in an aging population, rendering it as the country with the highest proportion of older adults. The number of annual deaths has exceeded 1 million since 2000, reaching 1.58 million in 2023 and projected to reach 1.68 million in 2040. It is estimated that over 1.5 million people will die annually for the next five decades, which is indicative of a high mortality society.[8] As death toll increases, it will become increasingly challenging for healthcare professionals to dedicate more time and attention to each inpatient, including investigating their relatives individually to determine appropriate care solutions, as they previously did.

[6.] Uemura, Kazumasa (2015) "1. Advance Directives and Living Will (General Rules)" [in Japanese] *Geriatrics and Gerontology International* Volume 52 Issue 3, 207–210, 207. https://www.jpn-geriat-soc.or.jp/publications/other/pdf/clinical_practice_52_3_207.pdf.

[7.] Sudore, R. L., H. D. Lum, J. J. You, et al. (2017) "Defining Advance Care Planning for Adults: A Consensus Definition: From a Multidisciplinary Delphi Panel" *Journal of Pain and Symptom Management* Volume 53 Issue 5, 821–832.

[8.] Japan, Ministry of Health, Labour, and Welfare (MHLW) (2020) "White Paper on the Health, Labour, and Welfare 2020" [in Japanese] 5. https://www.mhlw.go.jp/content/000735866.pdf; A research survey has revealed that 27% of funeral enterprises have indicated that there is a shortage of cremation capacity. Japan, Ministry of Health, Labour, and Welfare (MHLW) (2023) "Verification Research into Various Issues Related to Cemetery and Burial Laws, Including the Handling of Bodies Infected with COVID-19" [in Japanese]. https://mhlw-grants.niph.go.jp/project/159849.

Therefore, hospitals must develop a method to efficiently understand patients' intentions in end-of-life care.

Second, the number of newborns is anticipated to decline annually.[9] In 2023, the number of newborns was 0.73 million, while the number of neonatal deaths was 1.58 million. These demographic changes are triggering various societal shifts. The progression of an aging population alongside declining birth rates has created a situation in which the capacity to provide aged-care services is gradually becoming insufficient. This could potentially lead to limitations in aged care capability unless significant technological innovations occur.

Third, the proportion of older adults (aged 65 and over) living alone has been increasing.[10] Such individuals may be unable to rely on the provision of care from relatives for various reasons or may possess only limited assets. In accordance with Japanese legislation, responsibility for managing the affairs of older adults who die alone is delegated to the local governments of the municipalities in which they resided (i.e., Article 7 of the Act on the Treatment of Persons Who Have Contracted Disease or Died on a Journey of 1899). Consequently, local governments are required to gain an understanding of the actual circumstances of older adults who reside alone and to prepare for end-of-life care and death procedures.[11] Lack of uniform rules on family investigation and storage creates challenges. A study will examine local practices and issues under relevant laws.[12]

Fourth, there is a generational shift among older adults, with an increasing proportion of this population embracing the idea of making their own decisions. By 2025, the baby boomer generation has reached the age of 75 and above. In contrast to the preceding generation, this cohort, having been educated in the post-war democratic era, tends to possess a sense of individual autonomy and

---

[9.] Takao, Yasuo (2024) "Understanding Fertility Policy through a Process-Oriented Approach: The Case of Japan's Decline in Births" *Journal of Population Research* Volume 41 Issue 12, 1–27. https://doi.org/10.1007/s12546-024-09333-2.

[10.] By 2020, the proportion of older adults living alone had risen to 15.0% of men and 22.1% of women. By 2040, it is projected that the proportion will reach 26.1% of men and 29.3% of women. Cabinet Office of Japan (2024) "Annual Report on the Ageing Society 2024: Trends in Persons Aged 65 and over Living Alone: (Figure 1-1-9)" [in Japanese]. https://www8.cao.go.jp/kourei/whitepaper/w-2024/zenbun/06pdf_index.html; A 2024 projection by the National Institute of Population and Social Security Research predicts a rise in one-person households aged 65 and over. By 2050, 32 of 47 prefectures will surpass 20% of total households. A key challenge is protecting the lives and safety of older adults without family caregivers.

[11.] A *Yomiuri* Newspaper survey found a 30% rise in unclaimed bodies in 69 cities and wards between FY2017 and FY2022, including major cities and Tokyo's 23 wards. This increase outpaces the national trend, driven by more older adults living alone and relatives refusing to take them in. *Yomiuri* Online (2024) "Unclaimed Bodies up 30 per cent in Five Years, with an Increase in the Number of People Living Alone and the Refusal of Relatives to Take Them in...Yomiuri Survey" [in Japanese] (June 3, 2024).

[12.] The Japan Research Institute (2024) "Regarding the Implementation of the Social Welfare Promotion Project in FY2024" [in Japanese]. MHLW Delegated Research Project in FY2024. https://www.jri.co.jp/page.jsp?id=108519.

a desire to make decisions for themselves.[13] This generation is well versed in information and communication technology, and thus able to adapt to the future digitization of documents. It may therefore be the case that preparation for end-of-life care is more readily accepted.

Moreover, there is a consensus that the patient's autonomy and preferences should be respected. Nevertheless, it is not always a simple matter to ascertain the background of the individual in question in relation to their family members, and potential conflicts of interest may arise. This is evidenced by the fact that, for example, relatives are appointed as adult guardians by the family courts in 18.1% of cases, and legal or welfare professionals who are nonrelatives are appointed in the remaining 81.9%.[14] This is because the family courts wish to avoid appointing relative guardians who tend to use the principals' assets for themselves. In this context, a methodology that elucidates the person's intentions without relying on relatives is a valuable contribution.

In instances where family involvement presents challenges for whatever reason, or when older adults express a desire to prepare for their end-of-life independently, it may be necessary to take proactive planning. This gives rise to the question of how such preparations should be approached. In the absence of standard medical legislation in Japan, which is common in other modern nations, it is vital to consider how Japan should respond to future needs for ADs and ACP. However, focusing solely on Japan limits the discussion, as the relevant legal and regulatory frameworks remain underdeveloped. Therefore, we propose expanding the scope of the study to include East Asia, defined for the purposes of this study as Japan, the Republic of Korea ("South Korea"), Taiwan, and Singapore.

1.2 Importance of the East Asian Project

1.2.1 Social Factors to Require Proactive Measures in East Asia

The traditional values of filial piety, collectivism, family-centered responsibility, and the practices of healthcare professionals, which will be discussed in greater detail in Chapter 5, collectively elucidate why family members across East Asia

---

[13.] Takahashi, Yasushi (2024) "Reference 8: Necessity of Forecasting Future Demand for Medical and Welfare Facilities: Taking into Account the Rapid Change of the Elderly Population in the Later Stages of Life" [in Japanese]. A Survey Delivered at the 3rd Study Meeting on New Regional Medical Care Concept, etc. held on May 22, 2024.

[14.] Courts of Japan (2024) "Overview of Adult Guardianship Related Cases" [in Japanese]. https://www.courts.go.jp/toukei_siryou/siryo/kouken/index.html.

are involved in their parents' healthcare, particularly in end-of-life decision-making processes. Conversely, the social factors prevalent in East Asia require the implementation of proactive planning for end-of-life medical care among older adults, as evidenced in the Japanese context in the previous section. In particular, the population of East Asia is aging (see Figure 1.1),[15] which is resulting in an increase in the number of older adults who may experience cognitive decline, such as dementia.[16] At the present time, the medical sciences are unable to make a reliable prediction as to who will develop dementia in the future. Consequently, the entire population is at risk as the population ages. The prevalence of dementia

Figure 1.1: Trends in the Rate of Aging in the World

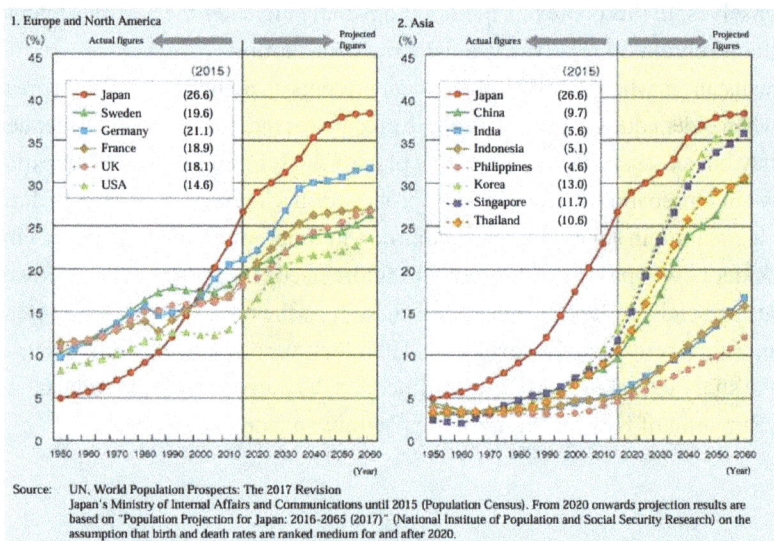

Source: UN, World Population Prospects: The 2017 Revision
Japan's Ministry of Internal Affairs and Communications until 2015 (Population Census). From 2020 onwards projection results are based on "Population Projection for Japan: 2016-2065 (2017)" (National Institute of Population and Social Security Research) on the assumption that birth and death rates are ranked medium for and after 2020.

Source: Cabinet Office of Japan

---

[15] Japan, Cabinet Office (2018) "Annual Report on the Ageing Society 2018." https://www8.cao.go.jp/kourei/english/annualreport/index-wh.html.

[16] This book uses "dementia," a syndrome involving impaired memory, thinking, behavior, and daily functioning (WHO). In the fifth edition of the Diagnostic and Statistical Manual of Mental Disorders (DSM-5), dementia, which formed a category called "Delirium, dementia, amnestic, and other cognitive disorders" in DSM-IV, falls under the new category of "major neurocognitive disorders" (American Psychiatric Association, 2013).The new psychiatric Diagnostic and Statistical Manual (DSM 5, 2021) renamed "dementia" as "major neurocognitive disorder" and added a new, less severe category of cognitive difficulty called mild cognitive impairment (or mild neurocognitive disorder).

rises exponentially with age, accompanied by a corresponding increase in the demand for dementia care.[17]

The annual number of deaths is increasing.[18] In East Asia, Japan has the highest mortality rate, followed by Taiwan, South Korea, and Singapore.[19] The number of newborns is expected to decrease annually. The East Asian region is situated at the lowest point in the global total fertility rate.[20] Furthermore, the proportion of older adults living alone is increasing, and family ties are weakening over time, as reported by the Yeung's study.[21] In some cases, long-distance employment has a detrimental impact on family relationships. These phenomena may have serious implications for asset management and end-of-life care for older adults. A comparable generational shift among older adults is anticipated in Taiwan and other East Asian countries, occurring in a manner analogous to that observed in Japan.[22]

It is, therefore, of the utmost importance that each country or area in East Asia implements proactive planning to address changes in social factors. This gives rise to the question of how the law and policy can respond to this social challenge and strike a balance between traditional aspects of family involvement and legislative and policy requirements. Moreover, how might we ensure that older adults experience life-ending events with dignity and reasonable satisfaction?

The challenges posed by aging populations and the increasing prevalence of dementia, which are common in East Asia, require a comprehensive approach that encompasses social, medical, legal, and policy dimensions. The research on proactive planning in East Asia demonstrates a complex interplay of cultural beliefs, levels of awareness, medical practice, and patient perspectives. It is, therefore, important to identify and address each of these influential factors to improve end-of-life medical care for older adults in the region.

[17.] In South Korea, the Dementia Management Act of 2011 and in Japan, the Basic Act on Dementia to Promote an Inclusive Society of 2023 were enacted to encounter dementia risk.

[18.] The global annual death toll is rising rapidly. Projections indicate it will grow from 60 million to 80 million by 2040 and surpass 100 million by 2060. Our World in Data (2024) "Deaths per Year (Chart)." https://ourworldindata.org/grapher/number-of-deaths-per-year. This chart is based on the World Population Prospects 2022, United Nations.

[19.] The World Factbook (2024) "Death Rate." https://www.cia.gov/the-world-factbook/field/death-rate/country-comparison/.

[20.] In 2024, the total fertility rate is estimated to be 1.4 in Japan (ranked 212th out of 227), 1.17 in Singapore (ranked 225th), 1.12 in South Korea (ranked 226th), and 1.11 in Taiwan (ranked 227th). The World Factbook (2024) "Total Fertility Rate." https://www.cia.gov/the-world-factbook/field/total-fertility-rate/country-comparison/.

[21.] Yeung, Wei-Jun Jean (2016) "Living Alone: The Trend of One-Person Households in Asia." chrome-extension://efaidnbmnnnibpcajpcglclefindmkaj/https://fass.nus.edu.sg/cfpr/wp-content/uploads/sites/17/2020/09/Aug16E.pdf.

[22.] On February 9, 2024, Sieh-Chuen Huang, Professor of Law and Vice Dean at the College of Law, National Taiwan University, delivered a lecture on Taiwan's social changes and testamentary law via Zoom.

1.2.2 The European Project of Advance Choices

To gain an understanding of the current situation in East Asia, it is necessary to compare it with the current situation in Europe, which served as a model for the East Asian countries and areas in terms of their legal system. The European Law Institute ("ELI"), based in Vienna, Austria, is engaged in a project entitled "Advance Choices for Future Disablement," which is scheduled to conclude in 2025, or at latest in 2026.[23] The project's objective is to draft a model law for advance choices in 2025, or at latest in 2026, accompanied by supporting materials. The project will provide European states with comprehensive assistance in the formulation of legislation pertaining to advance choices, dissemination of information to relevant parties, and promotion of their utilization by citizens.

The term "advance choices" is employed to describe instructions given, preferences recorded, wishes expressed, and information provided by a competent adult for making decisions in the event of their disablement.[24] These instructions may relate to a range of issues—including health, welfare, and personal matters—as well as economic and financial matters, and any legal act not expressly excluded by law from the scope of advance instructions.

This project is co-funded by the European Union ("EU"). Behind the ELI project, there are the facts that European countries and the EU have developed considerable amounts of legislations and policies, such as lasting powers of attorney (LPA), ADs, guardianship, and supported decision-making.[25] These are measures to support and protect the rights to self-determination and individual autonomy of vulnerable adults. Nevertheless, a notable degree of divergence persists in legislative methodology across Europe, attributable to the heterogeneous

---

[23.] The information on Advance Choices refers to those in the public domain. European Law Institute (ELI) (2024) "Advance Choices for Future Disablement." https://www.europeanlawinstitute.eu/projects-publications/current-projects/current-projects/advance-choices/.

[24.] Ibid; "Instructions given" are legally binding and referred to as "advance instructions." "Wishes made" express an individual's preferences, meant to be considered but not legally binding, including values, mottos, and beliefs, called "advance statements." The terms "preferences recorded" and "information provided" are introduced in the ELI project. This commentary is informed by the ELI Project Kick-Off Webinar on March 15, 2023 conducted by Adrian D Ward and other members, and the Law Society of Scotland's 2022 proposal: Law Society of Scotland (2022) "Human Rights Must Be at the Core of Proposals for Law Reform around Advance Choices and Medical Decision-Making." https://www.lawscot.org.uk/news-and-events/law-society-news/advance-choices-and-medical-decision-making/.

[25.] Sakurai, Yukio (2023) "Supported Decision-Making in the Japanese Context: Developments and Challenges" *The Journal of Aging and Social Change* Volume 13 Issue 1, 151–169. https://doi.org/10.18848/2576-5310/CGP/v13i01/151-169.

cultural milieu and the existence of discrete legal systems, namely civil law and common law. The ELI project states in their website as follows:[26]

> *The ELI project's objective is to facilitate advancements in advance choices through a comparative approach, thereby benefiting European citizens by promoting good practice and uptake with cross-border consistency, particularly in urgent situations. It will provide guidance to European states on how to enable citizens to make advance choices with certainty regarding their effects. Furthermore, the ELI project will enhance human and disability rights principles and improve cross-European compatibility. The anticipated outcome is draft model laws for advance choices, accompanied by supporting materials to aid legislation, educate the public, and encourage uptake.*

1.2.3 The East Asian Project of Advance Decision-Making

In contrast, in East Asia, the development of the legal system and the formation of policy regarding these matters are determined by individual countries or areas at different stages of development. These variations are reflected in the social backgrounds, legal systems, and levels of economic development of the countries and area. To illustrate, Hong Kong and Singapore are common law jurisdictions, whereas South Korea, Taiwan, and Japan are civil law jurisdictions based on the European continental model. These legal systems are distinctive and have their own historical background.

Moreover, given the divergence in traditions and local customs between Europe and East Asia, measures adopted in Europe may not always be well received or applicable in the East Asian context. There is a growing trend in East Asia toward a preference for human relationships over legal documents. This is evidenced by the relatively low uptake of adult guardianship systems, both statutory and enduring powers of attorney. This suggests that a separate set of considerations may be required in East Asia, distinct from those typically applied in Europe.

It is essential to consider the cognitive processes and behavioral patterns of individuals to identify effective methods of communication. This aspect presents a significant challenge. Although the distinctive thoughts and behavioral patterns of East Asians are typically perceived as a subjective impression, the underlying mechanisms remain inadequately elucidated within academic disciplines such

---

[26.] ELI (n 23).

as medicine, anthropology, and psychology. These characteristics are typically grouped under the umbrella term "culture." Prior research has discussed people's "legal consciousness" in general terms, but specific legal policies derived from this understanding have yet to be established.[27]

Historically, discussions on death have been considered taboo in East Asia due to the prevalence of ancient beliefs that it is inauspicious to speak openly about someone's death.[28] However, considering the social factors previously discussed, it becomes a practical necessity to enhance the social environment surrounding human death to ensure that everyone can experience death in a peaceful manner. This is a societal challenge that requires collective action to address a subjective matter, namely death. To achieve this, it is necessary to engage in empathy, understanding, and forward-thinking discourse.

Considering the pervasive societal challenge in East Asia, it is possible to share insights pertaining to legal and policy studies within East Asia and to explore avenues for regional collaborative study within the region. In contrast to Europe, it can be assumed that there is a distinct academic value in examining the differently named project "Advance Decision-Making for Future Disability in East Asia" ("East Asian Project") with a methodology that diverges from that of the ELI in Europe. The new concept of "advance decision-making" will be examined in Section 6.2 of Chapter 6.

1.3 Objective and Prior Research of the Study

1.3.1 Objective and Research Question of the Study

The objective of this study is to contribute to the ongoing debate on end-of-life medical care for older adults in East Asia, addressing a specific aspect of the

---

[27.] Sakurai, Yukio (2023) "Adaptation of Law and Policy in an Aged Society: Guardianship Law and People's Behavioral Pattern" *The Rest: The Journal of Politics and Development* Volume 13 Issue 2, 144–154. http://hdl.handle.net/10131/0002000015: A German researcher found that many Japanese individuals tend to distance themselves from the legal system, showing ignorance and indifference towards the law. This includes avoiding legal institutions like courts and having limited awareness of their rights, preferring vague moral guidance within a patriarchal social structure. Voss, Steffen (1992) "These Factors Have a Profound Impact on Contemporary Social Dynamics—Japanese Legal Consciousness: Especially Traditional Legal Consciousness" [in Japanese] *Japanese Language and Culture Training Program Report Collection, Hiroshima University* 77–81. https://ir.lib.hiroshima-u.ac.jp/00039306.

[28.] Cheng, S. Y., S. Y. Suh, T. Morita, et al. (2015) "A Cross-Cultural Study on Behaviors When Death Is Approaching in East Asian Countries: What Are the Physician-Perceived Common Beliefs and Practices?" *Medicine (Baltimore)* Volume 94 Issue 39, e1573. https://doi.org/10.1097/MD.0000000000001573. PMID: 26426631; PMCID: PMC4616852.

East Asian project. This represents a significant issue in the fields of health law and policy. The objective will be attained by adopting an interdisciplinary methodology, with a particular focus on the insights offered by law and policy studies. The research question is as follows:

(a) What proactive measures might older adults in East Asia adopt to prepare for their end-of-life medical care on a voluntary basis, despite the existence of local customs that regard the topic of death as taboo?

(b) How effectively might legislation and policy influence the decision-making process at the end of life, particularly in light of the fact that East Asian populations tend to prioritize family involvement over legal measures?

(c) How might the term "advance decision-making" be conceptualized to provide a comprehensive legal framework for end-of-life medical care in the East Asian context?

1.3.2 Prior Research of the Study

The principal prior studies pertinent to this book are as follows: Luisa Ho and Rebecca Lee published a book addressing financial planning from a comparative perspective; in the same publication, Terry Carney discusses guardianship and financial planning in Australia.[29] These studies were published based on how the law and policy of multiple states and areas can support and protect asset management for people with cognitive disability. The perspective that emphasizes individual autonomy forms the foundation of laws and policies, prioritizing an individual's will and rights.

In the context of healthcare decision-making, there are discussions by Mary Donnelly and Jonathan Herring in Europe, while some discussions are made at the medical law textbooks in Japan.[30] In private autonomy within individual lives or communities such as corporations, the prioritization of an individual's will and preferences or individual autonomy is not always guaranteed. In Japan, it is

---

[29.] Ho, Luisa, and Rebecca Lee (eds) (2019) *Special Needs Financial Planning: A Comparative Perspective.* Cambridge: Cambridge University Press; Carney, Terry (2019) "Adult Guardianship and Other Financial Planning Mechanisms for People with Cognitive Impairment in Australia" in Lusina Ho and Rebecca Lee (eds), *Special Needs Financial Planning: A Comparative Perspective.* Cambridge: Cambridge University Press. 3–29.

[30.] Donnelly, Mary (2010) *Healthcare Decision-Making and the Law: Autonomy, Capacity, and Limits of the Liberalism.* Cambridge: Cambridge University Press; Donnelly, Mary (2017) "Developing a Legal Framework for Advance Healthcare Planning: Comparing England & Wales and Ireland" *European Journal of Health Law* Volume 24 Issue 1, 67–84. https://doi.org/10.1163/15718093-12341412; Herring, Jonathan (2022) *Medical Law and the Ethics.* 9th ed. Oxford: Oxford University; Yonemura, Shigeto (2016) *Lectures on Medical Law.* Tokyo: NIPPON HYORON; Teshima, Yutaka (2022) *Introduction to Medical Law.* 6th ed. Tokyo: Yuhikaku Publishing. 48–49.

customary for familial opinions to be accorded greater weight than an individual's personal preferences, and for corporate interests to supersede individual autonomy. When contemplating relationships with others, individual autonomy is regarded as relative but is nevertheless deemed acceptable. This is known as relational autonomy, reflecting the individual's prioritization of relationships with others. Discussions on relational autonomy have been undertaken by Catriona Mackenzie and Shunsuke Akiba.[31]

In the context of international comparisons of ADs in end-of-life care, three studies merit particular attention: the first by Takehiro Morikawa, the second by Daisy Cheung and Michael Dunn, and the third by Satoshi Kodama.[32] The initial study offers an analysis grounded in policy science, which informs the formulation of AD policy. The second is a collection of articles focusing on ADs by local researchers from a wide range of Asian countries. This encompasses a vast geographical area, extending from Japan in the east to Turkey in the west. The third study comprises a research group study conducted in collaboration with East Asian researchers, with the aim of synthesizing ethical and legal considerations in end-of-life medical care across East Asia.

In the context of a country-by-country analysis, Tracey Chan presents a communitarian perspective on the Singaporean ACP.[33] Meanwhile, Daniel Fu-Chang Tsai addresses ADs in Taiwan from an Asian cultural perspective.[34] Norio Higuchi addresses the legal issues pertaining to end-of-life care in Japan, comparing the

[31.] Mackenzie, Catriona (2013) "The Importance of Relational Autonomy and Capabilities for an Ethics of Vulnerability" in Catriona Mackenzie, in Wendy Rogers and Susan Dodds (eds), *Vulnerability: New Essays in Ethics and Feminist Philosophy (Studies in Feminist Philosophy)*. Oxford: Oxford University Press. 33–59. https://doi.org/10.1093/acprof:oso/9780199316649.003.0002; McKenzie, Catriona (2019) "Feminist Innovation in Philosophy: Relational Autonomy and Social Justice" *Women's Studies International Forum* Volume 72, 144–151. https://doi.org/10.1016/j.wsif.2018.05.003; Akiba, Shunsuke (2021) "Self-Other Relationships and Relational Autonomy in Self-Determination regarding Medical Care" [in Japanese] *Bioethics* Volume 31 Issue 1, 46–54.

[32.] Morikawa, Takehiro (2020) "International Comparison of Institutional Frameworks for End-of-Life Medical Care and Aged Care" [in Japanese] *Annual Report on Public Policy Studies* Volume 14, 137–150; Cheung, D., and M. Dunn (eds) (2023) *Advance Directives across Asia: A Comparative Socio-Legal Analysis*. Cambridge: Cambridge University Press; Satoshi, Kodama, and Miho Tanaka (2024) "International Collaborative Research on Ethical and Legal Issues in End-of-Life Medical Care in East Asia" [in Japanese]. https://www.asian-eolc-ethics.com/; Tanaka, Miho, Satoshi Kodama, Ilhak Lee, et al. (2020) "Forgoing Life-Sustaining Treatment: A Comparative Analysis of Regulations in Japan, Korea, Taiwan, and England" *BMC Medical Ethics* Volume 12 Issue 1, 1–15.

[33.] Chan, Tracey (2019) "Advance Care Planning: A Communitarian Approach?" *Journal of Law and Medicine* Volume 26 Issue 4, 896–921. Chan, Tracey (2019) "Advance Care Planning: A Communitarian Approach?" NUS Centre for Asian Legal Studies Working Paper 19/06. NUS Law Working Paper No. 2019/020. https://ssrn.com/abstract=3459382.

[34.] Tsai, Daniel Fu-Chang (2023) "The Law and Practice of Advance Directives in Taiwan" in D. Cheung and M. Dunn (eds), *Advance Directives across Asia: A Comparative Socio-Legal Analysis*. Cambridge: Cambridge University Press. 75–89; Tsai, Daniel Fu-Chang (1999) "Ancient Chinese Medical Ethics and the Four Principles of Biomedical Ethics" *Journal of Medical Ethics* Volume 25 Issue 4, 315–321. https://doi.org/10.1136/jme.25.4.315.

legislation and practice in the U.S.[35] Saku Machino discusses patient self-determination and the law, focusing on end-of-life care in Japan while referring to German penal law.[36]

Similar research has been conducted in other disciplines, including gerontology, oncology, and humanity, outside the field of law and policy studies.[37] However, there is no research on the legal and policy realities and proposals regarding the development of advance decision-making, including ADs and ACP, specifically tailored to the characteristics of traditions, local customs, and relational autonomy in the East Asian context. The study of the East Asian project represents a novel and challenging endeavor.

1.4 Methodology

1.4.1 Methodology of the Study

This study draws upon the disciplines of law and policy studies, employing a comprehensive literature and research survey of East Asian researchers, as well as a detailed review of legal literature in both Japanese and English on matters pertaining to life and death. This study focuses on East Asia because Japan has not yet developed comprehensive legislation and policies regarding ADs and ACP for end-of-life medical care among older adults. The analysis continues to

---

[35.] Higuchi, Norio (2007) *Thinking about Medicine and Law* [in Japanese]. Tokyo: Yuhikaku Publishing; Higuchi, Norio (2008) *Continued: Thinking about Medicine and Law* [in Japanese]. Tokyo: Yuhikaku Publishing; Higuchi, Norio (2015) "Legal Issues on Medical Interventions in Terminally Ill Patients" [in Japanese] *Medical Care and Society* Volume 25 Issue 1, 21–34. https://doi.org/10.4091/iken.25.21; Higuchi, Norio, and Fusako Seki (eds) (2019) *Elder Law: Legal Basics for a Super-Aged Society* [in Japanese]. Tokyo: Tokyo University Press; Higuchi, Norio (2020) "Current Status and Issues of End-of-Life Care Legal Issues" *Japanese Journal of Geriatrics* Volume 2 Issue 5, 579–584.

[36.] Machino, Saku (1986) *Patient Self-Determination and Law* [in Japanese]. Tokyo: University of Tokyo Press; Machino, Saku (1996) "Patient Self-Determination vs. Doctor's Paternalism" [in Japanese] *Bioethics* Volume 6 Issue 1, 32–34; Machino, Saku (2000) "Self-Determination and Determination by Other" [in Japanese] *Journal of Medical Law* Volume 15, 44–52; Machino, Saku (2007) "Patients' Right to Self-Determination and Doctors' Duty to Treat: In the Wake of the Kawasaki Kyodo Hospital Case Appeals Court Decision" [in Japanese] *Criminal Law Journal* Volume 8, 47–53; Machino, Saku (2013) "Caring-From a Legal Point of View" *Sophia Bioethics* December 2013, 103–109.

[37.] Kawakami, A., E. W. Y. Kwong, C. K. Y. Lai, et al. (2021) "Advance Care Planning and Advance Directive Awareness among East Asian Older Adults: Japan, Hong Kong and South Korea" *Geriatrics & Gerontology International* Volume 21, 71–76. https://doi.org/10.1111/ggi.14086; Martina, Diah, Cheng-Pei Lin, Martina S. Kristanti, et al. (2021) "Advance Care Planning in Asia: A Systematic Narrative Review of Healthcare Professionals' Knowledge, Attitude, and Experience" *Journal of the American Medical Directors Association* Volume 22, P349.E1–P349.E28. https://doi.org/10.1016/j.jamda.2020.12.018; Pun, Jack K. H. (2022) "Communication about Advance Directives and Advance Care Planning in an East Asian Cultural Context: A Systematic Review" *Oncology Nursing Forum* Volume 49 Issue 1, 58–70. https://doi.org/10.1188/22.ONF.58-70.

focus on key theoretical frameworks, such as the vulnerability approach, safe-guarding laws, the concept of autonomy, and relevant ethical principles, building on the author's doctoral dissertation, "Value of Legislation Providing Support and Protection to Vulnerable Adults: Vulnerability Approach and Autonomy" (Yokohama National University, 2022).

A focus on Japan alone would entail significant limitations, given the absence of comprehensive legal frameworks or detailed guidelines in this field. By exploring the legal systems and policies surrounding ADs and ACP in other East Asian countries and areas with similar social contexts but more advanced legal structures, this study aims to provide insights that could inform future developments in Japan.

The input for this study was gathered from researchers within East Asia. To gain a comprehensive understanding of the subject matter, six scholars specializing in law and bioethics from South Korea, Taiwan, and Singapore were consulted. These consultations involved the submission of written responses to questionnaires (see Appendix 1) and discussions through email and a Zoom. Additionally, two Japanese experts in the fields of psycho-oncology and ethics engaged in a discussion with the author regarding the presented article topics. The author presented draft articles on various aspects of the study at international conferences throughout the research process. The findings from this work are incorporated into the present book.

Despite geographical distance, we collaborated with four Australian legal researchers from Melbourne, Brisbane, and Sydney, as well as one Italian researcher from Rome and one Scottish researcher from Edinburgh, who provided advisory support. The Australian network was formed through prior collaborations on field research related to ADs and ACP in February and March 2023 and in the previous visits, while the Italian contact was made in person in Rome on September 2, 2024. Both the Australian and Italian researchers provided feedback on the draft manuscript, and additional email exchanges were held with the Scottish researcher regarding advance choices in Europe.

This study's comparative analysis is based on two main axes: first, comparisons among East Asian countries and area, and second, comparisons of conceptual models between East Asia, the U.S., and Europe. The examination of ADs and ACP within East Asia highlights both similarities and differences, particularly concerning legislation and the role of families. Furthermore, analyzing conceptual models, especially those related to ADs, offers valuable insights. Through these two comparative axes, the study identifies distinctive characteristics of an East Asian model, contrasting it with the U.S. and European models.

1.4.2 Scope of the Study

The analysis is limited to older adults having decision-making ability and does not encompass those who lack this. It is essential to recognize that cases involving older adults without decision-making capacity, such as those necessitating substituted decision-making in healthcare, require distinct attention through guardianship or supported decision-making frameworks, which are the focal points of the doctoral dissertation. While advance decision-making encompasses a wide range of issues, this book will not delve into asset management in detail.[38]

The term "end-of-life medical care" is open to interpretation. The 2008 report by the Science Council of Japan provides a classification system that divides end-of-life care into three categories: acute (e.g., primarily emergency care), subacute (e.g., mainly focused on managing end-stage cancer), and chronic (e.g., care for frail older adults, individuals in a vegetative state, or those with dementia). This book focuses on subacute and chronic end-of-life care, as these are the most prevalent forms of care for the dying population in Japan at the present time.

The term "end-of-life medical care in East Asia" is a multifaceted concept that encompasses a range of complex elements, including legal, political, social, cultural, religious, and spiritual considerations. However, this book focuses on a select few aspects of the legal, social, and cultural factors to align with the book's objective and research question.[39] The subsequent stage will examine cases of greater complexity, such as the nuanced consideration of the patient's decision-making process.

1.4.3 Streamline of the Study

The book begins with an introduction (Chapter 1), followed by a review of theoretical discussions on the vulnerability approach, safeguarding law, the concept of autonomy, and ethical values in health care. This provides the basis for the study's theoretical framework (Chapter 2).

[38.] Sakurai, Yukio (2023) "A Study on the Use of Public Interest Corporations regarding Asset Management for Older Adults: Plans for Dealing with Issues in an Ageing Society" [in Japanese] Excellence Award in the First Thesis Contest of the Japan Association of Charitable Organization (JACO). http://doi.org/10.18880/00015170.

[39.] Dzeng, Elizabeth, Thomas Bein, and J. Randall Curtis. (2022) "The Role of Policy and Law in Shaping the Ethics and Quality of End-of-Life Care in Intensive Care" *Intensive Care Medicine* Volume 48, 352–354. https://doi.org/10.1007/s00134-022-06623-2.

Subsequently, the book presents an overview of historical, social, and legal aspects of ADs and ACP in both an international context and specifically within Japanese context, with a view to identifying benefits and issues (Chapters 3 and 4).

The book then proceeds to a comprehensive examination of ADs and ACP in East Asia, with a model comparison to the situation in the U.S. and Europe. Additionally, the East Asian cultural background that has led to the prevalence of family involvement in these matters is reviewed (Chapter 5).

The book devotes special attention to the features and challenges of the East Asian model, with the objective of improving the current situation. Furthermore, it examines prospective directions for advance decision-making in principal concepts, criteria and key provisions of legislation, as well as a potential avenue for legislative frameworks, and a socio-legal approach to a regional study in East Asia (Chapter 6).

The book concludes with a summary of the key findings and recommendations (Chapter 7).

CHAPTER 2

Theoretical Foundation

This chapter presents a theoretical perspective on the proposition by examining the vulnerability approach and safeguarding, alongside concepts of individual and relational autonomy. It explores how these frameworks interact in the context of advance decision-making, particularly in balancing protection and self-determination. Additionally, the chapter incorporates an East Asian values perspective, considering cultural and familial influences on end-of-life care decisions. Through this discussion, it aims to provide a nuanced understanding of how these theoretical approaches shape legal and ethical considerations in the region.

2.1 Vulnerability Approach and Safeguarding Law

2.1.1 Vulnerability Approach

The concept of vulnerability finds application in various academic fields, including philosophy, ethics, ecology, geography, physics, risk studies, and social sciences.[1] There is, however, no interdisciplinary unified concept. Each field should have its own definition, but it is challenging to explicitly define vulnerability in each academic field. Historically, the concept of vulnerability stemmed from philosophical discussions by Hannah Arendt[2] and Emanuel Levinas,[3] from the

---

[1] This part refers to Sakurai, Yukio (2022) "Value of Legislation Providing Support and Protection to Vulnerable Adults: Vulnerability Approach and Autonomy" Chapter 2. Doctoral Dissertation, Yokohama National University. http://doi.org/10.18880/00014834.

[2] Arendt, Hannah (1958) *The Human Condition*. Chicago: Chicago University Press.

[3] Levinas, Emmanuel (1961) *Totality and Infinity: An Essay on Exteriority.* Translated by Alphonso Lingis. Pittsburgh: Duquesne University Press.

natural sciences of ecology, geography, and risk studies in the 1970s, and from the social sciences of developmental studies by Amartya Sen.[4]

More recently, the concept of vulnerability in the social sciences has been explored by Martha Albertson Fineman. The notion of vulnerability is based on the understanding that people are vulnerable. Vulnerability suggests dependency on others, particularly in the cases of older adults and persons with disabilities who heavily rely on others. It is a simple and understandable concept that defines human nature and "the inescapable interrelation and interdependence that mark human existence."[5]

Such a general implication may include the idea that humans do not always have full capacity and autonomy. From the vulnerability approach, a general view is derived that vulnerable adults at risk of harm must be protected by law and policy. This view may clarify people's perception of the vulnerability approach, because vulnerability is a human characteristic, regardless of the relevant mental capacity of the principal (" the represented person" or " the person who is supported by others"). This is on a legal foundation based on the combination of civil law (i.e., guardianship in the capacity doctrine) and welfare law (i.e., abuse prevention in the vulnerable approach).

The vulnerability approach encourages respect for human rights, particularly equality as a universal value. As Fineman points out, "vulnerability can be embraced by people wanting to remove stigma from a designated group."[6] The notion of vulnerability is general but vague; thus, vulnerability alone is not enough for academic research and the construction of appropriate policy instruments.[7] Combining vulnerability with a rights-based approach may result in a greater understanding of the potential empowerment.

2.1.2 Safeguarding Law

With regard to safeguards or safeguarding, there is an idea of safeguarding law or policy that vulnerable adults or adults at risk of harm must be protected

---

[4] Honkasalo, Marja-Liisa (2018) "Guest Editor's Introduction: Vulnerability and Inquiring into Relationality" *Suomen Antropologi [Journal of the Finnish Anthropological Society]* Volume 43 Issue 3, 1–21. http://hdl.handle.net/10138/305956. https://doi.org/10.30676/jfas.v43i3.82725.

[5] Fineman, Martha Albertson (2012) " 'Elderly' as Vulnerable: Rethinking the Nature of Individual and Societal Responsibility" *Elder Law Journal* Volume 20, 101–142, 71. https://ssrn.com/abstract=2088159.

[6] Ibid., 112.

[7] Kohn, Nina A. (2014) "Vulnerability Theory and the Role of Government" *Yale Journal of Law & Feminism* Volume 26, 1–27. https://digitalcommons.law.yale.edu/yjlf/vol26/iss1/2.

by law and public policy from abuse.[8] This idea consists in the fact that older adults have fundamental human rights to protection from abuse and the state has an obligation to put in place law and public policy to combat elder abuse.[9] In general, vulnerability, adults at risk of harm, and safeguarding law or policy are seen in common law jurisdictions, and they are, in fact, differently made into legislation or policy by each individual country.

Previous studies on comparative law analysis in common law jurisdictions were focused on adult safeguarding laws in England, Scotland, Ireland, the U.S., Canada (mainly the province of British Columbia) and Australia (mainly the State of Victoria).[10] The definitions of "vulnerable adult," "at-risk adult," or "adult at risk" in safeguarding law or policy of the adult protection systems have a certain diversity according to country.[11]

While common principles are seen in the adult protection system in common law jurisdictions, namely, adult guardianship and elder abuse legislation are closely related like as the two sides of a coin. For example, in England, the same national judicial and administrative agencies—i.e., the Court of Protection and the Office of the Public Guardian—that administer adult guardianship under the Mental Capacity Act 2005 (MCA) are responsible for "care and support" for adults at risk of harm.[12]

In Australia, guardianship law reform in the states and special territories, including elder abuse legislation, are in progress. In the state of South Australia, elder abuse is dealt with by a neighboring agency of guardianship, i.e., the Adult Safeguarding Unit. The New South Wales (NSW) newly established an Aging and Disability Commissioner and launched a similar public policy to combat

---

[8.] This part refers to Sakurai, Yukio (2021) "Vulnerability Approach and Adult Support and Protection: Safeguarding Laws for Adults at Risk" *The Journal of Aging and Social Change* Volume 11 Issue 1, 19–34. https://doi.org/10.18848/2576-5310/CGP/v11i01/19-34; Mandelstam, Michael (2008) *Safeguarding Vulnerable Adults and the Law.* London: Jessica Kingsley Publishers.

[9.] Herring, Jonathan (2012) "Elder Abuse: A Human Rights Agenda for the Future" in Israel Doron and Ann M. Soden (eds), *Beyond Elder Law: New Directions in Law and Aging.* London: Springer. 175.

[10.] Montgomery, L., J. Anand, K. McKay, et al. (2016) "Implications of Divergences in Adult Protection Legislation" *Journal of Adult Protection* Volume 18 Issue 3, 1–16. https://doi.org/10.1108/JAP-10-2015-0032; Wayne, Michael Martin, Sabine Michalowski, Jill Stavert, et al. (2016) "The Essex Autonomy Project Three Jurisdictions Report: Towards Compliance with CRPD Art: 12 in Capacity/Incapacity Legislation across the UK". https://doi.org/10.13140/RG.2.2.10734.72002; Donnelly, Sarah, Marita O'Brien, Judy Walsh, et al. (2017) *Adult Safeguarding Legislation and Policy Rapid Realist Literature Review.* https://researchrepository.ucd.ie/handle/10197/9183.

[11.] Ibid. [Donnelly].

[12.] This is based on Section 42(1)(a) of the Care Act 2014. The MCA 2005 requires two conditions for incapacity to decide: the individual cannot understand, retain, or use relevant information, and this inability results from a mental impairment. Herring, Jonathan, and Jesse Wall (2015) "Autonomy, Capacity and Vulnerable Adults: Filling the Gaps in the Mental Capacity Act" *Legal Studies* Volume 35 Issue 4, 698–719, 701.

elder abuse. Which public agency is responsible for both guardianship and elder abuse is subject to the relevant state/special territory in Australia, but it should be noted that guardianship is regarded as one of the legal instruments for dealing with elder abuse.

Considering these legal developments in developed nations, the legal framework encompassing adult guardianship, supported decision-making, and elder abuse safeguards should be viewed as interrelated. This concept of law thereby constitutes a complex of laws to support and protect older adults from adults at risk. In this book, we refer to this legal framework as "adult support and protection legislation."[13] It is speculated that the approach of adult support and protection legislation can be applied in the public health and medical field.

2.2 Individual Autonomy and Relational Autonomy

This section presents a critical examination of the concept of autonomy, including both individual autonomy and relational autonomy, which constitutes a fundamental tenet of modern legal theory. It will then discuss how autonomy is situated within the context of the East Asian model.

2.2.1 Individual Autonomy

Autonomy is closely tied to right to self-determination.[14] Self-determination is said to identify "external, structural (social and political) conditions for individual autonomy, specifically in freedom conditions and opportunity conditions."[15] Catriona Mackenzie defines that self-determination is to have "the freedom and opportunity to make and enact choices of practical import to one's life, that is, choices of what to value, who to be, and what to do."[16] Some psychologists

---

[13.] The term "adult support and protection legislation" refers to a set of laws that provide legal advocacy for vulnerable adults. These laws protect them through the least restrictive measures, considering their will and preferences for as long as necessary.

[14.] The part "Individual Autonomy and Relational Autonomy" is based on the previously published article: Sakurai (n 1) 150–158.

[15.] Mackenzie, Catriona (2014) "Three Dimensions of Autonomy: A Relational Analysis" in Andrea Veltman and Mark Piper (eds), *Autonomy, Oppression, and Gender.* Oxford: Oxford University Press. 15–41, 25.

[16.] Ibid. MacKenzie remarks that "the promotion of autonomy is a matter of social justice." Mackenzie, Catriona (2008) "Relational Autonomy, Normative Authority and Perfectionism" *Journal of Social Philosophy* Volume 39, 512–533. 530.

state that the notion of autonomy is "regulation by the self."[17] Gerald Dworkin asserts that individual autonomy is "a second-order capacity of a person to reflect critically upon their first-order preferences, desires, wishes, and so forth and the capacity to accept or attempt to change these in light of higher-order preferences and values."[18]

Koji Sato argues, in part citing Robert Young's views in 1986,[19] that individual autonomy implies two aspects: the freedom to act without external constraints and individual self-determination in accordance with a chosen plan of life.[20] Considering these views on individual autonomy, it can be seen that the scope of autonomy may be broader than that of self-determination, and both autonomy and self-determination are regarded as universal values.[21] In history, the notion of individual autonomy has been argued and developed by Immanuel Kant and Kantian scholars, including John Rawls,[22] on the one hand, and by John Stuart Mill and utilitarian liberal philosophy scholars, on the other hand. Kantian scholars emphasize the moral and ethics of internal motives of human beings based on a human-centered approach.[23]

While Mill does not use the term autonomy but respects "the principle of individual liberty on the utilitarian bias that it is through liberty that human individuality develops."[24] Mary Donnelly remarks, based on Mill's insight, that "a view of autonomy as empowerment provides a better way of thinking about

---

[17.] Ryan, Richard M., and L. Edward (2006) "Self-Regulation and the Problem of Human Autonomy: Does Psychology Need Choice, Self-Determination, and Will?" *Journal of Personality* Volume 74 Issue 6, 1557–1585, 1557.

[18.] Dworkin, Gerald (Ed.) (1988) "The Nature of Autonomy" in *The Theory and Practice of Autonomy*. Cambridge: Cambridge University Press. 3–20, 20; Dworkin, Gerald (2015) "The Nature of Autonomy" *Nordic Journal of Studies in Educational Policy* (an unchanged republishing) Volume 2, Article: 28479.

[19.] Young, Robert (1986) *Personal Autonomy: Beyond Negative and Positive Liberty*. London: Routledge.

[20.] Sato, Koji (1990) "The Meaning of 'Self-Determination' in the Constitutional Studies" [in Japanese] *Legal Philosophy Annual Report* [1989] 76–99, 86–87.

[21.] Takikawa identifies three values in the concept of self-determination: an instrumental value, which views it as the best way to achieve well-being; a growth value, which sees it as a driver of personal growth; and a symbolic value, recognizing situations where autonomous decision-making is appropriate. The principle of self-determination does not always imply self-responsibility, as exceptions like incapacity and cases of intention or negligence exist. Takikawa, Hirohide (2001) "Between Self-Decision and Self-Responsibility: A Philosophy of Law Consideration" [in Japanese] *Law Seminar* September 2001, 32–35.

[22.] Rawls, John (2010) *A Theory Justice* [in Japanese]. 2nd ed. Translated by Takashi Kawamoto, Yuuko Kamishima, and Satoshi Fukuma. Tokyo: Kinokuniya Bookstore.

[23.] For example, Hasuo, Hiroyuki (2010) "The Structure of 'Autonomy' in Kant's Moral Philosophy: New Possibilities through Practice of Duty of Love" [in Japanese] *Civilization Structure Theory* Volume 6, 15–34.

[24.] Donnelly, Mary (2010) *Healthcare Decision-Making and the Law: Autonomy, Capacity, and Limits of the Liberalism*. Cambridge: Cambridge University Press. 914 and 1484.

autonomy than the traditional liberal view of autonomy as non-interference."[25] From a feminist point of view, there are some arguments by Martha Albertson Fineman against individual autonomy.[26] Fineman criticizes the autonomy myth, which she believes has caused the U.S. to fail in effective public policymaking.[27] Thus, Fineman wants to introduce to the U.S. public debate the alternative terms of "dependency" and "substantive equality." Fineman raises an argument on "vulnerability" to ask for state responsibility to protect vulnerable people.

In this regard, it can be understood that vulnerability is used as a conflicting concept against individual autonomy, since the "vulnerable theory [as a universal one] asserts that agency or [individual] autonomy should always be understood as particular, partial, and contextual."[28] Daniel Bedford comments that vulnerability has been positioned as "the other of the ideal of autonomy."[29] Christine Straehle states that the "normative and moral question behind vulnerability-based theories is a concern for individual autonomy and the conditions of individual agency."[30]

Considering the views above, it can be understood that individual autonomy is no doubt valuable, but sometimes may conflict with other values, including vulnerability. As Sato remarks, the idea of individual autonomy closely relates to the value of the community and thus is reasonably restricted by public welfare.[31] The question then is what public welfare is like. Here, it can be said that public welfare is "a device that coordinates conflicts between rights and conflicts between the public interest and rights"[32] or "the ultimate philosophy of domestic law"[33] that people in the community must respect and it should be deliberately clarified case by case in a democratic process.

[25.] Ibid. Donnelly states that the MCA 2005 is based on the traditional liberal view as noninterference.

[26.] Other viewpoints than feminist can be seen as "receptivity, dependency, and social and clinical psychology." O'shea, Tom (2012) "Critics of Autonomy" *Essex Autonomy Project: Green Paper Report* 1–26.

[27.] Fineman, Martha Albertson (2004) *The Autonomy Myth: A Theory of Dependency.* New York: The New Press.

[28.] Fineman, Martha Albertson (2017) "Introducing Vulnerability" in Martha Albertson Fineman and Jonathan W. Fineman (eds), *Vulnerability and the Legal Organization of Work.* New York: Routledge. 1–10, 8. https://doi.org/10.4324/9781315518572.

[29.] Bedford, Daniel (2020) "Introduction: Vulnerability Refigured" in Daniel Bedford and Jonathan Herring (eds), *Embracing Vulnerability, the Challenges and Implications for Law.* London: Routledge.

[30.] Straehle, Christine (2017) "Introduction: Vulnerability, Autonomy, and Applied Ethics" in Christine Straehle (ed), *Vulnerability, Autonomy and Applied Ethics.* London: Routledge.

[31.] Sato (n 20) 90–92.

[32.] Obayashi posits that public welfare can function in various ways, contingent on the circumstances. It may serve as a basis for limiting rights or as a criterion for evaluating the constitution. Obayashi, Keigo (2022) "What Is Public Welfare: Public Welfare as the Standard" [in Japanese] *Hougaku Seminar* Volume 807, 39–44, 44.

[33.] Odaka, Tomoo (1965) *The Ultimate in Law* [in Japanese]. 2nd ed. Tokyo: Yuhikaku Publishing. 228.

2.2.2 Relational Autonomy

2.2.2.1 Notion and Function of Relational Autonomy

The notion of autonomy includes a different approach—relational autonomy.[34] Relational autonomy is often advocated in the field of bioethics, specifically with the principal's family members or relatives when medical treatment or serious physical operations are deemed to be necessary.[35] Relational autonomy, however, is not limited to bioethics; it can be applied to any field,[36] but "to be in a network of relationships, with their dependent responsibilities."[37] Herring also states that "our decisions are rarely 'ours,' but are the results of consultation and discussion. They are made in the context of our relationships, reflecting the obligations we owe to those around us. This does not require us to abandon autonomy, but to rethink it in a deeply relational way."[38]

The notion of relational autonomy may imply a greater understanding of human relationships involving older adults, including healthcare and aged care.[39] Herring states that "dependency on others is an aspect of humanity"[40] and "vulnerabilities,

---

[34.] Ikeya posits that a perspective of universal vulnerability encourages the transformation of the prevailing notion of individual autonomy into one of relative autonomy. Ikeya, Hisao (2016) "Bioethics and Vulnerability" [in Japanese] *The Bulletin of Ryotokuji University* Volume 10, 105–128.

[35.] McKenzie remarks that "Relational theories of autonomy seem to have had greatest traction outside the discipline, or in sub-discipline, such as bioethics, applied ethics, and political philosophy where there is a (relatively) larger proportion of women." McKenzie, Catriona (2019) "Feminist Innovation in Philosophy: Relational Autonomy and Social Justice" *Women's Studies International Forum* Volume 72, 144–151. https://doi.org/10.1016/j.wsif.2018.05.003; Gómez-Vírseda, Carlos et al. review 50 articles regarding "relational autonomy" in the bioethics. Gómez-Vírseda, C., Y. de Maeseneer, and C. Gastmans (2019) "Relational Autonomy: What Does It Mean and How Is It Used in End-of-Life Care? A Systematic Review of Argument-Based Ethics Literature" *BMC Medical Ethics* Volume 20 Article No. 76, 1–15. https://doi.org/10.1186/s12910-019-0417-3.

[36.] Tahara notes that individual autonomy is frequently critiqued in contemporary discourse due to its perceived underestimation or denial of the value of concepts such as love, friendship, and interdependence, which are widely regarded as important by a high proportion of people. Subsequently, the concept of relational autonomy is explored. Tahara, Shotarou (2017) "What Should Autonomous Agents Be Like? From the Individualistic to the Substantive Conception" [in Japanese] *Waseda Rilas Journal* Volume 5, 193–203.

[37.] Herring, Jonathan (2010) "Relational Autonomy and Rape" in S. Day Sclater, F. Ebtehaj, E. Jackson, and M. Richards (eds), *Regulating Autonomy*. Oxford Legal Studies Research Paper No. 12. 13. Oxford: Oxford Legal Studies.

[38.] Herring, Jonathan (2016) *Vulnerable Adults and the Law*. Oxford: Oxford University Press (Kindle) 1998.

[39.] The topic of healthcare decision-making is frequently addressed in conjunction with the concept of relational autonomy, as discussed in the introductory section. Menon, Sumytra, V. A. Entwistle, and A. V. Campbell, et al. (2020) "Some Unresolved Ethical Challenges in Healthcare Decision-Making: Navigating Family Involvement" *Asian Bioethics Review* Volume 12 Issue 1, 27–36. https://doi.org/10.1007/s41649-020-00111-9; Morita, Tatsuya, Aya Enzo, Masanori Mori, et al. (2020) "Relational Autonomy in Advance Care Planning" [in Japanese] *Palliative Care* Volume 30 Issue 5, 399–402.

[40.] Herring, Jonathan (2014) "The Disability Critique of Care" *Elder Law Review* Volume 8 Article 2, 12; Herring states that "people are understood as relational, interconnected, and interdependent. The law's job is to uphold and maintain relationships and protect people from the abuses that can occur within them." Herring, Jonathan (2014) *Relational Autonomy and Family Law*. London: Springer Science & Business Media. 13.

care and identities become mutual and interdependent"[41] with the notion of relational autonomy. "The emphasis on caring relationships acknowledges that it is a huge simplification to separate people into carers and those cared for. In caring relationships, we are all in the merging of interests and selves."[42]

In relation to people with dementia, Terry Carney states that "[i]t is here that richer concepts of relational autonomy and vulnerability prove their worth in helping to understand the ethical, social and legal issues in dementia care—searching out and promoting relational harmonies while remaining vigilant to correct disharmonies such as abuse and neglect, or even the 'pathogenic' vulnerability manufactured by poor legal processes."[43]

The notion of relational autonomy may imply why people are motivated to care for other people in need. This may be because people recognize their mutual vulnerability and need care from others.

Relational autonomy is in part rooted in feminist studies and is proposed with the purpose of criticizing the concept of individualist autonomy and proposing a different approach. Considering the independent relationship of human beings in family, community, and society, the notion of relational autonomy is assumed to be crucial in practice. This is because one's pattern of human conduct and decision-making is largely influenced by family, community, and society.[44]

This general tendency illustrates one characteristic of humans living in a community. This relational autonomy, however, does not refer to a strictly defined concept of autonomy in theory, but to a loosely organized research trend that shares a research policy of incorporating relationships with others into autonomy research.[45] It is assumed that this tendency may hint that the notion of relational autonomy has something imperfect to be a general theory. The point of discussion

---

[41] Ibid. [The Disability Critique of Care] 15.

[42] Herring, Jonathan (2020) "Ethics of Care and Disability Rights: Complementary or Contradictory?" in Loraine Gelsthorpe, Perveez Mody, and Brian Sloan (eds), *Spaces of Care*. London: Hart Publishing. 180; From action theory of philosophy viewpoint, an interactive uncontrollability of care is discussed, which implies that the matter is not so simple. Hayakawa, Seisuke (2014) "Caring and Vulnerable Agency" *Studies on Action Theory* Volume 3, 1–10; Nishimura, Jun (2021) "Ethics of Care and Social Security Law: For the Conversion from the Benefit-Centered Law to the Support-Centered Law" [in Japanese] *Journal of Kanagawa University of Human Services* Volume 18 Issue 1, 9–18.

[43] Carney, Terry (2020) "People with Dementia and Other Cognitive Disabilities: Relationally Vulnerable or a Source of Agency and Care?" Sydney Law School Research Paper No. 20/17 *Elder Law Review* Volume 12 Issue 1, 1–21. https://ssrn.com/abstract=3561294.

[44] Braun, Joan (2020) "Legal Interventions to Protect Vulnerable Adults: Can Relational Autonomy Provide a New Way Forward?" *Elder Law Review* Volume 12 Issue 2, 1–25. https://www.westernsydney.edu.au/__data/assets/pdf_file/0017/1714220/PEER_REVIEWED_BRAUN_Article.pdf.

[45] Tahara, Shotaro (2022) "Substantive Conceptions of Autonomy: An Approach Based on Shared Characteristics" [in Japanese] *Bulletin of the Faculty of Humanities, Ibaraki University: Studies in Social Sciences* Volume 1, 55–76, 63.

is how to demonstrate the notion of relational autonomy in a legal framework.[46] The important decision-making areas that the principal should be able to freely execute without excessive interference must be considered, namely, voting, marriage, life or death decisions, and matters of creed or belief. The principal's own decision must be respected as an individual autonomous decision, which is a basic principle of human rights.

If the principal has little ability to decide on an important issue for some reason, then relational autonomy, as a support approach, should prevail as an alternative to individual autonomy.[47] Even in such a case, relational autonomy needs to be carefully examined by a third party as a witness to determine whether or not it is unduly influenced by others.[48] In the other important decision-making areas besides the above-mentioned ones, relational autonomy can be utilized according to some ethical guidelines to safeguard the principal's interests. This is because human relationships with others, including relatives, are not always as good as the principal likes, but may be harmful to the principal in the worst case.[49] It can be said that the weak point in relational autonomy is ambiguity whether there is a risk for undue or harmful influence on the principal for some reason, and the principal with intellectual/mental disability may not identify the risk by himself/herself.

As evidenced by illegal acts such as financial exploitation of relatives, there are cases where the person concerned and relatives may have a conflict of interest, or where some family members do not agree with the end-of-life care plan that the principal considers appropriate. For example, given the numerous instances where relatives, appointed as guardians by family courts, have abused their authority and exploited the assets of those under guardianship, the current rate of relatives being appointed as guardians stands at 18.1% of all cases.[50] Relational

---

[46.] Ohe, Hiroshi (1999) "Rights and Relationships" [in Japanese] *St. Paul's Review of Law and Politics* Volume 53, 149–178.

[47.] Wright, Megan S. (2020) "Dementia, Autonomy, and Supported Healthcare Decision Making" Pennsylvania State Law Research Paper No. 05-2019 *Maryland Law Review* Volume 79, 257–324.

[48.] Series notes that the MCA 2005 is based on two conflicting premises: autonomy as a function of an individual's psychological makeup and autonomy influenced by external circumstances. The MCA adopts a narrow "support" approach, while the CRPD offers new perspectives on how relationships can promote relational autonomy in legal capacity. Series, Lucy (2015) "Relationships, Autonomy and Legal Capacity: Mental Capacity and Support Paradigms" *International Journal of Law and Psychiatry* Volume 40, 80–91.

[49.] Lindsey, Jaime Tabitha (2018) "Protecting and Empowering Vulnerable Adults: Mental Capacity Law in Practice" Doctoral Dissertation, University of Birmingham. 1–341, 41.

[50.] Courts of Japan (2024) "Overview of Adult Guardianship Related Cases" [in Japanese]. https://www.courts.go.jp/toukei_siryou/siryo/kouken/index.html.

autonomy may be established in some instances, but not in others. In this sense, relational autonomy may lack universality in cases where a conflict of interest or disagreement among family members occurs.

2.2.2.2 Scope of Relational Autonomy

Why is relational autonomy challenging to understand? This difficulty in part may arise from the broad range of interpretations of relational autonomy, from cases where individuals completely depend on relations and lose individual autonomy to cases where individuals consider relations but make decisions based on individual autonomy. Due to this wide spectrum, there may be varying assumptions about relational autonomy among individuals, making it challenging to reach a consensus.

It can thus be posited that relational autonomy, as a functional concept, serves to facilitate coordination between individual autonomy and the surrounding stakeholders. Relational autonomy plays a role in facilitating early communication and in preventing relatives from overriding an individual's wishes through ADs or ACP. Family members should be aware of the principal's wishes and preferences regarding end-of-life medical care through ADs or ACP and understand them to prevent family indecision or arguments about the patient's treatment. Consequently, it does not support the decision by relatives but the decision by the individual.

This book will proceed with the assumption that relational autonomy is narrowly defined. It includes cases where individuals take relationships into account but make decisions based on individual autonomy. However, it does exclude cases where individuals are entirely dependent on relationships, resulting in a loss of individual autonomy. By explicitly defining relational autonomy in this manner, we can avoid confusion. In other words, this book will no longer discuss cases where individuals are entirely dependent on relationships and have lost individual autonomy, as these individuals have no opportunity to address ADs and ACP for themselves.

Relational autonomy is a notion to consider the nuanced human self and human relationships between people and between people and society, which are variable factors according to the surrounding environments. It can be concluded here that the notion of relational autonomy has some positive or negative implications to complement the area where individual autonomy falls short of, but relational autonomy is not an established general theory yet.

2.2.3 Autonomy in the East Asian Context

The discussions on autonomy have been conducted in accordance with Western values, irrespective of utilitarian, communitarian, or normative perspectives. East Asian countries, including Japan, have embraced Western ideologies and the legal systems founded upon them during the process of modernization from the nineteenth to the twentieth centuries. In East Asia, including Japan, the family is a fundamental social unit. Despite the lack of a strong legal system, mutual assistance based on kinship is deeply rooted. This is also seen in the Middle East and the Mediterranean region, related to regional lifestyles. Reliance on law, policy, or family varies between regions.

Each East Asian country has followed a distinct historical trajectory, resulting in a diverse array of development paths. This book will examine the modernization process and the establishment of Japan's legal framework as an example in East Asia.[51] Two significant events in Japanese history—the Meiji government's establishment in 1868 and the Meiji Constitution of 1989—along with post-World War II democratization, transformed the legal system. The former led to modern legislation like the Meiji Constitution and the 1898 Civil Code, establishing the emperor as head of state and citizens as subjects, and introducing parliamentary systems. The Civil Code's family system made the family the basic social unit, with the eldest son as the heir. After Japan's defeat in 1945, the family system was abolished in the 1947 Civil Code revision, replaced by individualistic principles influenced by the Supreme Commander for the Allied Powers.

Despite this, traditional practices, particularly in performing arts, crafts, and rural customs like family graves, continued. The old family system's influence persists in business activities.[52] While traditional customs have declined with generational changes, they remain in professions where they are integral. The constitutional monarchy, supported by the population, reflects the enduring value of traditional family systems. Understanding the historical influence on the current Civil Code is important. Surveys on public legal consciousness show nuanced responses due to different methodologies. Older adults aged 80 and above

---

[51.] Sakurai, Yukio (2023) "International Cooperation of Asian Law Systems beyond Diversity" *Political Reflection Magazine* Volume 9 Issue 3, 27–31; Oki, Masao (1983/2024) *Japanese Concept of Law: A Comparison with Western Concept of Law* [in Japanese]. Tokyo: University of Tokyo Press.

[52.] Todd, Emanuel (2022) *Où en sommes-nous? Une esquisse de l'histoire humaine* (Where Are We? A Sketch of Human History) [in Japanese]. Tokyo: Bungeishunju.

educated before and during WWII understand the value transition and family system reforms with complex emotions. Despite the Civil Code's individualistic approach, traditional family beliefs coexist, and state non-intervention in family matters is seen as reasonable.

In the context of the shifts in values and reforms to the legal system, the legal status of individual autonomy is not always clear. Furthermore, the legal status of the family remains ambiguous. From a commercial perspective, individualism is strictly observed. This is evidenced by the requirement for personal identification for transactions involving individual bank accounts, which cannot be accessed by family members without the establishment of a legal agency.

A contrasting approach is observed in medical institutions, where healthcare practitioners seek signatures on numerous consent forms from both older adults and their family members, referred to as informed consent, regardless of the legal authority of the family's representation. In instances where there are no close relatives available, efforts are made to locate distant relatives to obtain proxy consent for the principal's medical procedures. The concept of informed consent is said to have undergone a shift in its interpretation. Rather than being regarded as a confirmation of the patient's or their substitute's wishes in accordance with the patient's human rights, it is now perceived as a mere procedural requirement imposed by healthcare institutions to protect their own interests.

Judicial opinions on individual autonomy in medical contexts remain nuanced. Although there is no legislation that specifically regulates patient rights in medical care or defines family authority, the judiciary employs logic suggesting that "timely cooperation and consideration from family members and others would be in the patient's best legal interests" in the absence of clear legal provisions.[53] This implies that if family considerations do not contribute to the patient's legal protection, they may not be preferable.

Inaba posits that the foundations for self-determination are vulnerable, and thus self-determination in Japan is not well established as a legally protected right.[54] It is unreasonable to expect healthcare practitioners to make such determinations as would be made by judicial judges. Consequently, in practice, family intervention

---

[53.] Japan, the Supreme Court judgment, September 24, 2002, Judgment: Proportion of notification to families' duties; There is an opinion to agree with Supreme Court Judgement; Machino, Saku (2000) "Self-Determination and Determination by Other" [in Japanese] *Journal of Medical Law* Volume 15, 44–52.

[54.] Inaba, Kazuo (2008) "Patient Decision-Making and the Role of the Family from a Legal Perspective (Patient Decision-Making and the Role of the Family)" [in Japanese] *Journal of Philosophy and Ethics in Health Care and Medicine* Volume 26, 87–90.

occurs irrespective of whether it contributes to the legal protection of older adults, with no regulations in Japan to prevent such interventions.

Despite the ambiguity surrounding the issue, Japan has successfully navigated numerous legal challenges without significant litigation. This has led to minimal discussions on the legalization of individual autonomy and patient rights. Nevertheless, it cannot be guaranteed that this trend will continue, particularly considering the changing generations, and that the baby boomer generation will exhibit different behavioral patterns from the previous generation. It is anticipated that discussions on legal frameworks concerning individual autonomy, self-determination, and the legal authority of families will become increasingly necessary in the medical field.[55]

2.3 Value Model for the East Asian Project

This section sets forth the foundational value system that informs the provision of support and protection for older adults at the end of life.

2.3.1 Principal Values of the Legal Principles Dimension and Indicators' Matrix

The framework of values related to the adult support and protection legislation system is shown in Figure 2.1. This is the modified multidimensional model of elder law ("modified model"). The modified model is adapted by the author from the multidimensional model of elder law created by Israel Doron. If advance decision-making aligns with the same values as adult support and protection legislation, they can adopt the same modified model that the adult support and protection legislation employs. The question at hand is how the legal concept of advance decision-making can be represented within the modified model. Some comments on principle values, indicators, and dimensions are provided below.

[55.] Jinno, Reisei (2016) "Medical Practice and Family Consent" [in Japanese] *Hiroshima Law Review* Volume 12, 223–245; Mizuno suggests that Japanese legislation, including the Civil Code, primarily relies on the responsibility of individuals and their families, aiming to minimize national intervention in private autonomy. However, this approach is supported by a vulnerable judicial infrastructure, including Japan's courts and notary public system. Mizuno, Noriko (2023) "Conditions for Making Civil Law Work (1) (2)" [in Japanese] *Lawyers Association Journal* Volume 75 Issue 7/8, 1285–1297/1515–1540.

Figure 2.1: The Modified Multidimensional Model of Elder Law

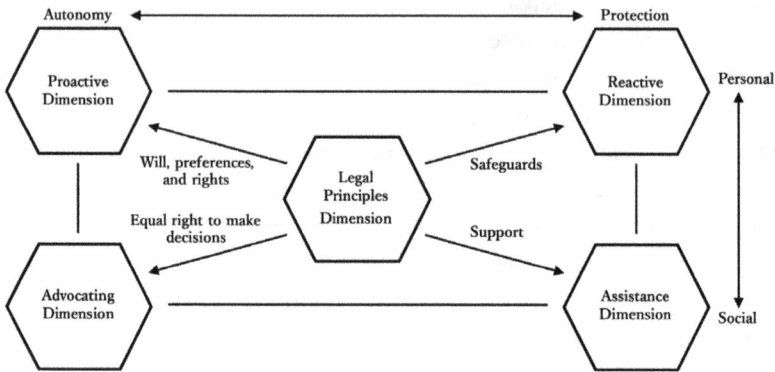

Source: Partly modified by the Author based on the Model of Doron
2003/2009[56]

It can be observed from the examples of both Japan and Australia that interna-tional consensus has almost been reached on the United Nations Convention on the Rights for Persons with Disabilities (CRPD), which 164 states/areas signed, and 193 entities have ratified as of September 2025. The Australian National Decision-Making Principles addressed in the ALRC Report 124 clearly reflect some principal values—namely, principle 1, *the equal right to make decisions*; principle 2, *support*; principle 3, *will, preferences and rights*; and principle 4, *safeguards*—that could be applied to the legal principles dimension of other countries, including Japan.

The matrix with autonomy and protection on the horizontal axis is key. It ac-knowledges the need for legal safeguards for vulnerable adults, shifting the focus from vulnerability to human rights. The capability approach values individual autonomy, self-determination, and freedom of choice, respecting diversity and promoting individual autonomy. Thus, the matrix is founded on these principles of vulnerability (protection) and autonomy.

Reviewing the matrix of personal and social on a vertical axis, discussions have focused on human internal motives. In our diverse society, relational autonomy, influenced by family and society, is crucial. This suggests the need to consider the

---

[56.] The multidimensional model of elder law was originally introduced in the article in 2003 with some amendments afterward. Doron, Israel (2003) "A Multi-Dimensional Model of Elder Law: An Israeli Example" *Ageing Inter-national* Volume 28 Issue 3, 242–259; Doron, Israel (2009) "A Multi-Dimensional Model of Elder Law" in Israel Doron (ed), *Theories on Law and Ageing: The Jurisprudence of Elder Law.* Berlin, Heidelberg: Springer. 59–74.

social aspect alongside the person. The social aspect includes equal transactions and necessary vertical interventions by public agencies. This combination of social and personal aspects leads to support for vulnerable adults, with measures to protect their interest and emphasize their decision-making rights and safety.

2.3.2 Principal Values of Four Dimensions

The term *reactive* refers to a response to properly react a vulnerable adult when he/she is identified or deserved a suspect.[57] The term *proactive* refers not only to appropriately responding to a vulnerable adult when they are identified or suspected to be at risk, but also taking preventive measures to mitigate potential harm.[58] The term *assistance* refers to any kind of support by relatives or third parties, whom they are assumed appropriate to vulnerable adults.[59] The term *advocacy* refers to any action by an individual or a corporation, or any public policy to empower vulnerable adults on minimum conflict of interests between people or between people and society.[60]

ADs and ACP are more about individual autonomy than protection when we look at the matrix with autonomy and protection on the horizontal axis. This means they fall under the *Proactive Dimension*, not the *Reactive Dimension*. When we look at the matrix of personal and social on a vertical axis, ADs and ACP cover both aspects because they involve the person, related parties, and the wider society. Therefore, they fall under both the *Proactive* and *Advocacy Dimensions*.

These *Proactive* and *Advocacy Dimensions* are connected, through the *Legal Principles Dimension*, with the values of the equal right to make decisions and will, preferences, and rights. Vulnerable adults should be advocated for and empowered to use, of their own accord, supported decision-making and other relevant measures, including ADs and ACP. It is desirable that adults use these self-advocating measures at their own accord, including estate planning and AD measures. This is to respect the autonomy and right to self-determination

---

[57.] The term "reactive" refers to "reacting to events or situations rather than acting first to change or prevent something." Cambridge Dictionary. https://dictionary.cambridge.org/ja/dictionary/english/reactive.

[58.] The term "proactive" refers to "taking action by causing change and not only reacting to change when it happens". https://dictionary.cambridge.org/ja/dictionary/english/proactive.

[59.] The term "assistance" refers to "help, especially money or resources that are given to people, countries, etc. when they have experienced a difficult situation". https://dictionary.cambridge.org/ja/dictionary/english/assistance.

[60.] Cocks, Errol, and Gordon Duffy (1993) *The Nature and Purposes of Advocacy for People with Disabilities.* Parth: Edith Cowan University Publications. 121. https://ro.ecu.edu.au/ecuworks/7172.

of the principal by advocating the equal right to making decisions, focusing on his/her uniqueness as an individual, but with consideration of social relationship as well.

2.3.3 Policy Orientation in East Asia

The discussion elucidates the interrelationship between the values and dimensions intrinsic to Western-style legal and policy frameworks. ADs and ACPs prioritize individual autonomy, thereby facilitating the *Proactive Dimension* and *Advocacy Dimension* and promoting self-advocacy and supported decision-making. The encouragement of participation in measures such as estate planning and ADs serves to uphold individual autonomy and strives for equitable decision-making. The legal system of the West, shaped by the ideals of the Enlightenment, is founded upon the protection of individual freedoms and rights.

In this context, the protection of individual freedoms and rights is enshrined in legislation, with a particular emphasis on the minimization of external interference. The establishment of legal protection for rights is undertaken with the objective of safeguarding individual human rights. In this context, decisions are frequently based on legal legitimacy rather than moral judgment. In the context of end-of-life medical care, the patient's right to make decisions is of the utmost importance. Documents such as living will and ADs are frequently acknowledged by legal systems.

In East Asia, traditional values, as espoused by Confucianism, Taoism, and Buddhism, form the basis of social norms. Individual actions and decisions frequently emphasize *toku* (德, virtue), which can be defined as moral excellence and harmony in human relationships. In this context, the values of harmony and obligations within the family and community are accorded primacy, superseding individual freedoms and rights.

There is a tendency to adhere to moral guidelines rather than legal mandates. Consequently, in the context of end-of-life medical care, traditional values frequently prioritize the preferences of the family and the maintenance of social order. The virtue approach in East Asia emphasizes relationships and harmony. While the legal protection of rights in the West emphasizes individual autonomy and the protection of rights. These approaches are fundamentally distinct, which has a considerable impact on the manner in which end-of-life medical care for the elderly is addressed.

To facilitate a discussion of the context in relation to the modified model, the following analysis is offered for consideration. The distinctive value system of East Asia requires the implementation of legislation and policy that is in accordance with this cultural context. In comparison to Western orientations, East Asians tend to prioritize the social aspects of life. This is currently reflected in their alignment with the *Reactive Dimension*, which is influenced by traditional death taboos. It is therefore imperative that policies facilitate a transition from the *Reactive Dimension* to the *Proactive Dimension* without altering the social orientation of the population.

To facilitate this transition, it is essential that measures are put in place that offer visible benefits, thereby enabling older adults and its stakeholders to understand the merits and providing an incentive for a shift from the *Reactive Dimension* to the *Proactive Dimension*. Moreover, it is of the utmost importance that governments and relevant institutions foster trust through the enactment of laws and policies that guarantee social justice and fairness. The increasing number of older adults in East Asia who live alone and may lack family support underscores the necessity for a transition from the *Assistance Dimension* to the *Advocacy Dimension*.

It is therefore necessary for the government to intervene to address issues such as loneliness, poverty, and self-neglect, as these could otherwise lead to social unrest. Healthcare administration and legislation in East Asia often favor Western-style laws due to academic influences, which creates a gap between policymakers and the general populace. It is therefore crucial to be aware of this gap to avoid policy failures,[61] as evidenced by attempts to counter declining birthrates in Japan and South Korea.[62]

Guiding public policy under the governance of a democratic constitution and the rule of law presents a significant challenge. The only viable approach to provide merits and incentives is to instill confidence that government-advocated policies will universally benefit individuals and stakeholders. Achieving this objective necessitates comprehensive verification and unceasing experimentation to transform setbacks into triumphs.

To date, no government in East Asia has fulfilled these prerequisites. It is hypothesized that collaborative implementation among East Asian countries

---

[61.] Masahiro, Yamada (2020) *Why Did Japan's Measures to Counteract Declining Birthrates Fail? The True Reasons behind the Avoidance of Marriage and Childbirth* [in Japanese]. Tokyo: Kobunsha.

[62.] Kim, M. (2024) "South Korea's Birthrate Is 0.72, Marking the Lowest Level for the Eighth Consecutive Year: Accurate Understanding of the Youth's Mindset and Effective Measures Implementation Needed" [in Japanese] NLI Research Institute, March 4, 2024. https://www.nli-research.co.jp/report/detail/id=77782?site=nli.

and areas will yield more assured and expeditious outcomes than pursuing this journey individually in a single country or area. This book focuses on East Asia as a case study to explore the potential for academic collaboration in the region.

2.4 Notes on Law and Bioethics in Healthcare

This section will examine the way the legal and ethical frameworks of healthcare are integrated as the foundation for its operations, and how they are modified in the context of the East Asian model, with reference to the views of researchers in the field.

Considering the ongoing discourse on autonomy and the East Asian model, it is imperative that healthcare integrate legal and ethical frameworks as the foundation for its operations. The establishment of a normative system is a crucial step in the development of modern healthcare administration. The explicit definition of law and ethics provides a framework for navigating their complexities. The "law" is a component of normative discourses that are considered valid solely based on their enactment,[63] whereas "ethics" is regarded as a field of knowledge that is valid in and of itself, irrespective of whether it has been formally codified. Another normative discourse, "justice," examines the righteousness of "law" and "ethics."[64]

The history of medicine has evolved from a focus on folklore to a scientific approach, with the introduction of autopsies in the nineteenth century. Notwithstanding these advances, the treatment of patients remains a challenging endeavor, with medical ethics playing a pivotal role, as exemplified by the Hippocratic Oath. The formation of modern states has resulted in the emergence of diverse legal systems, including civil and criminal law, as well as specific regulatory frameworks, such as those governing healthcare. The Constitution represents the pinnacle of this legal framework. Laws may be classified as statutory ("hard law"), case law, or policy directions ("soft law"). Natural law constitutes a foundational aspect.

[63.] In accordance with the Cabinet of Japan decision of September 13, 1963, entitled "On the Arrangement of Draft Laws Submitted to the Cabinet," any items that are defined as legal matters in accordance with the relevant legislation and which have a direct bearing on the rights and duties of citizens must be prescribed by law. Oishi, Makoto (2006) "The Cabinet Legislation Bureau's Function in Forming National Order" [in Japanese] *Public Policy Studies* Volume 6, 7–16.

[64.] Nakano, Toshio (2002) "Law and Ethics" [in Japanese] *Sociology of Law* Volume 56, 1–15.

The hierarchy of healthcare laws is established by each state's constitution, statutory laws, medical laws, regulations, guidelines, and bioethics. In instances where legislation or regulatory frameworks are lacking, bioethics, with the support of clinical ethics committees and ethical education, can play a role in addressing these gaps. The four principles of bioethics—autonomy, non-maleficence, beneficence and justice—are of critical importance in the context of American-style bioethics. In contrast, the principles of European-style bioethics encompass four key concepts: autonomy, dignity, integrity and vulnerability.[65]

These three or four principles may give rise to considerations of influence on third parties. Desirable law and ethics in healthcare involve the creation of norms through an iterative process, with international coordination bodies like the World Health Organization ("WHO") influencing national systems. Traditional values exert a profound influence on behavior and thought patterns, particularly in the context of end-of-life care. The adoption of Western legal systems by East Asian countries during the process of modernization may not always align with local customs, particularly in matters of domestic and social life influenced by religion and tradition.

It is therefore imperative that legal systems consider regional traditions and values. It is of the utmost importance that legislation be designed in a manner that accommodates local customs, with the establishment of guidelines that facilitate future amendments. The effective provision of end-of-life care requires collaboration and information exchange between countries and areas. The pursuit of a balance between legal and ethical considerations represents a shared objective, with ethics finding common ground at the national level, while hard and soft laws vary by country or area, allowing shared issues and solutions. Furthermore, as social environments evolve over time and medical technology advances, the design of law and ethics must evolve in tandem.

In Japan, Tetsuro Shimizu puts forth three ethical principles: The first principle is that of human respect, which entails treating others as individuals with inherent dignity and worth. The second is the principle of benefit, which requires that actions be taken with the intention of benefiting others and avoiding harm. The third is the principle of social appropriateness, which stipulates that actions

---

[65] Beauchamp, T. L., and J. F. Childress (2001) *Principles of Biomedical Ethics*. 5th ed. Oxford: Oxford University Press; Okinaga, Takako (2022) "Bioethics Theory" [in Japanese] in Takayoshi Tsukada and Kazuhiko Maeda (eds), *Bioethics and Medical Law*. 3rd ed. Tokyo: Iryokagakusha. 39–40.; Fox, Renée C. (1990) *The Evolution of American Bioethics: A Sociological Perspective: Social Science Perspectives on Medical Ethics*. Dordrecht: Springer; Yonemura, Shigeto (n.a.) "For the Cooperation of Medical Science, Ethics and the Law" [in Japanese] The Graduate School of Law, The Tohoku University. chrome-extension://efaidnbmnnnibpcajpcglclefindmkaj/ https://web.tohoku.ac.jp/hondou/files/psj-4.pdf.

should be aligned with the norms and expectations of the social context.[66] The meanings of the three principles are largely consistent with those proposed by Beauchamp. However, Shimizu expresses them in Japanese, which facilitates comprehension for the Japanese audience.

While Norio Higuchi presents a discussion on the necessity for the application of both hard and soft law to the field of healthcare. This is based on the understanding that there is currently a lack of clarity regarding the extent to which legislation should apply in the context of Japanese medicine. Furthermore, Higuchi puts forth the argument that there are discrepancies between the perspectives of lawyers and healthcare practitioners on the matter of the law. Consequently, it is not advantageous for both parties to legislate as extensively as possible in the field of healthcare.[67]

In this discussion, Shigeaki Tanaka addresses the role of legal involvement in bioethics from a legal theory perspective.[68] Tanaka's analysis concentrates on the interconnection between self-determination, or individual autonomy, and social consensus. While respect for the individual's right to self-determination is of primary importance in the legal response to bioethics, it is evident that the consent of those involved, social consensus, and public decision-making have an interactive influence on each other.

The involvement of law in bioethics serves to facilitate consensus-building between public and private forums, enabling the mutual coordination of the elements.[69] Tanaka identifies three categories of legalization in bioethics: autonomous legislation (i.e., legislation and judicial precedents), administrative legislation (i.e., administrative guidelines), and self-governing legislation (i.e., self-regulation of academic societies and industry, ethics committees of universities, research, and medical institutions).

Tanaka puts forth the proposition that the immediate objective is to activate the multilayered and multidimensional consensus-building forums, including various voluntary forums, with the aim of strengthening consensus-building channels

---

[66.] Shimizu, Tetsuro (2013) "Origin and Essence of Caring in Healthcare: A Logical Investigation" [in Japanese] *Journal of Japan Academy of Nursing Science* Volume 33 Issue 2, 101–103.

[67.] Higuchi, Norio (2005) "The Role of Legalization and Norms in Medicine: Under- and Over-Law" [in Japanese] in H. Shiroyama and T. Yamamoto (eds), *Environment and Life: Melting Boundaries Transcending Law* volume 5. Tokyo: University of Tokyo Press. 139–180. Higuchi, Norio (2022) "Reading the World Medical Association's Code of Ethics (Latest 2022 Edition)" *Law Association Journal* Volume 140 Issue 8, 1013–1040.

[68.] Tanaka, Shigeaki (2004) "On the Legal Involvement in Bioethics" [in Japanese] in Shigeaki Tanaka (ed), *Perspectives on Modern Law: Aspects of Self-Determination*. Tokyo: Yuhikaku Publishing. 131–175; Inoue, Shigeru (1981) *Philosophy of Law* [in Japanese]. Tokyo: Iwanami Shoten Publishers.

[69.] Ibid.

based on a bottom-up approach from clinical settings.[70] This challenge may result in a shift away from the conventional administrative-led top-down approach. The perspective proposed by Tanaka aligns with the "practical approach," which will be further elucidated in Section 6.1 of Chapter 6.

The legislative framework in the medical field in Japan is not yet sufficiently developed.[71] In lieu of legislation, administrative guidelines and notices have been employed with greater frequency. It is thus imperative to develop a reasonable combination of legal and nonlegal materials in the medical field in order to respond effectively to social changes. These should include administrative guidelines, recommendations from academic societies, ethical committee recommendations (i.e., materials for reasoning outside of legal provisions, case law, and legal principles), and materials on ethics in the medical domain. While the weight of each regulatory framework differs by country or area in East Asia, the basic design of the regulatory combination is seen to be the same.

In particular, in East Asia, in addition to the aforementioned legal and nonlegal materials, as well as ethics in the medical domain, traditional values such as *toku* (virtue) exert considerable influence in the social domain. This can be defined as optimal moral conduct and the establishment of harmonious human relationships. In this context, the values of harmony and obligations within the family and community are accorded primacy, superseding individual freedoms and rights in legal, nonlegal, and ethical matters. This is the context in which the shared, underlying characteristics and background factors pertaining to legislation and policy in East Asia can be understood.

[70.] Ibid.

[71.] In response to the question of why medical law has not been sufficiently legislated, Megumu Yokono offers the following explanation at the online seminar held on December 17, 2023 at Kyoto University: There is minimal debate on the law, which is typically left to the domain of medical ethics; there is no Court of Human Rights system, in contrast to the European context, and there is limited external pressure; There is a dearth of interest, not only among politicians but also among citizens; the legislative approach to matters of a private nature is characterized by a lack of robust enforcement; there is also a lack of a legal infrastructure; while the views of legal scholars and ethicists are given due consideration, the opinions of the public are largely ignored.

CHAPTER 3

ADs and ACP in the International Context

This chapter explores the creation and evolution of ADs globally, analyzing their limitations and potential improvements in various legal and healthcare contexts. It examines how different countries have addressed challenges in AD implementation, highlighting efforts to enhance their effectiveness and accessibility. The discussion then shifts to a review of ADs in Asia, considering regional legal frameworks, cultural attitudes, and policy developments. Additionally, the chapter explores the global discourse on voluntary assisted dying (VAD), situating it within the broader ethical and legal landscape of end-of-life decision-making.

3.1 Origins and Types of Advance Directives

3.1.1 Historical Background of ADs

A review of the historical context reveals that the relationship between physicians and patients was a pivotal issue during the American civil rights movement of the 1960s. The prevailing view was that patients should not be compelled to accept the decisions of physicians but should have the right to choose their own medical treatment. This shift in perspective was driven by the growing recognition among physicians that obtaining informed consent[1] from patients before performing invasive medical procedures was crucial.

While the patient's medical consent is of great importance, it is crucial to recognize that in the event of the patient losing their mental capacity to make

---

[1.] "Informed consent" involves a healthcare provider explaining the risks, benefits, and alternatives of a procedure to a patient. The patient must have the necessary knowledge and capacity to make an autonomous decision about the procedure. In the United States, informed consent is both an ethical and legal duty of healthcare practitioners, based on the patient's right to control their medical treatment. National Library of Medicine (2023) "Informed Consent". https://www.ncbi.nlm.nih.gov/books/NBK430827/.

decisions for any reason, they will no longer be able to provide medical consent. To address this issue, a legal document was created that allows the patient to express their wishes in advance and to give instructions to physicians even if they lose the mental capacity to make decisions. Louis Kutner, who proposed such a legal document, stated the following passage in a 1969 article:

> The suggested solution is that the individual, while fully in control of his faculties and his ability to express himself, indicate to what extent he would consent to treatment.[2] The document indicating such consent may be referred to as "a living will," "a declaration determining the termination of life," "testament permitting death," "declaration for bodily autonomy," "declaration for ending treatment," "body trust," or other similar reference.....The document would be notarized and attested to by at least two witnesses who would affirm that the maker was of sound mind and acted of his own free will. The individual could always carry the document on the person, while the spouse, a physician, a lawyer or confidant would have the original copy.

ADs were created because the development of medical technology such as ventilators has made it possible to maintain life support for patients who have lost consciousness, so it is necessary to decide whether to maintain life-support measures for patients in a prolonged vegetative state. This is because a medical dispute has arisen as to whether to continue or suspend treatment.[3]

3.1.2 Karen Ann Quinlan Case and Afterword

A representative medical dispute in the U.S. is the Karen Ann Quinlan case (i.e., Judgment of the Supreme Court of New Jersey, March 31, 1976). Karen (age 21 at the time), who ingested alcohol and drugs, suffered serious brain damage, fell into a coma, and entered a persistent vegetative state. Then, a lawsuit was filed by her family in court asking for the treatment to be suspended. In the 1976 judgment, based on the person's right to privacy, if the person's prognosis cannot

---

[2.] The paragraph refers to Kutner, Louis (1969) "Due Process of Euthanasia: The Living Will, a Proposal" *Indiana Law Journal* Volume 44 Issue 4, 539–554, 551. https://www.repository.law.indiana.edu/ilj/vol44/iss4/2/.

[3.] Ishida, Hitomi (2020) "Legal Aspects of ACP" [in Japanese] *Takaoka Law Review* Volume 38, 123–157. https://doi.org/10.24703/takahogaku.38.0_123; Kamei, Ryuta (2015) "Patient Advance Directives: Focusing on the Relationship with Civil Law" *Chiba University Law Review* Volume 30 Issue 1–2, 370 (277)–324 (323).

be expected to recover, the person has the right to refuse life support, and the court determined the following points.[4]

- Discharge Thomas R. Curtin, Esquire, as Karen Quinlan's guardian and thank him for his service. Appoint Joseph Quinlan as her guardian with the authority to choose her treating physicians.
- If Karen's guardian and family agree, and her attending physicians conclude there is no reasonable possibility of her emerging from her coma to a cognitive state, they should consult with the hospital's ethics committee.
- If the ethics committee agrees, the life-support system may be withdrawn without civil or criminal liability for any participant, including the guardian, physicians, and hospital.

The State of New Jersey prosecutors did not appeal this decision, and the judgment became final (April 6, 1976). Pursuant to this ruling, Karen was removed from life support (May 16, 1976) and transferred from St. Clare's Hospital in Denville, NJ, to a hospice Morris View Nursing Home (June 9, 1976). Karen continued to live on her own for nine years and died on June 11, 1985.[5] This medical dispute was settled by a court granting a refusal of medical treatment based on the patient's right to refuse the physician's life-support treatment, but the patient continued to live on her own for a considerable period after the life-support machine was removed. It can be said that her life expectancy far exceeded the expectations of her physicians.

As an impetus, each state in the U.S. enacted a natural death act, such as the California's Natural Death Act of 1976, which stipulates that a person can choose to die naturally based on their own will under certain conditions. A living will loses its legal effect when the principal's capacity to make decisions declines and the person becomes unable to explain the contents of the living will.[6] For this reason, the living will turned out to be legally useless in practice.

[4.] JUSTIA US Law, In Re Quinlan, 70 NJ 10 (1976), 355 A.2d 647, The Matter of Karen Quinlan, an Alleged Incompetent. The Supreme Court of New Jersey. Decided March 31, 1976. https://law.justia.com/cases/new-jersey/supreme-court/1976/70-n-j-10-0.html.

[5.] United Press International (UPI) (1985) "Chronology of Karen Ann Quinlan's Life" *UPI Archives*, June 12, 1985. https://www.upi.com/Archives/1985/06/12/Chronology-of-Karen-Ann-Quinlans-life/2454487396800/.

[6.] In Japan, an alternative interpretation of Article 111 of the Civil Code argues that a power of attorney contract is void upon the delegator's death. In contrast, the power of attorney remains valid even if the delegator loses capacity. This interpretation follows the older German civil code and differs from the approach in Anglo-American law.

Therefore, a document was developed in which the legal effect of the mandate contract persists even after the mandator's capacity to decide has diminished. This is called durable power of attorney, and it is a legal document that appoints an agent in advance to make legal decisions for asset management on behalf of the principal and is valid until the principal dies.

It is said that a similar legal document for medical directives is called an AD. The ADs spread to every state in the U.S., and legislation to regulate ADs was developed. Although the introduction of ADs has not resolved, medical disputes regarding the pros and cons of life-sustaining treatment, the individual's wishes have a certain influence on medical treatment decisions by ADs.

In the case of CRUZAN by *Cruzan v. Harmon*, 760 S.W. 2d 408 (MO. Banc 1988), the Supreme Court of Missouri, En Banc, ruled that parents or other legal guardians lack authority to require that food and water be withheld from a comatose daughter who has no cognitive brain function but is neither dead nor terminally ill.[7] In light of this ruling, the majority opinion was that a decision to cease treatment for a patient lacking legal capacity must be based on clear evidence that the individual in question has previously made such a decision. ADs play a role in supporting this.

Then, advance medical directives have spread from the U.S. to all over the world, and according to a recent survey, in Eurasia, from East Asia to Turkey, countries and areas without ADs legislation and guidelines are Saudi Arabia, Pakistan, Macao, China, and Japan. In East Asia, South Korea, Taiwan, Hong Kong, and Singapore have systems of ADs.

South Korea and Taiwan, influenced by the U.S., have been active in enacting end-of-life care legislation (i.e., South Korea: Hospice and Palliative Care Act and 2016 Decision on Life-Extending Treatment for Terminal Patients; Taiwan: Hospice and Palliative Care Act 2000/Patients Autonomy Act 2019). Singapore has the Advance Medical Directives Act 1996. In recent years, the number of users of LPA has increased, and there are plans to integrate the digital data of EPA and ACP so that healthcare professionals can effectively use ACP in the future. Hong Kong has guidelines for ACP.

In Europe, each country has ADs legislation, but its contents are not uniform. Therefore, the European Law Institute (ELI; Vienna) is proceeding with a project aiming to create a European model law for advance choices in Europe.

[7.] Casetext "Cruzan, by Cruzan v. Harmon". https://law.justia.com/cases/missouri/supreme-court/1988/70813-0. html; Masuda, Yuichiro, and Akihisa Iguchi (1998) "The Current Status of the 'Patient's Right to Die' in the US: With a Focus on the Advance Directive" [in Japanese] *Overseas Social Security News* Volume Spring Issue 118, 29–44; Weinmeyer, Richard (2013) "Legal Constraints on Pursuit of a 'Good Death'" *Virtual Mentor* Volume 13 Issue 12, 1056–1061. https://doi.org/10.1001/virtualmentor.2013.15.12.hlaw1-1312.

3.2 Limitations and Criticisms of ADs and ACP

3.2.1 SUPPORT Study

In 1989–1994, a large-scale fact-finding survey of ADs for 9,105 critically ill older patients in the U.S. (i.e., Study to Understand Prognoses and Preference for Outcomes and Risks of Treatments [SUPPORT]) was conducted.[8] Phase I of the study found that healthcare professionals were not very proactive in preparing ADs for end-of-life care. Therefore, when healthcare professionals were given training on the preparation of ADs at Phase II, the rate of preparation of ADs improved, but there was almost no actual result of fulfilling the wishes of patients. Increasing opportunities for patient–physician communication has been advocated to improve the outcome of medical procedures for patients but is insufficient to change the established practices of healthcare practitioners.

The observational phase of the study concluded that greater individual and societal involvement and more aggressive and stronger measures are needed to improve the treatment of critically ill older patients. The flaw with ADs is that even though the AD system has been enacted, knowledge of ADs is not shared equally among patients, healthcare professionals, and related parties, and conventional medical treatment practices continue in medical settings. Behind this is an irreversible gap in position and perception between healthcare professionals and patients, and various factors that arise from this gap have led to the implementation of ADs not being as successful as expected.

Furthermore, it has become apparent that ADs frequently encounter a conflict of interest regarding medical law and ethics in clinical settings. ADs are legally recognized documents, and medical doctors are obliged to respect the patient's expressed wishes. However, medical doctors are permitted to refuse to carry out the patient's expressed wishes if they have a conscientious objection or consider them to be medically inappropriate.[9]

The National Institute on Aging (U.S.) states that "An advance directive is legally recognized but not legally binding. It is important to note that while your healthcare provider and proxy will endeavor to respect your ADs, there

---

[8.] Connors, Alfred F., Jr., N. V. Dawson, N. A. Desbiens, et al. (1995) "A Controlled Trial to Improve Care for Seriously Ill Hospitalized Patients: The Study to Understand Prognoses and Preferences for Outcomes and Risks of Treatments (SUPPORT)—The SUPPORT Principal Investigators" *JAMA* Volume 274 Issue 20, 1591–1598. Erratum in: *JAMA* Volume 275 Issue 16, 1232. PMID: 7474243.

[9.] Sabatino, Charles (2015) "Myths and Facts about Health Care Advance Directives" *Bifocal* Volume 37 Issue 1. https://www.americanbar.org/groups/law_aging/publications/bifocal/vol_37/issue_1_october2015/myths_and_facts_advance_directives/.

may be circumstances in which they are unable to adhere to your wishes in their entirety."[10] Medical doctors are bound by the law and medical ethics, including medical society guidelines, the institution's policy, and their accepted healthcare standards. In the event of a conflict between a medical decision and an AD, the medical decision prevails by law or medical ethics. Medical doctors make decisions based on the updated diagnosis of the patient, which may differ from the patient's initial expectations. This demonstrates the inherent limitations of ADs.

3.2.2 The Advancement of ADs

It has been improved that ADs include "Do Not Attempt Resuscitate" ("DNAR"), which instructs in advance not to resuscitate a person in the event of cardiopulmonary arrest, and an advance statement, which illustrates the person's beliefs and values in documents. Although advance statements are not legally binding, they may be useful in estimating the person's intentions based on the beliefs and values expressed in the statements when considering the choice of life-support measures.

In addition, Physician Orders for Life-Sustaining Treatment ("POLST") has been proposed, in which physicians take the lead in listening to the intentions of patients and their family members and determining the policy for life-sustaining treatment for patients in advance, and standard formats have been developed for this purpose.

In all healthcare institutions in La Crosse County with a population of 50,000, the State of Wisconsin, the U.S., comprehensive interventions have been implemented since 1993. Consequently, there has been an increase in the frequency of creating ADs. Within this context, the implementation of POLST is being advocated. This is called a "Respecting Choices" study.[11] Amid these attempts derived from ADs, a procedural method was devised that focuses on the decision-making process of both physicians and patients given the relationship between them. This is called ACP.

[10.] National Institute on Aging (NIA) (2022) "Advance Care Planning: Advance Directives for Health Care" October 31, 2022. https://www.nia.nih.gov/health/advance-care-planning/advance-care-planning-advance-directives-health-care.

[11.] Forlini, J., and L. Goldberg (2014) *"Respecting Choices*: A Case Study for Incorporating Advance Care Planning into Person and Family-Centered Health Care Delivery" *Health Policy Brief—National Academy of Social Insurance* Volume 9, 1–3. https://www.nasi.org/wp-content/uploads/2014/02/Health_Policy_Brief_09.pdf.

ACP is defined as "the ability to enable individuals to define goals and preferences for future medical treatment and care, to discuss these goals and preferences with family and healthcare providers, and to record and review these preferences if appropriate."[12] It refers to a series of processes that review the preparation of legal documents in anticipation of aging by the person concerned. This is the method recommended by elder law that has been developed in the U.S. since the 1980s.[13] A characteristic of ACP is that the patient, his/her family members, and the healthcare professionals form an agreement through discussion, rather than the physician or the patient/family members unilaterally preparing legal documents. It emphasizes a decision-making process based on the trust of the parties involved.

In medicine, this is called shared decision-making, and it advocates a process in which physicians discuss and jointly decide on medical treatments with their patients. However, looking at the current situation, in the countries/areas that have implemented ADs and ACP systems, the utilization rate of these methods is not as high as expected. A report in the State of Victoria, Australia, states that many people other than the patients fill out ADs on behalf of the patients, and it is sometimes unclear whether the ADs reflect the patients' wishes, resulting in confusion in hospitals.[14] Even in the U.S., where the utilization rate of ADs is said to be as high as about 37%,[15] there is an opinion that the ACP does not make sense.[16] In Taiwan, the usage rate of ADs is only 3.1% of the national population in 2018.[17]

---

[12] Rietjens, J. A. C., R. L. Sudore, M. Connolly, et al. (2017) "Definition and Recommendations for Advance Care Planning: An International Consensus Supported by the European Association for Palliative Care" *Lancet Oncology* Volume 18 Issue 9, 543–551. PMID: 28884703. https://doi.org/10.1016/S1470-2045(17)30582-X.

[13] Seki, Fusako (2018) "End-of-Life Care in the United States: Decision-Making Support Seen in Hospice Care" [in Japanese] *Comparative Law Research* No. 80, 7–25.

[14] Buck, Kimberly, L. Nolte, M. Sellars, et al. (2021) "Advance Care Directive Prevalence among Older Australians and Associations with Person-Level Predictors and Quality Indicators" *Health Expectations* Volume 24 Issue 4, 1312–1325. https://doi.org/10.1111/hex.13264.

[15] Yadav, Kuldeep N., N. B. Gabler, E. Cooney, et al. (2017) "Approximately One in Three US Adults Completes Any Type of Advance Directive for End-of-Life Care" *Health Affairs* Volume 36 Issue 7, 1244–1251.

[16] Morrison et al. mention that "ACP does not improve end-of-life care, nor does its documentation serve as a reliable and valid quality indicator of an end-of-life discussion." Morrison, R. Sean, D. E. Meier, R. M. Arnold, et al. (2021) "What's Wrong with Advance Care Planning?" *JAMA* Volume 326 Issue 16, 1575–1576. https://doi.org/10.1001/jama.2021.16430.

[17] Tsai, Hsiao Ying (2022) "The Influence of Familism on Taiwan's Advance Care Planning (ACP) for End-of-Life" *Journal of the Japanese Society of Nursing Ethics* Volume 14 Issue 1, 48–51. https://www.jstage.jst.go.jp/article/jjne/14/1/14_20211011/_pdf.

3.3 Comparison and Evaluation of ADs across Asia

In greater Asia covering from Japan to Turkey, countries without legislation or guidelines regarding ADs are Saudi Arabia, Pakistan, Macau, China, and Japan.[18] A book has been published based on the international conference on ADs over Asia organized by the editors and held online between September 30 and October 2, 2020. The book categorizes jurisdictions into three categories as described at Table 3.1: "well-regulated" (jurisdictions with AD legislation), "semi-regulated" (jurisdictions with quasi-legislation such as guidelines), and "nonregulated" (jurisdictions without AD legislation or guidelines).

Table 3.1: Types of Advance Directives in Greater Asia

Typology	Definitions	Applicable Country/Area
Well-Regulated	Jurisdictions with a clear set of legal rules on or encompassing ADs.	Israel, Singapore, South Korea, Taiwan, Thailand, India
Semi-Regulated	Jurisdictions with other forms of regulation on ADs, including regulations via official regulatory documents and practical guidelines or other forms of guidance from professional societies.	Hong Kong, Iran, Malaysia, Philippines, Turkey
Non-Regulated	Jurisdictions where there might be, at best, broad principles contained in legislation or guidelines around healthcare that stress the importance of patient preferences in general terms, but no regulation or guidance related that connects to ADs specifically.	Japan, China, Macau, Pakistan, Saudi Arabia

Source: Cheung and Dunn (2023).[19]

[18.] Cheung, D., and M. Dunn (eds), (2023) *Advance Directives across Asia: A Comparative Socio-Legal Analysis.* Cambridge: Cambridge University Press. 311.

[19.] Ibid., 13–14.

Notwithstanding Japan's categorization as a nonregulated entity with a nonexistent, clearly defined set of guidelines for ADs, efforts to respond to the needs of older adults are ongoing and distinctive. Healthcare professionals are not bound by regulatory constraints and dedicate their time to listening to the requests of terminally ill older adults for medical care and consulting with their families or the managers of care facilities for older adults. They demonstrate a growing interest in ADs and ACP, and known as a "life conference," are increasingly incorporating these concepts into their medical practice.

A significant number of local governments in Japan have introduced recommendations for the completion of an "ending note" or "end-of-life planning note," which is a nonlegal personal document designed to clarify the wishes of older adults. In some cases, local governments have provided templates of ADs to citizens, with the aim of encouraging their voluntary preparation. In Yokosuka City, for instance, city officials have been visiting the homes of older adults who live alone and have no relatives to rely on, offering consultation and support for funerals, burials, and living will.[20] Nevertheless, the question of the legalization of ADs has yet to be openly debated at the national level.

Some Asian countries have established ADs, which function to some extent. Consequently, differences in traditional background between Asia and Western countries may have a limited impact on medical care and asset management. In other words, legislators and/or the government can introduce ADs and associated proactive planning in legislation or policy if they consider it to be a priority. This can be attributed to the influence of governmental and legislative policy.

While a study conducted in the state of New South Wales (NSW), Australia, a country with a multicultural society, revealed that the cultural background indicated by the region of birth of the individual in question resulted in variations in the rate of preparation of ADs and the description of the person themselves or a third party. This discrepancy pertains to the rate of preparation.[21] This suggests that patients or care consumers are subject to the influence of cultural factors associated with their region of birth.

ADs or ACP need to clarify "who will operate it, for what purpose, and how." In the U.S., where this system was devised, it would be organized as the parties entrust lawyers to prepare legal documents in order to realize individual autonomy,

---

[20.] Yokosuka City (2023) "Yokosuka City Ending Plan Support Business" [in Japanese]. https://www.city.yokosuka.kanagawa.jp/2610/syuukatusien/endingplan-support.html.

[21.] Sinclair, Craig, M. Sellars, K. Buck, et al. (2021) "Association between Region of Birth and Advance Care Planning Documentation among Older Australian Migrant Communities: A Multicenter Audit Study" *The Journals of Gerontology: Series B* Volume 76 Issue 1, 109. https://doi.org/10.1093/geronb/gbaa127.

but in Japan, it can be summarized that the parties repeatedly consult with relatives, medical doctors, and other people around them, and record their wishes verbally or in nonlegally binding documents (i.e., ending note or end-of-life planning note) to obtain the best choice. The ultimate difference between the two lies in whether the document used is legally binding. After observations, it can be assumed that each nation's people have their own method, regardless of whether it is legally binding or not, to clarify the will and preferences of the individual in their end-of-life care.

3.4 International Response to Voluntary Assisted Dying

3.4.1 Recent Development of VAD

This book does not address the issue of Voluntary Assisted Dying (VAD) in ADs or ACP. VAD is a discrete topic, though it is occasionally referenced in discussions pertaining to end-of-life decisions. This passage offers a concise overview of recent developments in VAD.[22] In the international context, the responses of medical doctors to assisted dying vary by country.[23] In contrast to Singapore, which criminalizes both suicide and assisted dying (Article 308 of the Penal Code, up to 10 years imprisonment and fine), the latter is also prohibited in Article 202, the Penal Code of Japan.

A number of countries, states, and regions have enacted legislation pertaining to this issue. These include over 10 U.S. states including Oregon in 1996, the Netherlands in 2001, Belgium in 2002, Luxembourg in 2009, and Canadian provinces in 2016, as well as the Australian State of Victoria in 2017, Queensland and Taiwan in 2018, New Zealand and Western Australia in 2019, South Australia and Tasmania in 2021, Spain and New South Wales in 2022, Portugal in 2023, and the Australian Capital Territory (2024).

In certain countries, case law has permitted what is known as "unselfish assisted suicide" (Switzerland, 2019), while in others, constitutional courts have ruled that physicians may assist patients in dying (Italy, 2019; Austria, 2020; Colombia, 2022). Since 2016, VAD has been disseminated across countries by means of legislative or judicial enactment. Table 3.2 provides a summary of the responses of developed countries to the forms of assisted dying.

[22.] A debate is currently underway in Japan regarding the potential introduction of legislation to regulate VADs: Asai, A., T. Okita, Y. Shimakura, et al. (2023) "Japan Should Initiate the Discussion on Voluntary Assisted Dying Legislation Now" *BMC Medical Ethics* Volume 24 Issue 1, 5. https://doi.org/10.1186/s12910-023-00886-0.

[23.] SWI Swissinfo.ch (2023) "Which Countries Adopt Euthanasia?" [in Japanese] January 31, 2023. https://www.swissinfo.ch/jpn/society/%E5%AE%89%E6%A5%BD%E6%AD%BB%E3%81%8C%E8%AA%8D%E3%82%81%E3%82%89%E3%82%8C%E3%81%A6%E3%81%84%E3%82%8B%E5%9B%BD%E3%81%AF%E3%81%A9%E3%81%93/47739244. White, B. P. (Ed.) (2025) *Research Handbook on Voluntary Assisted Dying Law, Regulation and Practice.* Edward Elgar Publishing.

Table 3.2: Countries' Responses to Voluntary Assisted Dying

Typology	*Countries / States / Area*
Legislation	Oregon (1996),[24] Netherlands (2001), Belgium (2002), Luxembourg (2009), Canada (2016), Victoria (2017), Queensland (2018), New Zealand / West Australia (2019), South Australia / Tasmania (2021), Spain / NSW (2022), Portugal (2023),[25] and the Australian Capital Territory (2024)[26]
Judicial Precedent	Switzerland (2019 Acceptance of "unselfish assisted dying," publication of academic guidelines)
Decision of the Constitutional Court	Italy (2019),[27] Austria (2020),[28] and Colombia (2022)[29]
Bill rejected by parliament	England and Wales (2013/2015)[30, 31]
Illegal	Singapore (Article 308 Penal Code)

Source: Created by the author based on reference materials.[32]

---

[24] American situation: Suzuki, Carol M. (2019) "The Pursuit of Dignified Death for Competent Terminally Ill Persons in the United States" *Journal of Clinical Ethics* Volume 7, 60–73.

[25] In Portugal, an assisted dying bill was passed in parliament in 2019, but the president vetoed it and failed to make it into law in 2021. Finally, it was enacted in 2023. Japan, The National Diet Library, "Short Message [Portuguese] Legalization of Euthanasia" [in Japanese] Reference to Foreign Legislation No. 297-1 [in Japanese].

[26] Jeanneret, R., and S. Prince (2024) "Nurses and Voluntary Assisted Dying: How the Australian Capital Territory's Law Could Change the Australian Regulatory Landscape" *Journal of Bioethical Inquiry* Volume 21, 393–399. https://doi.org/10.1007/s11673-024-10370-y.

[27] In 2017, Italy introduced legislation on informed consent and ADs for health treatments, including lifesaving ones. On September 25, 2019, the Italian Constitutional Court ruled (242/2019) allowing individuals meeting certain criteria to request assisted dying. This led to Italy's first case of voluntary assisted dying, following the Court's decision. Delogu, G., D. Morena, V. Tortorella, et al. (2024) "First Case of Medically Assisted Suicide in Italy Set New Legal Perspectives" *Clinical Therapeutics* Volume 175 Issue 1, 7–10. https://doi.org/10.7417/CT.2024.5026. PMID: 38358470.

[28] The Austrian Constitutional Court ruled on December 11, 2020 that it is unconstitutional to ban all forms of assisted dying, while maintaining aiding suicide as a crime under the Austrian Criminal Code.

[29] In Colombia, euthanasia for terminally ill patients was decriminalized in 1997. In July 2021, euthanasia was also decriminalized for terminally ill patients experiencing severe physical and mental distress. In May 2022, the Constitutional Court approved assisted dying, allowing patients to take a lethal drug prescribed by a doctor to commit suicide.

[30] During the 2015 debate on the Assisted Dying Bill in the British Parliament, religious organizations, including the Church of England and Jewish, Islamic, and Sikh groups, collectively sent a letter to oppose the bill's passage. Herring, Jonathan (2022) *Medical Law and Ethics*. 9th ed. Oxford: Oxford University Press. 560–621, 604.

In 2020, the Federal Constitutional Court of Germany delivered a noteworthy ruling, establishing the right to assist voluntary dying for others. The German Federal Penal Code, Article 217, stipulates that the provision of assistance to another individual with the intention of facilitating his/her own death for financial gain is prohibited. On February 26, 2020, the Federal Constitutional Court ruled that the aforementioned section of Article 217 is unconstitutional and void. This signifies that the Federal Basic Acts recognize the rights to assist in the voluntary dying of another person for financial gain.[33]

In East Asia, in South Korea, the ruling and opposition parties were engaged in deliberations regarding an assisted dying bill, although consensus has yet to be reached. Several countries that have not yet enacted legislation on VAD have nevertheless introduced other forms such as living will, ADs, and ACP. Taiwan has enacted legislation concerning ADs and ACP; however, it has not legalized VAD yet.[34]

The acceptance of foreign nationals for VAD is at the discretion of a nonprofit organization run by Swiss medical doctors. Consequently, it is reasonable to posit that the case law interpretation of "unselfish assisted suicide" may become more rigorous in the future. As euthanasia tourism becomes more prevalent, other countries with more lenient legislation may consider implementing different regulatory frameworks, one that prohibits and another that permits. It has been suggested that international nongovernmental organizations (NGOs), such as Dignitas and Go Gentle Australia, are driving the legislative and legal developments surrounding VAD in various countries.

3.4.2 A Case Study in the State of Victoria

It is a challenge to evaluate how VAD is implemented in each country based on laws, case law, and decisions of the Constitutional Court without examining its

---

[31.] The Terminally Ill Adults (End of Life) Bill 2024–25 has its second reading on November 29, 2024. The text of the bill has not yet been published. UK Parliament (2024). https://commonslibrary.parliament.uk/research-briefings/cbp-10123/. The VAD bill of England and Wales was approved by parliament on November 29, 2024. However, it still requires the approval of the House of Lords. Following its enactment, a two-year implementation period has been set aside for preparation, and it will take time for the bill to become operational. *The Guardian* (2024) "What Happens Next after MPs' Vote in Favour of Assisted Dying Bill?" November 29, 2024. https://www.theguardian.com/society/2024/nov/29/what-happens-next-assisted-dying-bill.

[32.] Tanaka, Miho, and Satoshi Kodama (2021) "Outline of Legal Systems and Data regarding Euthanasia in Foreign Countries Version 1" [in Japanese] Japan Medical Association Research Institute Working Paper. https://www.jmari.med.or.jp/result/report/post-3303/.

[33.] Tayama, Teruaki (2024) "Judgement of the Federal Constitutional Court on 26 February 2020" [in Japanese] *Quarterly Comparative Guardianship Law* Volume 21, 3–71.

[34.] Tsai (n 17); Buletsa, S. B. (2019) "Features of Euthanasia in Eastern Asia Countries" in *Jurisprudence Issues in the Development of Legal Literacy and Legal Awareness of Citizens*, edited by Sabina Grabowska, Joanna Marszałek-Kawa, and Tetiana Kolomoiets. Chapter 2, 17–37. Liha Press. http://catalog.liha-pres.eu/index.php/liha-pres/catalog/view/59/660/3554-1; In Japan, some medicine researcher and clinicians ask for consideration of VAD act. see Asai (n 22).

track record. Therefore, the legislative case of the State of Victoria, Australia is briefly extracted.[35]

The rationale for examining Victorian legislation here is that the Act is perceived as aiming to facilitate VAD in a strictly cautious and conservative manner, with certain reasonable requirements for patients and medical doctors. This character-ization is perceived as being more aligned with the characteristics of East Asian people. Victoria's VAD Act of 2017 was enacted on November 29, 2017, and came into force on June 9, 2019.[36] The law is modeled after the law of the state of Oregon, U.S., with comprehensive safeguards and rigorous review procedures.[37]

VAD is for competent Victorians aged 18 or over who have lived in Victoria for at least 12 months. It is a statutory requirement for persons suffering from an incurable, advanced, and progressive disease or condition that is causing intolerable suffering.[38] Therefore, non-Victorian citizens and older adults with dementia who do not have adequate decision-making capacity are not eligible to access the law. The patient's medical condition is judged by two medical doctors, including one specialist, and cases where the patient's death is expected within six months are considered.

A third-party independent body, the Voluntary Assisted Dying Review Board, monitors and reviews activities under the law. From June 2019 to June 2023, a total of 912 deaths were attributed to the ingestion of prescription drugs, with an average of 218 deaths per annum.[39] Since June 2019, 2,203 individuals have qualified for assisted voluntary dying, 1,527 of whom have been issued permits, 912 of whom have died under the Act. Following the enactment of this law, five other states in Australia successively enacted VAD laws within five years.[40]

[35.] Regarding legislative process of the VAD law, see Willmott, L., and B. P. White (2021) "The Challenging Path to Voluntary Assisted Dying Law Reform in Australia: Victoria as a Successful Case Study" in L. Willmott and B. P. White (eds), *International Perspectives on End-of-Life Law Reform*. Cambridge: Cambridge University Press.

[36.] Ries, Nola M., and Elise Mansfield (2022) "Supported Decision-Making: A Good Idea in Principle but We Need to Consider Supporting Decisions about Voluntary Assisted Dying" in Daniel J. Fleming and David J. Carter (eds), *Voluntary Assisted Dying: Law? Health? Justice?* Canberra: ANU Press. 49.

[37.] Interview with an officer of Victorian Department of Health and Human Services by the author (Melbourne, March 12, 2019).

[38.] The State of Victoria is currently undertaking the legislated five-year review, which is operational. Once the Centre for Evaluation and Research Evidence has conducted targeted stakeholder consultations and the review has concluded, the Minister for Health will present a report containing the key findings to both Houses of Parliament in 2024. Australia, Department of Health Victoria (2024) "Voluntary Assisted Dying" April 30, 2024. https://www.health.vic.gov.au/voluntary-assisted-dying/about.

[39.] Australia, Victorian Voluntary Assisted Dying Review Board (2023) "Annual Report: July 2022 to June 2023." chrome-extension://efaidnbmnnnibpcajpcglclefindmkaj/https://www.safercare.vic.gov.au/sites/default/files/2023-08/VADRB%20Annual%20Report%202022-23.pdf.

[40.] Minami, Takako (2022) "Progress of Voluntary Assisted Dying Legislation and the Characteristics of State Legal Systems in Australia" [in Japanese] *Journal of Kagawa Prefectural College of Health Sciences* Volume 13, 19–27. http://doi.org/10.50850/00000337.

Victoria's Act sets out strict requirements for VAD laws and provides oversight by the state government and independent third parties to prohibit any assisted dying that does not meet the requirements of the Act. In other words, self-determination of patient-assisted dying is prohibited except for those who participate in this Act. It can be said that the right to self-determination of assisted dying is strictly restricted by the Act.

The results of an interview survey with family caregivers of the patients revealed several specific barriers to connecting with the system.[41] Community awareness initiatives are essential, given that VAD is still a relatively new concept in Victoria.

Although the VAD Act provides patients with a degree of clarity, it is still in conflict with the definition of "suicide" as used in sections 474.29A and 474.29B of the Criminal Code in Australia.[42] In the case of *Carr v Attorney-General (Cth)* [2023] FCA 1500 (Carr), the Federal Court of Australia Justice Abraham upheld a broad interpretation of suicide, affirming that consulting on VAD via carriage services remains a criminal offense, even under the VAD Act. Furthermore, providing method-specific suicide information remains prohibited.

It is imperative that VAD receives significant attention from stakeholders, including patients, families, and medical doctors at the highest level. The implementation of the VAD in the Australian State of Victoria has been referenced, with the other Australian states and the special territory subsequently enacting similar legislation. It is notable that these legislative measures exhibit certain nuanced distinctions in terms and conditions. Consequently, it would be beneficial to observe their subsequent developments in the other states for comparison with those in the State of Victoria within Australia.

[41.] The aforementioned barriers can be classified into four categories: (i) unaware VAD is a legal option, (ii) failing to identify VAD eligibility, (iii) unclear or unachievable next steps, and (iv) patients forced to initiate VAD discussions due to legal limits on doctors. White, Ben P., Ruthie Jeanneret, and Lindy Willmott (2023) "Barriers to Connecting with the Voluntary Assisted Dying System in Victoria, Australia: A Qualitative Mixed Method Study" *Health Expectations* Volume 26 Issue 6, 2695–2708. https://doi.org/10.1111/hex.13867.

[42.] Law Council of Australia (2024) "Full Medical Not a Given When Deciding to End One's Life" *The Canberra Times*, January 19, 2024. https://lawcouncil.au/media/news/opinion-piece-full-medical-not-a-given-when-deciding-to-end-ones-life; Kennedys Law (2024) "Lessons from Victoria's Voluntary Assisted Dying Laws" September 13, 2024. https://kennedyslaw.com/en/thought-leadership/article/2024/lessons-from-victoria-s-voluntary-assisted-dying-laws/.

CHAPTER 4

ADs and ACP in the Japanese Context

This chapter examines Japanese legislation on life and death, along with key health policy issues, to provide a clearer understanding of the country's legal and policy framework. It highlights the unique challenges Japan faces, as its legislation on end-of-life medical care remains among the least developed in East Asia. The discussion explores how ADs and ACP are addressed within this context, focusing on both legal provisions and the role of nonlegislative measures such as professional guidelines and institutional policies. By analyzing these factors, the chapter sheds light on the gaps and ongoing efforts to improve end-of-life decision-making in Japan.

4.1 Laws Concerning Human Life and Death in Japan

This section examines the current laws in Japan concerning human life and death, with the aim of clarifying the legal definitions of these matters and identifying areas not dealt with laws.[1] According to Article 3(1) of the Civil Code of Japan, individuals acquire rights from birth. However, exceptions exist, such as when a fetus is considered "born" under specific articles of the Civil Code.[2] The birth of a child requires a notification to the city office within 14 days, which must include a birth certificate (Article 49(1) of the Family Register Act of 1947).

While the Civil Code does not contain provisions on death, it is argued by law scholars,[3] and generally understood, that an individual loses his or her

---

[1] Sakurai, Yukio (2024) "The Role of Law and Bioethics in Human Life and Death: Japanese Medical Law in End-of-Life Care" *Australian Journal of Asian Law* Volume 25 No. 1, 89–105. https://ssrn.com/abstract=4964356.

[2] Refers to Article 721: Compensation for Damages Based on Tort, Article 886: Inheritance, and Article 965: Bequests of the Civil Code of Japan.

[3] For example, Yoshida, Hisashi, and Mamoru Kaida (1963) "Death under Civil Law (1)" [in Japanese] *The Chuo Law Review* Volume 70 Issue 9, 696.

rights upon death. The determination of death involves medical practices under the Medical Practitioners' Act, which requires physicians to confirm death through specific criteria and issue a death certificate. If a patient is eligible for organ donation, a doctor will determine brain death and follow the prescribed procedures for organ donation. Since the Act on Organ Transplantation has changed the conventional concept of human death in certain conditions, the basic principle of the Act is that "donation of organs for use in transplantation must be voluntary" (Article 2(2)).

In cases of anticipated home deaths, it is essential to notify the primary care physician (Article 20 of the Medical Practitioners' Act of 1948). Deaths at home or in elderly facilities may necessitate ambulance calls, and emergency transportation is initiated based on specific conditions. If there is suspicion of a crime or suicide, deaths must be reported to the police (Article 21), leading to a request for a death certificate. Notifications, including the death certificate or autopsy report, must be submitted to the city office within a specified period (Articles 86 and 87 of the Family Register Act).

Special circumstances, such as ward deaths or infectious diseases, are addressed through legal provisions (Article 873-2 of the Civil Code, art 12 of Act on the Prevention of Infectious Diseases and Medical Care for Patients with Infectious Diseases of 1998). The rising trend of the elderly living alone without relatives poses social challenges such as the lack of relatives to care for these elderly, and the absence of individuals who can infer the elderly's wishes and preferences when they develop dementia and lose mental capacity. Declarations of disappearance are made when an individual's life or death status is unknown for a relevant period.[4]

A multitude of legislative and regulatory instruments pertain to the domains of human life and death. A significant proportion of these regulations belong to administrative procedures related to life and death events. In the case of a relative's death, it is expected that the relevant procedures will be handled by the deceased's relatives or their representatives within a specified time frame. The completion of various procedures and inheritance matters following a person's death can be a lengthy and labor-intensive process. Recent trends indicate an increase in petitions for adult guardianship in family courts tar

[4] If an individual's life or death is unclear for seven years (ordinary disappearance) or for one year after a peril has passed (perilous disappearance), family courts can declare them legally disappeared (Article 30 of the Civil Code, Article 94 of the Family Register Act). This declaration establishes a legal presumption of death for the person.

geting the elderly with dementia and no relatives, which highlights emerging societal concerns.[5]

A concise examination of pertinent legislation in this section elucidates the notion that the dimensions of human life and death extend beyond the personal realm to encompass societal considerations. As the number of individuals approaching death continues to grow, the burden on those engaged in procedures related to human death, as well as on administrative entities, is becoming increasingly intense.

Conversely, there is a dearth of a specific legal framework that encompasses aspects such as supported decision-making in healthcare and AD systems for end-of-life scenarios. A specific legal framework goes beyond the general principles of civil law, with the objective of incorporating the will and preferences of individuals approaching death concerning the management of their property and medical care in Japan.

4.2 Issues of Healthcare Policy in Japan

4.2.1 Rising Medical Expenses for Older Adults in End-of-Life Care

Japan's healthcare system is founded upon a universal health insurance system that is integrated into a social insurance system. Private medical institutions are responsible for the provision of approximately 80% of healthcare services, while public institutions account for only approximately 20%. Similarly, the public insurance systems of Japan, Germany, and France are characterized by a markedly higher proportion of public medical institutions within their respective healthcare delivery systems.[6]

In contrast, the United Kingdom and Sweden have a tax-based system, with healthcare provided by public healthcare institutions that serve as gatekeepers. In the U.S., the provision of healthcare is predominantly the responsibility of private healthcare institutions, operating under private health insurance schemes

---

[5.] Courts of Japan (2024) "Overview of Adult Guardianship Related Cases" [in Japanese]. https://www.courts. go.jp/toukei_siryou/siryo/kouken/index.html.

[6.] Shimazaki, Kenji (2020) *Japan's Healthcare: Systems and Policies: Revised and Expanded Edition* [in Japanese]. Tokyo: University of Tokyo Press. 29; Shimazaki, Kenji (2013) "The Path to Universal Health Coverage: Experiences and Lessons from Japan for Policy Actions" Japan International Cooperation Agency (JICA); Naoki, Ikegami, and J. C. Campbell (1996) *Medical Care in Japan: Control and a Sense of Balance* [in Japanese]. Tokyo: Chuokoron-Shinsha.

by their insurance policy. The exceptions to this are Medicare, which provides healthcare for the elderly and persons with disabilities under a social insurance scheme, and Medicaid, which provides healthcare for low-income individuals under a tax scheme.

The objective of health policy in Japan is to guarantee that all citizens have equitable access to quality healthcare at the lowest possible cost burden. This entails three key considerations: (i) the quality of medicine, (ii) equality of medical access, and (iii) minimal cost burden.[7] Japan's healthcare system has demonstrably achieved all three, making it a unique model globally. However, this has led to significant national healthcare expenditure as the population has aged.

In the year 2021, Japan's healthcare expenditure increased by 4.8% in comparison with the previous year.[8] The mean expenditure per capita was ¥358,800 (this equates to US$2,392), representing a 5.3% increase. Healthcare spending constituted 8.18% of GDP, representing an increase from the previous year's figure of 7.99%.

An analysis of end-of-life care indicates that (i) medical expenses surge around six months before death, (ii) hospitalization costs dominate this period, and (iii) expenses decrease with older age at death.[9] The costs of end-of-life care for patients with ischemic heart disease, hypertension, and diabetes tend to increase significantly in the period preceding death. In contrast, cancer-related costs tend to spike approximately six months before death. The high costs of end-of-life care in Japan often reflect the provision of unnecessary treatments under the national health insurance system, influenced by patient or family preferences.[10]

[7.] Ibid. [2020] 20.

[8.] The expenditure data, broken down by age group, showed the following: ¥2.42 trillion (US$16.13 billion) for individuals aged 0–14, ¥5.37 trillion (US$35.80 billion) for those aged 15–44, ¥9.94 trillion (US$66.27 billion) for those aged 45–64, and ¥27.30 trillion (US$182.00 billion) for those aged 65 and above. The average expenditure for those under 65 was ¥198,600 (US$1,324), while individuals aged 65 and above spent an average of ¥754,000 (US$5,027). Japan, Ministry of Health, Labour, and Welfare (2023) "Overview of National Medical Expenses for Fiscal Year 2021" [in Japanese] chrome-extension://efaidnbmnnnibpcajpcglclefindmkaj/https://www.mhlw.go.jp/toukei/saikin/hw/k-iryohi/21/dl/data.pdf.

[9.] Suzuki, Wataru (2015) "Statistical Considerations on the Potential Reduction of End-of-Life Medical Expenses Using Receipt Data" [in Japanese] Doctoral Dissertation, Gakushuin University.

[10.] MHLW Grants System (2009) "Integrated Data Infrastructure Construction and Utilization for Continuous Examination and Planning of Municipalities and Insurers' Health, Medical, Long-Term Care, and Welfare Policies" [in Japanese]. https://mhlw-grants.niph.go.jp/project/16067; Japan's medical-legal system encourages doctors to provide artificial nutrition and hydration via percutaneous endoscopic gastrostomy tubes. There is a need for education on end-of-life care to challenge this automatic assumption among doctors. Aita, Kaoruko, M. Takahashi, H. Miyata, et al. (2007) "Physicians' Attitudes about Artificial Feeding in Older Patients with Severe Cognitive Impairment in Japan: A Qualitative Study" BMC Geriatrics Volume 7, 22. https://doi.org/10.1186/1471-2318-7-22.

The lack of specific regulations governing end-of-life care in Japan results in a reliance on discussions between healthcare professionals, patients, and families. Individuals aged 75 or older typically cover 10%–30% of medical expenses, with monthly caps. This system allows for extensive use of medical services, with minimal financial burden on individuals. Healthcare practitioners have little incentive to cease end-of-life care if they can justify it. The Japan Medical Association (JMA) provides substantial political contributions to ruling parties, thereby supporting them. Healthcare professionals must balance their medical conscience with the commercialization of healthcare.

Japan's public health insurance system requires rigorous verification and improvement of clinical practices, though such analyses are rarely reported. Japan's healthcare system is a hybrid of social insurance system and commercial medicine, with approximately 80% of services provided by private entities and approximately 20% by public institutions.[11] The government sets clinical and pharmaceutical fees, making the system complex and challenging to comprehend.[12] The Ministry of Health, Labour, and Welfare of Japan (MHLW), which is responsible for public healthcare insurance, is overseen by officials with medical licenses. Policies are often decided within this exclusive group, with minimal public input.

The politicization and commercialization of the healthcare sector run by the government has resulted in a lack of capacity within the administrative, legislative, and judicial institutions of Japan to self-correct. This has led to the exploitation of older adults by private medical institutions for end-of-life care. The advancement of healthcare discussions and addressing these issues requires the implementation of political reform through opposition parties and the utilization of accurate empirical data and analysis. Otherwise, the Japanese economy is on the brink of collapse due to the unsustainable costs associated with providing healthcare and aged care.

[11.] As of March 2020, public hospitals made up 18.5% of hospitals nationwide and 28.7% of beds. In areas with few private healthcare facilities, public hospitals are crucial, offering services like emergency, pediatric, perinatal, disaster, and psychiatric care, along with advanced medical procedures not always available in private hospitals. Public hospitals include national, regional, and public medical facilities, many affiliated with the Red Cross.

[12.] The Central Social Insurance Medical Council ("*Chuikyo*") is an advisory body to the MHLW, responsible for recommending official prices, such as medical fees and drug prices, to the Minister. The Council discusses agenda items prepared by the MHLW secretariat. Under the Social Insurance Medical Care Council Law, it consists of 20 members: eight representing insurers, insured individuals, and employers; eight representing physicians, dentists, and pharmacists; and four representing the public interest. Each member's term is two years.

4.2.2 Relationship between Physicians and Patients

A majority of respondents (62.3%) indicated support for legislation that would establish immunity from liability for physicians in cases where life-prolonging treatment is discontinued.[13] Additionally, nearly half of respondents reported that they lacked specific guidelines for end-of-life care, a figure that has remained relatively unchanged since a similar survey was conducted 10 years ago. The survey also found that 63.1% of respondents noted discrepancies between patients' wishes and those of their families. This discrepancy often arises when patients desire a natural death, while their families advocate for life extension.

The lack of more specific and clearer end-of-life care guidelines places healthcare professionals in a challenging position, as they are often deeply involved in decisions. This involvement can lead to inconsistencies in the view of older adults and other stakeholders. This can be frustrating for healthcare professionals, though it is commercially beneficial for hospitals.

Recently, some healthcare professionals have faced legal issues due to inappropriate conduct,[14] leading to administrative penalties that are perceived as lenient. In addition to criminal and civil lawsuits, the Medical Examining Board convenes twice a year to impose administrative penalties for illegal actions by healthcare professionals.[15] In this regard, stricter penalties are needed to maintain patient trust.

Conversely, there has been a rise in patient or family dissatisfaction leading to violence or harassment.[16] Traditionally, patients respected healthcare professionals, however, now openly express dissatisfaction, sometimes violently.[17] A 2023 Fukuoka Medical Association survey identified unreasonable patient

---

[13.] A survey conducted by the healthcare web magazine m3.com in November 2023, involving 509 physicians, revealed significant communication challenges in end-of-life care. m3.com (2024) "Survey on End-of-Life Care for Older Adults" [in Japanese] (January 13, 2024). https://www.m3.com/news/series/iryoishin/12962.

[14.] Kimura, Mitsue (2004) "Trends and Legal Basis of Administrative Sanctions against Physicians" [in Japanese] *Tokyo Metropolitan University Law Journal* Volume 45 Issue 1, 31–48.

[15.] The Medical Ethics Board issues recommendations on administrative sanctions for various healthcare professionals, including physicians, dentists, nurses, midwives, physiotherapists, and others. Its responsibilities include overseeing national examinations for medical professions and certifying anatomical qualifications under the Autopsy Law of 1949.

[16.] Japan Nursing Association (2024) "Measures against Violence in Medical Settings" [in Japanese]. https://www.nurse.or.jp/nursing/shuroanzen/n_harassment/index.html.

[17.] This trend is seen globally, especially post-COVID-19. Boyle, Patrick (2022) "Threats against Health Care Workers Are Rising: Here's How Hospitals Are Protecting Their Staffs' " AAMC August 18, 2022. https://www.aamc.org/news/threats-against-health-care-workers-are-rising-heres-how-hospitals-are-protecting-their-staffs.

demands and harassment, which disrupts medical care and affects staff.[18] Such behaviors in healthcare settings are referred to as "patient harassment." This is exacerbated by the COVID-19 pandemic, results from strained trust and reduced routine care,[19] and social media fuels grievances. Such harassment causes trauma among healthcare providers, leading to staffing shortages and criticism of hospital management. Addressing this requires collaboration with medical associations, authorities, and law enforcement.

In Japan, there is a pressing need to establish clear guidelines for patients as consumers, rather than healthcare professionals, in end-of-life care. This is due to the lack of definitive regulations in this area, which has resulted in ambiguity and uncertainty in medical practice.[20] It is imperative to acknowledge that the current era requires a shift toward more effective and inclusive approaches.[21] The relationship between physicians and patients must be re-established in accordance with the needs of the modern age.[22]

4.2.3 National Strategies and Legislation Against Dementia

As the global population ages, it is anticipated that the number of individuals living with dementia will exceed 130 million by 2050.[23] In response, the WHO has designated dementia as a global priority, urging member states to develop and update national strategies. These strategies aim to enhance the quality of life for those with dementia and their caregivers, incorporating elements such

---

[18.] Fukuoka Medical Association (2023) "Special Feature: Nuisance Behaviors in Healthcare Settings" [in Japanese] *Medical Information Chamber Report No. 261*, September 29, 2023. https://www.city.fukuoka.med.or.jp/jouhousitsu/.

[19.] II, Michiko, Moriyama, Masako, and Sachiko Watanabe (2023) "Patient Behavior during the COVID-19 Pandemic and Impacts on Medical Institution Revenue" *Public Policy Review* Volume 19 Issue 1, 1–39.

[20.] The Japan Geriatrics Society (2019) "Proposals for Promoting ACP" [in Japanese] chrome-extension://efaid-nbmnnnibpcajpcglclefindmkaj/https://www.jstage.jst.go.jp/article/geriatrics/56/4/56_56.411/_pdf; Goto, Yuri (2020) "Definition of the End of Life in Passive Euthanasia and the Justification and Grounds for Discontinuing Treatment: In the Wake of the Fussa Hospital Dialysis Discontinuation Incident" *Law Journal* Volume 98, 95–131.

[21.] The concept of "voluntary stopping of eating and drinking" (VSED) is presented for discussion: Yukawa, Keiko, and Takuya Matsushige (2023) "Issues in End-of-Life Care and Organizing and Prospecting Ethical and Legal Issues of Voluntary Stopping of Eating and Drinking (VSED) in Japan" *Journal of the National Institute of Public Health* Volume 72 Issue 1, 22–30. https://www.niph.go.jp/en/journal-en/data-72-1-e72-1-en/.

[22.] Machino, Saku (1996) "Patient Self-Determination vs. Doctor's Paternalism" [in Japanese] *Bioethics*, Volume 6 Issue 1, 32–34.

[23.] "Dementia" is referred to as "a syndrome in which there is deterioration in memory, thinking, behavior, and the ability to perform everyday activities." WHO (2021) "Dementia" (January 27, 2021). https://www.who.int/news-room/fact-sheets/detail/dementia.

as human rights protection. A dementia-inclusive society is one that adapts to the needs of people with dementia and their caregivers.

In Japan, dementia affects approximately 15% of individuals aged 65 and above, with nearly half of those aged 85 and above affected.[24] In September 2023, Japan had 36.23 million older adults, with 4.43 million having dementia and 5.59 million having mild cognitive impairment (MCI). By 2040, the older adult population is projected to reach 39.21 million, with 5.84 million affected by dementia and 6.13 million by MCI.[25] These conditions have a significant impact on families and society, resulting in substantial social costs.[26]

Japan's comprehensive dementia policies commenced in the late 1980s and have since evolved through the Orange Plan (2012), New Orange Plan (2015), and the Dementia Policy Promotion Outline (2019). With a focus on "coexistence" and "prevention,"[27] the Diet passed the Basic Act on Dementia to Promote an Inclusive Society (Act No. 55 of 2023) on June 4, 2023. The Act becomes effective on January 1, 2424.[28]

The aims of the Act are to safeguard the dignity and comfort of individuals with dementia, establish government headquarters for dementia-support policies, develop a comprehensive plan, raise awareness, and promote innovative products and services. Furthermore, the Act includes educational initiatives for employers with the objective of facilitating continued employment for those under the age of 65 with dementia. Additionally, it emphasizes the training of specialized caregivers and the improvement of medical facilities.

While initial responses were encouraging, the absence of concrete government action plans has introduced an element of uncertainty. The concept of supported decision-making is not yet firmly established, as the public remains influenced

---

[24.] Kotera, Shoichi (2019) "Dementia: Situation, Policies and Issues" [in Japanese] *The Reference, National Diet Library,* Volume 826, 29–58.

[25.] The updated projection of the dementia population was presented at the Second Dementia Policy Promotion Stakeholders Meeting held by the Cabinet Secretariat of Japan on May 5, 2024. The data indicated a decline in the number of dementia cases and an increase in the number of Mild Cognitive Impairment (MCI) cases. Japan, Ministry of Health, Labour, and Welfare (2022) "Future Estimates of the Number and Prevalence of Dementia and Mild Cognitive Impairment (MCI) among Elderly People" [in Japanese]. https://www.mhlw.go.jp/content/001279920.pdf.

[26.] It is estimated that societal costs related to dementia will reach 4.14% of GDP by 2025. Sado, Mitsuhiro, et al. (2014) "Study on the Economic Impact of Dementia in Japan: Summary of FY 2014 and Collaborative Research Reports" [in Japanese]. Comprehensive Research Project on Dementia Measures. https://mhlw-grants.niph.go.jp/niph/search/NIDD00.do?resrchNum=201418007A.

[27.] "The promotion of the adult guardianship system" was described in (1) the Promotion of Dementia Barrier-Free of the Outline to Promote Dementia Policy Program. Cabinet Office (2019) "The Outline to Promote Dementia Policy Program" [in Japanese] (June 18, 2019) 24. https://www.mhlw.go.jp/stf/seisakunitsuite/bunya/0000076236_00002.html.

[28.] Umeda, Sayuri (2023) "Japan: Diet Passes Dementia Basic Act" Law Library of Congress. https://www.loc.gov/item/global-legal-monitor/2023-09-07/japan-diet-passes-dementia-basic-act/.

by the values of reliance on authority and paternalism. The ongoing challenges include addressing stigma, promoting awareness, establishing early diagnosis and support systems, and preventing human rights violations. There is a need for enhanced mechanisms to support autonomy in decision-making, including medical consent.

A shift toward guardianship focused on well-being rather than asset management is essential. As other countries emphasize end-of-life and palliative care for dementia, Japan should consider similar measures. Moreover, Japan has the potential to facilitate global collaboration and serve as a model for other countries by sharing its experiences with dementia initiatives, provided that its public policy is logical and coherent.[29]

4.3 Legal and Ethical Framework for ADs and ACP

4.3.1 Policy of the Ministry of Health, Labour, and Welfare of Japan (MHLW)

In Japan, the MHLW has convened a review meeting of experts on medical care at the end of life approximately every five years since 1987, in advance of the demographic shift that has accompanied the aging of the population.[30] Since 1992, a public awareness survey regarding end-of-life medical care has been conducted. The emergence of issues regarding life-prolonging treatment has resulted in the first two rulings known as euthanasia cases being issued (see Table 4.1).[31]

Although these rulings do not elucidate the rationale behind the illegality of euthanasia, they have become widely known to the public through media reports. Consequently, it can be posited that social recognition of euthanasia has been gained in relation to the occurrence of incidents that contravene medical ethics regarding life-sustaining medical treatment for patients, as well as the reasons that physicians should exercise caution in their work.

[29.] Baba, Hiroko, M. N. Aung, A. Miyagi, et al. (2024) "Exploring the Contribution of Japan's Experience in Addressing Rapid Aging in Asia: Focus on Dementia Care" *Global Health and Medicine* Volume 6, 19–32. 2023–01124. PMID: 38450119 PMCID: PMC10912802. https://doi.org/10.35772/ghm.2023.01124.

[30.] Tsutsumi, Tsubasa (2018) "Revision of the Guidelines for Medical and Care Decision-Making Process in the Final Stage of Life" [in Japanese] *Aging and Health* Volume 87, 10–13. https://www.tyojyu.or.jp/kankoubutsu/pdf/Aging%26Health_No.87_light.pdf.

[31.] Machino, Saku (2013) "Caring-From a Legal Point of View" *Sophia Bioethics* December 2013, 103–109. A general acceptance of the autonomy of healthcare professionals is observed.

Table 4.1: Overview of the Euthanasia Cases in Japan

Case	Facts	Legal Consequences
Tokai University Hospital, Kanagawa (April 1991)	At the request of the patient's eldest son, who was suffering from cancer, medical treatment, including intravenous drip, was stopped. Further, the family expressed a desire for the patient to be at ease and taken home quickly. The patient was administered drugs, such as potassium chloride via injection, leading to death.	Yokohama District Court Judgment (March 1995): Convicted of murder, sentenced to two years imprisonment with a two-year probation.
Kawasaki Kyodo Hospital, Kanagawa (November 1998)	In a case of bronchial asthma attack, the attending physician removed the artificial respirator from an unconscious patient. Observing the patient appearing to struggle with breathing, the attending physician ordered a nurse to administer a muscle relaxant via intravenous injection, resulting in the patient's death.	Yokohama District Court Judgment (March 2005): Convicted of murder, sentenced to three years imprisonment with five years' probation. Tokyo High Court Judgment (February 2007): Convicted of murder, sentenced to one year and six months imprisonment with three-year probation. Supreme Court Judgment (December 2009): Dismissed.

Case	Facts	Legal Consequences
Imizu City Citizens' Hospital, Toyama (Reported in 2006)	Since 2000, the head of the surgical department and others removed artificial respirators, causing the deaths of seven patients (four males, three females) in an end-of-life state based on the wishes of their families.	Not prosecuted.

Source: Created by the author based on data from the MHLW[32]

Law scholars have been engaged in discussions pertaining to the suspension of life-sustaining treatments from a legal perspective.[33] For example, an article that discusses the acceptability of discontinuing treatment has been published.[34] This book compares the "patient's right to self-determination" and the "limitation of the physician's obligation to treat" to determine whether to suspend life-sustaining treatment. It accepts the doctor's discretion within the limited scope of the decision to be made by the doctor while considering the subjective circumstances of the patient.

[32.]Japan, Ministry of Health, Labour, and Welfare (2006) " 'Terminal Medical Care' 5th Social Security Council Special Subcommittee on Medical Care for the Elderly" [in Japanese] December 12, 2006. https://www.wam.go.jp/wamappl/bb11GS20.nsf/0/23ce16303dbc18bb4925724300097c6b/$FILE/shiryou1.pdf.

[33.] Machino, Saku (2007) "Patients' Right to Self-Determination and Doctors' Duty to Treat: In the Wake of the Kawasaki Kyodo Hospital Case Appeals Court Decision" [in Japanese] *Criminal Law Journal* Volume 8, 47–53; Inaba, Kazuo (2007) "Chapter 10 Laws and Precedents at the End of Life" in Takao Takahashi and Atsushi Asai (eds), *Japanese Bioethics: Retrospective and Prospects Kumamoto University Bioethics Collection 1* [in Japanese]. Fukuoka: Kyushu University Press. 209–239; Kai, Katsunori (2009) "Rulemaking and Legal Issues in End-of-Life Medical Care" [in Japanese] *Journal of Medical Law* Volume 24, 81–87; Kai, Katsunori (2010) "Chapter 10. Euthanasia and Death with Dignity in Japanese Law" *Journal International de Bioéthique* Volume 21 Issue 4, 135–147; Inada, Akiko (2012) "Supreme Court Decision on the Kawasaki Kyodo Hospital Case: Third (3rd) Decision December 7, 2009" [in Japanese] *Criminal Case* Volume 63, Issue 11, 1899. *Kochi University Review of Social Science* No. 105, 47–69; Tasaka, Akira (2013) "Permissibility of Discontinuing Treatment" [in Japanese] *Shimane Law Review* Volume 56 Issue 4, 101–119; Tatsui, Satoko (2013) "Norms Surrounding End-of-Life Care" in Katsunori Kai (ed), *End-of-Life Care and Medical Law Medical Law Course Volume 4*. Tokyo: Shinzansha Publisher. 216–233; Miho, Tanaka, and Kodama Satoshi (2020) "Ethical Issues around the Withdrawal of Dialysis Treatment in Japan" *Asian Bioethics Review* Volume 12 Issue 1, 51–57. https://doi.org/10.1007/s41649-020-00109-3.

[34.]Ibid., [Machino].

4.3.2 2007 Guidelines

In 2006, the MHLW changed its policy on end-of-life medical care following the medical incidents at Imizu Municipal Hospital in Toyama Prefecture (see the last case in Table 4.1), where the ventilators were removed from a total of seven terminally ill patients. In 2007, the MHLW published "Guidelines for Process of Medical Decision-Making in the End-of-Life" (2007 Guidelines) that deals with the need to: (i) discuss how to proceed with end-of-life care with the medical and care team rather than with the doctor alone; (ii) help those who care for the person tell the medical and care team what the person wants and wishes, and help the team decide on end-of-life care; and (iii) improve palliative care.

The 2007 guidelines elucidate that "active euthanasia," which encompasses the deliberate administration of pharmaceuticals or analogous agents with the intention of inducing the patient's demise, is not encompassed by the guidelines and is not legally permissible.[35] Following the publication of the 2007 guidelines, it would appear that healthcare professionals have demonstrated a willingness to adhere to the principles set out in the guidelines in their clinical practice. There is no evidence to suggest that any physician has been prosecuted for actions related to end-of-life medical care, and instances of judicial intervention in medical incidents have been limited.[36]

In accordance with the 2007 guidelines and subsequent guidelines issued by the medical community, Norio Higuchi, who chaired the review panel for the 2007 guidelines, states that the discontinuation of life-prolonging treatment is no longer a criminal offense.[37] If this remark suggests that the 2007 guidelines were drafted with the intention of affording healthcare professionals freedom of choice in end-of-life care, and that this freedom of choice can then be enjoyed by the patient as long as medical ethics allow, then this would constitute a practical solution.

Conversely, this interpretation could facilitate the withdrawal or withholding of life-sustaining treatment by healthcare professionals at their discretion. The existence of a national health insurance system ensures the financial guarantee

---

[35]Higuchi, Norio (2015) "Legal Issues on Medical Interventions in Terminally Ill Patients" [in Japanese] *Medical Care and Society* Volume 25 Issue 1, 21–34. https://doi.org/10.4091/iken.25.21.

[36]Japan, Ministry of Health, Labour, and Welfare (2018) "61st Medical Division Meeting of the Social Security Council" [in Japanese] Minutes for the Meeting held on April 11, 2018. https://www.mhlw.go.jp/stf/shingi2/0000212218_00001.html.

[37]Higuchi, Norio (2024) "5. Understanding the Laws and Guidelines Surrounding End-of-Life Care" in Kaoru Aida (ed), *ACP Concepts and Practice*. Tokyo: University of Tokyo Press.

of the patient's treatment, rendering the latter scenario unlikely. Akashi Tanaka states, the MHLW devised a guideline promoting communitarian consensus for end-of-life care, recognizing patients' social context, while the JMA stressed liability exemption, underscoring a hurdle to a unified libertarian stance among healthcare professionals.[38]

Although social factors necessitate the implementation of proactive measures to prepare for end-of-life care, the Japanese legal system lacks specific legislation regulating the use of ADs and ACP in healthcare settings. At present, there are no legal provisions governing the process of obtaining consent for medical treatment or the use of substituted decision-making in medical contexts. In 2007, a clause was incorporated into Article 1(4), Paragraph 2 of the Medical Care Act, which requires healthcare professionals to provide patients with sufficient explanations and to facilitate comprehension among those receiving medical care. However, the clause lacks specificity regarding the implementation of this policy.

4.3.3 2018 Guidelines

In 2018, the MHLW implemented a partial revision of the 2007 guidelines and issued "The Guidelines for the Process of Medical and Care Decision-Making in the End-of-Life" (2018 Guidelines).[39] The 2018 guidelines include two additional points on top of the 2007 guidelines. They are: (iv) in preparation for the future terminal stage, it is recommended that the patient repeatedly discuss end-of-life care with family members, etc., and (v) in some cases, it is important to identify a reliable person who will make medical decision-making on the patient's behalf.[40]

A legal practitioner has put forth the argument that the 2018 guidelines cannot be classified as soft law due to their dearth of sufficient detail and clarity.[41] Cheung and Dunn (2023) categorize Japan as "non-regulated" in ADs, as evidenced in Section 3.3 of Chapter 3. The 2018 guidelines have been designed for the

---

[38.]Tanaka, Akashi (2023) "Rulemaking and Consensus of Bioethical Problems: Historical Analysis of Japanese End-of-Life Care Policies" [in Japanese] *Bulletin of the Department of General Education, Tokyo Medical and Dental University* Volume 53, 71–82.

[39.]Japan, Ministry of Health, Labour, and Welfare (2018) "Revision of Guidelines for Process of Medical Care Decision-Making in End-of-Life" [in Japanese] March 14, 2018. https://www.mhlw.go.jp/stf/houdou/0000197665. html; The English version of the 2018 Guidelines is available: Kodama, Satoshi (2024) "Guideline on the Decision-Making Process for Medical and Nursing Care at the Last Stage of Life". https://www.cape.bun.kyoto-u. ac.jp/wp-content/uploads/2019/10/MHLW_Process_Guideline_English.pdf.

[40.]Ibid.

[41.]Uchida, Hirofumi (2021) *Medical Law and the Rights of Patients and Medical Workers* [in Japanese]. Tokyo: Misuzu Shobo, 22–23.

examination and decision-making procedures of healthcare professionals and social workers and are not intended for the public. Furthermore, the 2018 guidelines do not explicitly address ADs and ACP. Consequently, Japan's end-of-life medical care would be in a state of legal absence, lacking both hard and soft laws.

The 2018 guidelines permit a degree of ambiguity in their interpretation. In Japanese legal scholarship, "ambiguity" is crucial, particularly in decision-making and interpreting legal frameworks. It is viewed as a flexible tool, allowing legal rulings to adapt to changing social contexts and norms. While ambiguity enables expert interpretation, it may confuse the public, leading to misunderstandings of the law's intent. This creates a tension between expert authority and public understanding, with increasing emphasis in Japan on prioritizing public interest over expert control.

The following questions and answers (a) to (h) demonstrate typical examples of this ambiguity, as the implications in question are not explicitly indicated in the 2018 guidelines.[42]

(a) *Please outline the procedure to be followed if the patient does not discuss their choices with their relatives.*

In many cases, patients do not mention their choices and leave the decision-making process to their relatives. The attending medical doctors will engage in a discussion with the patient's relatives regarding the patient's care. If the relatives are unable to reach a decision, the doctors will make the decision based on what they consider to be in the patient's best interests. The hospital's clinical ethics committee is responsible for determining whether their established guidelines necessitate involvement in the decision-making process.

(b) *Please advise which relatives should be consulted.*

Please note that the 2018 guidelines do not define relatives. In this context, it is reasonable to assume that relatives have a good understanding of the patient's wishes. Otherwise, they will be unable to respond to the doctor's queries.

(c) *In what circumstances is it advisable to appoint a representative?*

The 2018 guidelines do not provide guidance on the appointment of a proxy. Nevertheless, in all cases, doctors would appreciate the appointment of a proxy, particularly in situations where the patient is approaching the end of

---

[42.] These questions and answers (a) to (h) are derived from email correspondence between Gianluca Montanari Vergallo (University of Rome La Sapienza) and the author in August 2024.

their life. Medical professionals specializing in cancer treatment highlight the importance of a proxy in both medical decision-making and financial management, which can be critical during extended hospitalization.

(d) *Please advise as to the consequence of the patient not appointing a proxy.*
This is a relatively common occurrence. The doctors will request that the next of kin coordinate the views of the relatives. Should this prove ineffective, the doctors will decide based on what they consider to be in the patient's best interests. It is the responsibility of the hospital's clinical ethics committee to determine whether their established guidelines require involvement in the decision-making process.

(e) *How to resolve a conflict of opinion between a doctor and a patient's family.*
It is standard practice for medical doctors to take the time to explain the recommended course of treatment to the patient's family and to ensure their satisfaction. While observing these family members, the doctor will persistently try to gain their understanding. However, should this prove unsuccessful, the doctor may decide after going through the clinical ethics committee or other procedures.

(f) *How should the situation be handled if some family members accept medical treatment and others refuse it?*
The most effective solution is for the relatives to consult with each other. Should this prove ineffective, the doctor may decide to take the matter to the clinical ethics committee or pursue other avenues.

(g) *If the doctor chooses not to follow the 2018 guidelines, does he have to justify his decision?*
To comply with the relevant regulations, the doctor must seek approval from a clinical ethics committee or, in hospitals, an alternative. They must also take responsibility for keeping a detailed record of the procedure involving the patient's relatives and nursing staff. This is to facilitate an external review of the circumstances of the event and to avoid litigation.

(h) *Please provide an overview of the decision-making processes in which social workers are involved.*
It should be noted that social workers and adult guardians, if applicable, are not involved in decision-making processes regarding medical care, as they do not have the requisite legal authority required to do so. In the absence of the aforementioned, their role is to provide support to the patient and their family, as well as to local healthcare practitioners, except for decisions pertaining to the patient's medical care.

4.3.4 Life Conference and Relevant Measures

The MHLW subsequently encourages citizens to convene a "life conference" (a kind of ACP) in which older adults in which older adults engage in a discussion with family members and other close friends regarding a portion of ACP for end-of-life care. This is risk communication with stakeholders that encourages people to make autonomous decisions during end-of-life care, thereby reducing the risk that their will and preferences will not be respected.

However, the concept of the "life conference" is not widely known to the public. A survey conducted by the MHLW (June 22, 2023) revealed that 72.1% of respondents were unaware of the concept of a life conference. There is a distinctive tradition of avoiding contemplation of the demise of a close relative and of perceiving discourse about preparing for death in the presence of older adults as an ominous portent. Consequently, relatives are often reluctant to engage in discussions with older adults regarding end-of-life care and asset management.

In the context of legal theory, three conditions must be met for medical treatment to be considered lawful.[43] Primarily, the objective of the medical practitioner must be the administration of treatment in accordance with medical indications. Secondly, the method of medical treatment employed must be deemed reasonable from the standpoint of contemporary medical practice. Thirdly, the patient must have provided consent. Regarding the third criterion, namely the patient's consent, the concept of informed consent has become firmly established in Japan. For informed consent to be deemed effective, the patient must possess the capacity to consent, which is defined as the ability to recognize their condition, its significance, the content of the medical treatment, and the degree of risk involved.

In cases where the patient's intention is unclear, medical institutions have adopted the practice of obtaining written consent from the patient's relatives or guarantor to mitigate the risk of subsequent litigation.[44] The 2018 guidelines, however, do not stipulate the criteria for determining the decision-making capacity of the patient in question or the degree of family members who can provide consent on their behalf. This leaves the decision to the discretion of the medical professionals, family members, and other relevant parties. This is one of the reasons why the practice of seeking medical consent from relatives or guarantors has become commonplace in medical institutions.

---

[43] Teshima, Yutaka (2022) *Introduction to Medical Law*. 6th ed. Tokyo: Yuhikaku Publishing. 48–49.

[44] Hoshi, Takako (2019) "The Urgent Need to Establish a Legal System for Medical Consent" [in Japanese]. Japan Research Institute, Research Focus No. 2019-028.

A growing number of service providers are offering *Lifetime Support Services for the Elderly*, which help on behalf of family members and relatives with procedures related to hospitalization and admission to nursing homes, support for daily living activities such as shopping for daily necessities, and post-mortem affairs such as funerals and the disposal of property after death. As this business is characterized by the inclusion of post-mortem services and the lengthy contract period, there is a significant requirement for the protection of users.

In June 2024, the Cabinet Office of Japan presented a set of guidelines on legal provisions to be complied with and matters to be noted across relevant ministries and agencies.[45] While this social issue is of significant importance, it will not be addressed in further detail in this book. Advance directives in Japan are summarized in Table 4.2.

Table 4.2: Advance Directives in Japan

Item	Japan
Relevant Laws on ADs	No specific law (governed by the 2018 guidelines)
Content of ADs	Withholding/withdrawal of life-sustaining treatment
Designation of Proxy	Not specified but recommended
Criteria for Proxy	Not specified
Criteria for Withholding Treatment in the Absence of ADs	Agreement between attending healthcare professionals or medical/care team and family
Criteria for Discontinuation in Cases of Incapacity, Lack of ADs, and No Family Presence	Decision of the attending healthcare professionals or the medical/care team (Principle is to adopt the best treatment policy for the patient)
Supported Decision-Making	Encouragement of consultation with the primary care healthcare professionals
Information-Sharing System for ADs	Recommendation to store it at home or with family, and to provide a copy to the primary care medical professional or caregiver

Source: The author

---

[45] Japan, Ministry of Justice (2024) "Guidelines for Lifelong Support Businesses for the Elderly, etc." [in Japanese]. https://www.moj.go.jp/MINJI/minji07_00358.html.

4.4 Relational Autonomy-Based Approach to ADs

4.4.1 Draft Principles to Be Considered

In the absence of legislation pertaining to ADs, medical consent, and substituted decision-making for medical treatment, what guidelines should be considered?

Firstly, regarding judicial precedents, the case of Kawasaki Kyodo Hospital, in which the decision of the Supreme Court and the Tokyo High Court judgment were presented, serves as a reference point. In the 2007 Tokyo High Court judgment case, the case was analyzed from both the "patient's self-determination approach" and the "medical practitioner's duty of care approach." The judgment states that the issue of death with dignity must be fundamentally resolved by the enactment of a death with dignity law or the formulation of alternative guidelines.[46] From this perspective, it is evident that the 2018 Guidelines will serve as a pivotal reference point, assuming the role of a guiding principle in lieu of a legally enforceable statute.

Furthermore, the 2009 Supreme Court ruling stated that the victim was in a coma at the time of the incident and that the endotracheal tube was removed at the request of the victim's family, who had given up hope of recovery.[47] From the evidence presented, it is evident that the extubation was not conducted in accordance with the appropriate medical information available regarding the victim's condition. It is therefore not possible to conclude that the extubation was based on the presumed intention of the victim.

In light of the aforementioned considerations, it can be posited that the act of extubation does not fall within the parameters of legally permissible treatment cessation.[48] An alternative interpretation of these statements is that it is legally permissible for a physician to extubate a patient if they have conveyed appropriate information to the family members about the victim's medical condition and their act is based on the patient's will or presumed will.[49]

---

[46] Japan, Tokyo High Court (2007) "Decision for the Kawasaki Kyodo Hospital Case on February 28, 2007" [in Japanese]. https://www.courts.go.jp/app/hanrei_jp/detail3?id=35145.

[47] Japan, The Supreme Court (2009) "Decision for the Kawasaki Kyodo Hospital Case on December 7, 2009" [in Japanese]. https://www.courts.go.jp/app/hanrei_jp/detail2?id=38241.

[48] Ibid.

[49] Kai, Katsunori (2021) "The Scope of Patients' Advance Directives and Self-Determination (Rights)" [in Japanese] in Makoto Tadaki and Gunnar Dutge (eds), *Comprehensive Research on End-of-Life Care, Euthanasia, and Death with Dignity*. Tokyo: Chuo University Press. 111–127.

It is therefore considered essential to have procedures that may satisfy these two conditions: The physician is expected to convey appropriate information to the patient, family, and other relevant parties. Additionally, the physician's actions are to be based on the patient's intention or presumed intention. This would encourage the patient to have a written AD and the physician to record the decision-making process through discussions with the patient, family, etc. in the medical record, and convey appropriate information to them accordingly.

Secondly, as part of the administrative response, it would be beneficial to consider the operational guidelines of the Tokyo Fire Department. If the Tokyo Fire Department receives a request for an ambulance and the emergency team arrives at the scene, if a family member declares the principal's intention not to want cardiopulmonary resuscitation for the person in cardiopulmonary arrest, the emergency team will contact the family physician, etc. In such a case, the emergency team will then proceed to interrupt cardiopulmonary resuscitation, provided that certain conditions are met.

Subsequently, the emergency team will transfer the patient to the care of their family physician or other designated family members. The aforementioned "certain conditions" are as follows: (i) an adult on an ACP who is in cardiopulmonary arrest; (ii) the patient is in the final stages of life; (iii) the patient does not want to perform cardiopulmonary resuscitation; (iv) matching the current symptoms with the symptoms assumed in the patient's decision-making.[50]

In other words, if there is a written AD and the content of the AD is confirmed by telephone contact with a family physician or a similar medical professional, the patient who does not want cardiopulmonary resuscitation will be treated in accordance with the patient's AD. It is of utmost importance that there is a written AD and that it is fully understood by a family physician.

The preceding two analyses can be synthesized to derive the following draft principles.

- In accordance with the 2018 Guidelines, the individual, family members, and their physician engage in discourse pertaining to the individual's end-of-life medical treatment, formulate written ADs, and undertake procedures with the objective of confirming the individual's intention or presumed intention based on the individual autonomy approach.

[50.] Japan, Tokyo Fire Department (2019) "Responding to Victims Who Do Not Want Cardiopulmonary Resuscitation" [in Japanese]. https://www.tfd.metro.tokyo.lg.jp/lfe/kyuu-adv/acp.html.

- If the physician provides the patient and their family members with appropriate information and performs all possible medical treatments, and further medical treatments are considered to be clinically meaningless, the physician may seek the judgment of the clinical ethics committee and make decisions such as discontinuing treatment, recording the process details in the medical records, and so forth. It is crucial that the decision made by the healthcare professionals is reasonable when viewed through the lens of their duty of care, and that it is perceived by a third party as exceeding the scope of their duty to treat.

4.4.2 Nonlegal Support Measures

The approach of Japan to ADs for end-of-life care differs from that of other countries that have developed legislation in this area. Although there is no legally binding enforcement, a movement conducted by local governments is spreading across Japan to encourage older adults to fill out "ending notes" or "end-of-life planning notes" that document the wishes of older adults at the end of life.[51]

A 2022 survey revealed that 8% of respondents aged 50–80 had written an ending note, with this figure increasing with age, to reach 13% of those aged 70 or older. A 2021 survey found that approximately 60% of those with an ending note had written one, with this figure reaching 60% of those aged 60 and over. A greater proportion of those aged between 30 and 59 had written an ending note (70.5%) than those aged 60 and over (60.5%).[52]

Besides ending notes, some local government and physicians' associations have developed their own AD templates with the intention of encouraging older people to complete their own ADs.[53] Some local governments provide assistance

---

[51.] These notes originated with Masaji Ishihara, the founder of Sekisei in Nagoya, who created a funeral preparation booklet as a sales promotion. Published in 1991 under the title "My Ending: My Preparation Note," it became widely popular in Japan. The term "end-of-life activities" first appeared in a weekly magazine in 2009 and gained traction among younger generations in 2011 through the documentary "Ending Note," directed by Asami Sunada; Musashino International Association (MIA) (2024) "End of Life Planning Notes". https://mia.gr.jp/en/foreigner/retirement; *Tsunagari* (2024) "List of Municipalities Distributing Ending-Notes [free distribution]" [in Japanese]. https://sougi-lab.com/shukatsu/endingnote-municipalities/.

[52.] Mobile Marketing Data Labo (2022) "Parent-Child Comparison Survey on End-of-Life Planning and Asset Management for Seniors" [in Japanese]. https://mmdlabo.jp/investigation/detail_2134.html; NPO Ra-Shi-Sa (2021) "Nationwide Survey on End-of-Life Awareness" [in Japanese]. https://www.ra-shi-sa.jp/_rashisa/wp-content/themes/rashisa/pdf/20210903_shukatsu-ishiki-survey.pdf.

[53.] Handa City (2023) "Handa City Version of 'My Advance Directive about Medical Care'" [in Japanese]. https://www.city.handa.lg.jp/hoken-c/kenko/iryo/hoken/jizensijisho.html; Chihiro, Tsuchiya, N. Mine, T. Matsumoto, et al. (2024) "Introduction and Operation Report of the Nagasaki City Medical Association's Advance Directive 'My Wishes'" [in Japanese] *Journal of Japanese Association for Home Care Medicine* Volume 5 Issue 3, 29–39. https://doi.org/10.34458/jahcm.5.3_29.

in preparing post-mortem affairs for older adults who receive welfare assistance and have no relatives to care for them.[54] At large-scale hospitals, such as university hospitals, the details of a patient's wishes regarding cardiopulmonary resuscitation or active life-prolonging treatment upon admission are confirmed in writing.[55]

In a national response, a subcommittee of the Ministry's Central Medical Insurance System Council (known as *Chuikyo*) deliberated on the potential for guiding patients to ACP through healthcare professionals, in conjunction with the revision of medical insurance fees.[56] The Subcommittee members expressed a positive opinion regarding the recommendation to conduct an ACP at life milestones.[57] This proposal has attracted attention as a potential move by the medical administration toward revising medical fees in 2024.

4.4.3 Necessity of Governmental Actions for Legislation

The response of the Japanese government to ADs and ACPs can be seen to be characterized by a notable absence of action, with the responsibility for action being delegated to the public. This inaction policy was clarified in the interpellation at the Diet held on April 1, 2024, Prime Minister Fumio Kishida and the relevant minister Keizo Takemi were questioned about the necessity of considering the Dignified Death Bill and the ADs system, with reference to recent trends in various countries. In response, it was stated as follows:[58]

> *The concept of a dignified death is contingent upon the prevailing national attitudes toward life and ethics. Given the diversity of these attitudes across countries, it would be unwise for Japan to pursue legalization based on the examples set by other nations. Instead, there is a need for a more nuanced public debate on this issue. It would be prudent for the government to avoid prematurely pushing*

[54] Yokosuka City (2023) "Yokosuka City Ending Plan Support Business" [in Japanese]. https://www.city.yokosuka.kanagawa.jp/2610/syuukatusien/endingplan-support.html.

[55] Niigata University General Hospital (2022) "Guidelines in End-of-Life Care" [in Japanese]. https://www.nuh.niigata-u.ac.jp/wp-content/uploads/2022/03/tmc_guideline.pdf.

[56] Japan, Ministry of Health, Labour, and Welfare (2023) "Opinion Exchange Meeting for Simultaneous Remuneration Revision in 2024 (3rd Session)" [in Japanese] (May 18, 2023). https://www.mhlw.go.jp/stf/shingi2/0000164258_00003.html.

[57] ACP has become a standard practice among healthcare professionals, albeit in a Japanese manner. In the event of an older adult being hospitalized, they and their relatives are required to complete a document indicating whether they wish to withhold life-sustaining treatment.

[58] The Account Settlement Committee in the House of Councillors, the 213rd Diet held on April 1, 2024. Japan, Diet Proceedings Search System. https://kokkai.ndl.go.jp/#/.

> *discussions on this topic, particularly given the limited public understanding on the matter. The promotion of the "life conference" would benefit from a more considered approach.*

However, some healthcare professionals have expressed difficulty in comprehending the legal framework surrounding end-of-life care in Japan, particularly in relation to the lack of clarity surrounding the scope of exemption for medical procedures performed by medical personnel in end-of-life care.[59] This has led to concerns among legal researchers that the current legal situation is not conducive to the provision of optimal care for patients at the end of their lives.[60]

The results of the 2018 questionnaire survey indicate that while a high proportion of healthcare professionals and the public support the concept of ADs, they are not in favor of their legalization.[61] It is hypothesized that this is because healthcare practitioners do not want ADs to be made legally compulsory as an additional burden, but the reasons for the public's opposition to ADs being legalized remain unclear. This leads to the question of whether MHLW's "Survey on Awareness of Medical Care at the End of Life" accurately reflects public opinion.

A lack of comprehensive understanding of ADs hinders the ability to engage in substantial discussions on the subject. However, only a minority of Japanese people have seen a template of ADs. In the survey by the MHLW, phrases such as "actually creating a document" and "believing that a law should be enacted to decide on treatment policies according to the document" are used in the questionnaire.

The survey was completed by a diverse range of respondents, including the public, physicians, nurses, and caregivers. The survey assumes that respondents can comprehend the nature of the document and the legal implications of the question. However, it is necessary to consider whether this assumption is valid. When conducting the survey, if the respondents are unfamiliar with the terms "document" and "law," and if no sample of the document or explanation of the

---

[59] Tsukamoto, a physician, puts forth the proposition of implementing the U.S. court system, which would grant permission upon request from the patient, family, or relevant stakeholder in cases where such authorization is necessary. Tsukamoto, Yasushi (2022) *Medicine and Law II* [in Japanese]. Tokyo: Shogakusha. 166–173.

[60] Ogata, Ayumi (2022) "The Right to Self-Determination and Legal System Design regarding Medical Care at the Final Stage of Life: From a Criminal Legal Perspective" [in Japanese] *Chukyo Lawyer* Volume 36, 1–22; Ogata, Ayumi (2024) "The Right to Live Life to the Fullest and the Right to End It: Focusing on the Kyoto ALS Contract Murder Case" [in Japanese] *Chukyo Lawyer* Volume 40, 25–46; Ikka, Tsunakuni (2019) "Law and Ethics of End-of-Life Care: What Is Permissible, What Is Not Permissible, and Its Basis" [in Japanese] *Hospital* Volume 78 No. 7, 508–513.

[61] Japan, Ministry of Health, Labour, and Welfare (2018) "Survey Report on Awareness regarding Medical Care in End of Life" [in Japanese]. March 2018. https://www.mhlw.go.jp/toukei/list/dl/saisyuiryo_a_h29.pdf.

nature of the law in question is provided, the proportion of negative reactions may be high. This might be the reason why people in general tended to react negatively to issues that they were unfamiliar with.

Given that Japan lacks established formats for ADs or laws concerning ADs, it is necessary to provide respondents with examples of documents and law for consideration. Without such information, the outcomes of the specific questionnaires may not be entirely reliable. Given that this survey is conducted on a regular basis and has a significant impact on healthcare policy, it is advisable for the MHLW to exercise the utmost caution.

It would be beneficial to refer to the optional format for ADs stipulated in Article 11 of the U.S. Health-Care Decisions Act of 2023 (see Appendix 2). Given the straightforward nature of the format for ADs, it is reasonable to posit that Japanese citizens would be able to complete them with relative ease. Considering past operational shortcomings, the format of ADs has been improved to enhance usability.

It can be assumed that Japanese people are reluctant to accept government intervention in matters of a personal nature, such as end-of-life decisions. Furthermore, the procedure for creating ADs is perceived as cumbersome, and there is a concern that the uniform implementation of the law may not be capable of considering individual circumstances and the wishes of family members. The current situation in Japan suggests that the legal definitions related to life and death lack flexibility, imposing standardized requirements on citizens and potentially restricting individuals in unexpected ways.[62]

Consequently, the personal wishes of those seeking ADs and relevant legislation are overlooked. It could be argued that differing interpretations of expectations and concerns about legal regulations fundamentally influence the existence or absence of ADs. It is unlikely that ADs will become legal in Japan unless the misconception that laws inherently restrict individuals is addressed.

It would appear prudent to establish guidelines for ADs rather than legislation, to accumulate experience in their practice, and to improve the formats and methods of use. The rationale for the promotion of ADs and ACP for end-of-life care can be attributed to the direct interaction of medical and nursing care settings with patients and older adults, as well as to the involvement of local governments in these matters.

[62.] Higuchi (n 35); Ikka, Tsunakuni (2011) "The History and Current Status of Medical Basic Law" [in Japanese] *Annual Report of Medical Law* Volume 26, 16–38; Ikka, Tsunakuni (2023) "Medical Jurisprudence on End-of-Life Care and Terminal Sedation" [in Japanese] in Tatsuya Morita and Shimon Tashiro (eds), *Questioning the Grey Zone of Sedation and Euthanasia: Perspectives from Medicine, Nursing, Bioethics and Law.* Tokyo: Chugai Igaku-sha. 211–230.

Local governments are encouraged to create ADs, which are not legally binding. Depending on how they are devised, these can be expected to have the de facto effect of indicating the person's intentions to their next of kin and healthcare professionals.

In conclusion, the distinction between Japan's approach and those of other developed countries that have enacted legislation lies in the question of whether the documents utilized are legally binding. To clarify the will and preferences of older adults at the end of life, it is of the utmost importance to develop and implement ADs and ACP that are in accordance with the traditions and local customs of the people concerned, regardless of whether they are legally binding or not.

It is proposed that two crucial aspects should be the focus of attention. Firstly, there is a necessity for citizen awareness about end-of-life care as their own issues. Secondly, there is a need for the evolution of the 2018 guidelines for healthcare professionals, which should be updated and include greater detail. These two aspects may propose changes to legislation to incorporate patient rights, responsibilities of healthcare professionals and advance care directives into the framework of medical law in Japan.

4.4.4 A Relational Autonomy-Based Approach

Considering the preceding discussion on relational autonomy, it is now appropriate to examine the approach to ADs in the Japanese context. ADs may take a variety of forms, including oral and written instructions, instructions drafted by the individual, and instructions drafted by family members. They may also be simple or detailed.

In other developed countries, legislation has been enacted to delineate the parameters for the formulation of ADs and their legal ramifications, thereby facilitating their appropriate administration. This is done to clarify the rights of individuals and the obligations of healthcare practitioners. However, the legislation pertaining to ADs in other countries is diverse and not unified, thus allowing for a degree of flexibility in its implementation.

The concept of prioritizing the individual's will and preferences is known as "individual autonomy" and forms the foundation of laws and policies in Western countries.[63] This concept was incorporated into Japan along with Western

---

[63.] Donnelly, Mary (2010) *Healthcare Decision-Making and the Law: Autonomy, Capacity, and Limits of the Liberalism*. Cambridge: Cambridge University Press; Donnelly, Mary (2017) "Developing a Legal Framework for Advance Healthcare Planning: Comparing England & Wales and Ireland" *European Journal of Health Law* Volume 24 Issue 1, 67–84. https://doi.org/10.1163/15718093-12341412; Herring, Jonathan (2022) *Medical Law and the Ethics*. 9th ed. Oxford: Oxford University Press.

legal systems, humanities, and social sciences when modern legal systems were established in the late nineteenth century.

Although Japan's current legal system has evolved in accordance with the Constitution of Japan, the underlying idea of the individual's autonomy and will remains unchanged. This approach is pervasive in fundamental legal codes such as the Civil Code, Commercial Code, and Criminal Code. Conversely, in the context of private autonomy, such as individual life and the communities of certain groups, the primacy of the individual's autonomy and will may not always be accorded.

In Japan, the opinions of family members and the interests of the group head are often given greater weight than the individual's will and autonomy. In considering relationships with others, individual autonomy may be relativized. However, in certain instances, this is not only acceptable but even preferable. This perspective, which posits that individuals prioritize relationships with others, is referred to as "relational autonomy."[64] In order to overcome the challenges posed by ADs based on individual autonomy, there is a movement to utilize ACP based on relational autonomy. This involves discussions between individuals, families, healthcare practitioners, and others over time.

MHLW has created 2018 Guidelines for medical care decision support for patients in the end-of-life stage, leaving the details of implementation to the discretion of healthcare practitioners, who are expected to apply their insights and ethical considerations in this context. For the public, the recommendation is to hold a "life conference" involving the individual and their family members. In Japan, there is a lack of awareness that ADs and ACP are instruments to safeguard the rights of individuals. Furthermore, the utilization of these tools remains limited.

It is necessary to devise ADs and ACPs or alternative measures that consider relational autonomy rather than individual autonomy and are acceptable to the Japanese people.[65] It seems reasonable to posit that a similar consideration would apply to Asian countries and areas. In consideration of relational autonomy, a relatively gentle approach, exemplified by an "ending-note" or "end-of-life

[64] Mackenzie, Catriona (2013) "The Importance of Relational Autonomy and Capabilities for an Ethics of Vulnerability" in Catriona Mackenzie, Wendy Rogers, and Susan Dodds (eds), *Vulnerability: New Essays in Ethics and Feminist Philosophy (Studies in Feminist Philosophy)*. Oxford: Oxford University Pres. 33–59. https://doi.org/10.1093/acprof:oso/9780199316649.003.0002; Mackenzie has conducted research into the concept of relational autonomy; McKenzie, Carorina (2019) "Feminist Innovation in Philosophy: Relational Autonomy and Social Justice" *Women's Studies International Forum* Volume 72. https://doi.org/10.1016/j.wsif.2018.05.003.

[65] Asagumo, Anri (2022) "Relational Autonomy, the Right to Reject Treatment, and Advance Directives in Japan" *Asian Bioethics Review* Volume 14 Issue 1, 57–69.

planning note," which is not legally binding but demonstrates the individual's wishes and preferences through written statements, has gained traction.

Nevertheless, there are numerous instances where family members or nursing home managers are unaware that the older adult has made a note or have expressed wishes that are contradictory to the older adult at hospitals. In such cases, health-care practitioners are often uncertain as to how to proceed, and their decisions are often influenced by their personal characteristics. In the contemporary era, numerous hospitals have established ethics committees, which collectively make decisions. However, these committees cannot address every case.[66]

A further question concerns the allocation of responsibility for the older adult in both ACP and asset management. The Japanese guardianship system is designed to permit the adult guardian to assume responsibility solely for asset manage-ment, and ACP is not a duty for the adult guardian. Physicians and nurses are often overwhelmed by the demands of their roles, and medical social workers, who are assigned to large-scale hospitals, are similarly constrained by limited resources. Consequently, the number of medical social workers is insufficient to provide comprehensive support to all patients.

It then becomes evident that a novel system, or one that is newly combined with aged care, is required to provide support to older adults in the community. Many retired individuals from their business at the age of 60–65 can contribute to such support work, receiving remuneration for a period of 5–10 years. These individuals can then succeed in this business from one generation to the next. To realize this concept, it is necessary to undertake further detailed consideration, which should include an examination of the existing welfare policy and measures, or alternatively, a revision of the welfare system to accommodate these methods at the state or local level.

4.5 ACP Studies in Japan

This section presents four Japanese ACP study projects and offers insights into decision-making for older cancer patients. In Japanese society, where family-centered decision-making is highly valued, there are significant chal-lenges in applying Western concepts of ACP directly to Japan. Consequently, a

---

[66.] It has been reported that small and medium-sized hospitals are less likely to adopt policies set by ethics committees. Given the high number of end-of-life care cases for the elderly, it is common practice, unless exceptional circum-stances arise, to defer to the medical team or department head's judgment rather than the ethics committees. Ikka, Tsunakuni (2013) "Reconsideration of Hospital Ethics Committee" [in Japanese]. *Bioethics* Volume 23 No. 1, 23–30.

study project was initiated with the objective of developing a consensus-based definition and behavioral guidelines for ACP and supported decision-making that would be suitable for Japanese contexts.

4.5.1 ACP Definition in a Modified Delphi Method

Atsushi Miyashita conducted a modified Delphi method with a group of 56 interdisciplinary Japanese experts from 2020 to 2022. The objective was to develop items regarding the definition, content, target audience, and behavioral guidelines for Japanese-based ACP. Consequently, ACP is defined as "an individual's thinking about and discussing with their family and other people close to them, with the support necessary of healthcare providers who have established a trusting relationship with them, preparations for the future, including the way of life and medical treatment and care that they wish to have in the future."[67]

Although this concept is not yet at a stage where it can be put into practice, the study does make several noteworthy points. Firstly, the study focuses on the relationship between the individual and their family members, attempting to reconcile the two values of individual autonomy and relational autonomy. Secondly, the trusted partner does not utilize the terms "proxy" or "representation" to refer to the individual who provides support to the principal. Instead, it is assumed that the principal's will and preferences are understood by the trusted partner. In other words, the trusted partner is the principal's supported decision-maker. Thirdly, they do not guarantee the format of a legal document. The method is considered flexible if it can accurately convey the principal's will and preferences. The above concepts represent the consensus of Japan's interdisciplinary experts and are consistent with the outlines discussed in this book.

4.5.2 MHLW's Commissioned ACP Research

Furthermore, research commissioned by the MHLW from 2021 to 2023, entitled "Research to Enhance End-of-Life Care for Older Adults with Dementia according to Differences in Treatment Settings" has been done.[68] The impact of the

---

[67.] Miyashita, Jun, S. Shimizu, R. Shiraishi, et al. (2022) "Culturally Adapted Consensus Definition and Action Guideline: Japan's Advance Care Planning" *Journal of Pain and Symptom Management* Volume 64 Issue 6, 602–613. https://doi.org/10.1016/j.jpainsymman.2022.09.005.

[68.] Japan, Ministry of Health, Labour, and Welfare (2021) "Research Survey for Enhancement of End-of-Life Care for Dementia Patients according to Different Treatment Venues: In Light of the Impact of the COVID-19 Epidemic" [in Japanese]. https://mhlw-grants.niph.go.jp/project/157717.

COVID-19 pandemic is considered in the context of this research. The objective of this study is to develop guidelines and informational booklets for end-of-life care for older adults with dementia, based on evidence and tailored to the diverse treatment settings (i.e., hospitals, aged care facilities, and residential homes). Hisayuki Miura (National Center for Geriatrics and Gerontology) has served as the research representative and overseen the research activities of healthcare professionals and aged care researchers, based on the end-of-life care survey in hospitals, aged care facilities, and homes.

The content provides guidelines based on an interdisciplinary approach, drawing on the expertise of medical, nursing and social welfare professionals, rather than a legal perspective. The results were disseminated through the publication of the book *ACP Thinking and Practice: Clinical Ethics of End-of-Life Care* and the organization of a March 2024 webinar by the co-authors of the book that was sponsored by the Graduate Research Centre for Death Science, University of Tokyo.[69]

The booklet on decision support for people with dementia addresses end-of-life care, supported decision-making and surrogate decision-making to facilitate its implementation in a manner that aligns with Japanese cultural nuances, rather than merely replicating the U.S. approach. In addition to a theoretical analysis of ACP, the book presents the concept of ACP in an accessible manner, with numerous illustrative examples of ACP in medical institutions, nursing homes, and the home. This is done to facilitate the practice of ACP based on Japanese cultural characteristics.

4.5.3 Research on the Effective Decision-Making Support Program to Enhance the Quality of Cancer Care for Older Adults by National Cancer Center

The National Cancer Center's Explanatory Oncology Research and Clinical Trial Center developed a decision-making support program for older cancer patients, published in 2020.[70] When treating older cancer patients, it is crucial to consider comorbidities, living conditions, and cognitive impairments, such as dementia.

[69.] Aida, Kaoruko (ed) (2024) *ACP Thinking and Practice: Clinical Ethics of End-of-Life Care* [in Japanese]. Tokyo: University of Tokyo Press; Shimizu, Tetsuro (2015) "Supporting Patients and Their Families to Make Informed Decisions: Shared Decision-Making and Advance Care Planning" [in Japanese] *Medicine and Society* Volume 25 Issue 1, 35–48.

[70.] National Cancer Center, Explanatory Oncology Research and Clinical Trial Center (2020) "A Guide to Decision-Making Support for Cancer Treatment for Older Adults" [in Japanese]. https://www.ncc.go.jp/jp/epoc/division/psycho_oncology/kashiwa/research_summary/050/020/index.html; Ogawa, Asao (2019) "End-of-Life Care for Dementia" [in Japanese] *Journal of Psychiatry* Volume 121, 289–297.

It is a common misconception that older patients, even those with cognitive impairments, should not be respected and should not be allowed to make their own treatment decisions. A wide range of treatment options can significantly impact on the quality of life of older patients. Therefore, it is essential that patients and their families are fully informed before proceeding.

The guide outlines the way healthcare professionals should make decisions for older cancer patients, assess their decision-making capacity, and provide appropriate support. According to government guidelines, patients' cognitive abilities should be utilized, even in dementia cases. It is the responsibility of healthcare professionals to ensure that patients are adequately informed about their options and supported in making their own decisions.

The findings of the study indicate that ACP can be enhanced by incorporating the preferences and wishes of older cancer patients. In this context, it can be posited that healthcare decision-making support and ACP are interrelated in the relationship between healthcare professionals and patients and their families.

This study aims to comprehensively clarify the cancer treatment challenges of older patients, as well as the medical needs of patients and their families. It will develop an effective decision-making support program for implementation at cancer treatment collaboration hospitals. Finally, it will confirm the feasibility and standardize the program.

The research team conducted a study on decision-making support for older cancer patients in Japan, with the objective of developing technology to enhance it. The research team identified that older patients frequently experience a decline in their ability in their daily activities and an increase in unexpected readmissions following treatment. This highlights the necessity to align treatment with patient values and consider long-term actions. Despite the availability of extensive treatment information, there is a dearth of long-term support and patient involvement in decision-making.

This study represents the first comprehensive analysis of these challenges. The team developed a decision-making support guide and tested a program, which demonstrated high satisfaction despite time constraints.

4.5.4 Online Seminar by Yokohama National University

The Regional Collaboration Promotion Organization in Yokohama National University[71] hosts online seminars that engage participants from a range of

---

[71.] This institution was established in April 2017 and has since become a principal agent for regional collaboration between the university and the local community.

academic disciplines. Before the captioned seminar, preliminary discussion was made between medical graduate students as healthcare practitioners, which is summarized in Table 4.3.

Table 4.3: A List of Comments Organized by End-of-Life Topic

Challenges	Specific Issues	Countermeasures
Awareness of Death	-It is challenging to discern that this is the terminal phase of life, particularly in instances of nonmalignant tumors. -Define the final stage of life.	-Promote research to determine the final stage of life even in non-cancer diseases. -Education about death is necessary; it should be a mandatory subject in junior high school health and physical education classes -It is beneficial to commence moral education in elementary school, which will facilitate the development of an understanding of how to live one's limited life.
Position of the Person	-Death is rarely discussed. -The individual's and the family's wishes may change. -Many people are unaware of the potential benefits of life-prolonging treatments. This can result in patients being unable to accurately imagine end-of-life care.	-The creation of an environment where individuals can express their wishes to their families. -The establishment of a culture where the topic of ACP is discussed on each birthday. This would facilitate the process of initiating conversations about ACP. -It is necessary to designate a steward to support the individual's decision.

Challenges	Specific Issues	Countermeasures
		-It would be beneficial to provide a guide to assist individuals in including pertinent details regarding medical care at the end of life in their ADs. -ADs are more readily comprehensible when presented with specific options.
Position of Family Members	- Children (family members) are unable to accept their parents' aging. - Many people lack knowledge about life-prolonging treatments, which makes it difficult for family members and others to accurately imagine end-of-life care.	-It is inadvisable to permit your family to determine a policy by stating, "I will not do this." -Palliative care is relatively straightforward to comprehend for families.
Position of Healthcare Professionals	-Due to the effects of dementia, it is not possible to confirm the individual's wishes. Consequently, families may request all medical treatment, including CPR. -Family members may request aggressive treatment against the individual's wishes. -It is challenging to halt an unwanted treatment once it has been initiated. -It is essential to distinguish between medical care for living and medical care for dying.	-It is of the utmost importance to establish an ACP. -It would be of significant benefit to medical staff if the individual's intentions were clearly defined. -It is crucial to gather the voices of patients' families and healthcare professionals, and to consider past court decisions. -Medical personnel should endeavor to communicate information in a timely manner when the situation changes. - The legal validity of the patient's wishes (issues such as voluntary assisted dying).

Challenges	Specific Issues	Countermeasures
Position of Medical Administration	- There is a shortage of resources to provide care for patients at home and in chronic care hospitals, where they can receive care with the reassurance of a dedicated team.	- Policies to ensure the activities listed on the left are financially viable. - The desired medical care differs depending on the patient's position and situation. It would be beneficial if the patient's wishes could be reflected in the medical information platform.

Source: The author

The inaugural online seminar—entitled "Are You Delegating or Planning in Advance?"—was held under the auspices of the institution's Legal Unit. A discussion on the management of older adults' assets and medical care was held on July 15, 2023. Subsequently, the second online seminar on the theme of "Decision Support in Healthcare—Advance Care Planning for People with Dementia" took place on November 12, 2023.[72] The author presented the keynote report for the inaugural seminar, while Asao Ogawa (physician and director of the Department of Psycho-Oncology at the National Cancer Center Hospital East) delivered the keynote report for the second seminar.

The two seminars were attended by 15 professionals from various fields, including physicians, public health practitioners, social workers, lawyers, and university faculty members. The discussions held during the five-hour seminars can be summarized in the following points, which serve as responses to the questions posed in this book.

- It is of the utmost importance to recognize death as a societal issue and to create a social environment where everyone can experience a peaceful death [all professions].

[72.] Yokohama National University, Regional Collaboration Promotion Organization (2023) "Unit for the Improvement of Legal Services for Kanagawa Residents—Hosted the First Online Seminar" (July 15, 2023). https://www.chiiki.ynu.ac.jp/news/000225.html; Yokohama National University, Regional Collaboration Promotion Organization (2023) "Unit for the Improvement of Legal Services for Kanagawa Residents—Hosted the Second Online Seminar" (November 12, 2023). https://www.chiiki.ynu.ac.jp/news/000269.html.

- It is beneficial to draft documents that reflect the intentions of older adults regarding end-of-life medical care through ADs, as this can be advantageous for both the individuals and healthcare practitioners. Although these documents lack the legal binding force of an end-of-life planning note or an ending note, their existence can serve as a valuable reference for healthcare practitioners if recognized by family members and attending physicians (physicians, lawyers, social workers).
- It is currently feasible for hospitals and local governments to provide templates for ADs, accumulate practical experience in document creation, and improve operational practices in the field. It is recommended that professional societies and universities provide advice and support to hospitals and local governments (physicians, lawyers, university faculty).
- In the initial stages, it is anticipated that policies that will provide incentives for medical and caregiving professionals will be introduced to encourage patients to engage in ACP, potentially through additional reimbursement. Nevertheless, it is of the utmost importance to implement policies and awareness campaigns that will eventually lead the public to engage in ACP on a voluntary basis (physicians, social workers, university faculty).
- Considering the increasing prevalence of dementia among older adults, it is recommended that the government support the implementation of awareness projects, including the creation of ADs and ACP training during regular check-ups for individuals in their 50s (physicians, lawyers, public health practitioners).

CHAPTER 5

ADs and ACP in the East Asian Context

This chapter examines the legislation and practices of South Korea, Taiwan, and Singapore regarding ADs and ACP, drawing on insights from local law scholars to provide a comprehensive overview. A comparative analysis identifies common regional characteristics while assessing the effectiveness and implementation of ADs and ACP across these countries. The discussion further delves into four seemingly conflicting conceptual directions that shape the development of ADs and ACP in East Asia. Through careful deliberation, the chapter proposes ways to reconcile and harmonize these differing perspectives, aiming to create a more cohesive framework.

5.1 Responses of South Korea, Taiwan, and Singapore to ADs and ACP

5.1.1 Observation of South Korea

5.1.1.1 Aging Society of South Korea

The national population of South Korea is estimated to be approximately 51.56 million people (Korea Statistics Agency, 2023). In 2023, the population aged 65 and overconstituted 18.4% of the total population. South Korea is expected to become a super-aged society by 2025, with older adults making up 20.6% of the population.[1] This proportion is forecasted to rise to 30.1% in 2035, 35.3% in 2040, 40.2% in 2050, 43.8% in 2060, and 46.4% in 2070.

By 2040, South Korea's aging population is predicted to surpass Japan's, reaching 34.8%, slightly higher than Japan's 34.4%.[2] The population by religion

---

[1] South Korea, Statistics Korea (2023) "2023 Statistics the Aged". https://kostat.go.kr/board.es?mid=a20111030000&bid=11759.

[2] Japan, Cabinet Office (2023) "Annual Report on the Ageing Society FY2023" [in Japanese]. https://www8.cao.go.jp/kourei/whitepaper/w-2023/zenbun/05pdf_index.html.

in South Korea is estimated as follows (Korea Statistics Agency, 2015): Buddhist (approximately 7.62 million people), Protestant (approximately 9.68 million people), Catholic (approximately 3.89 million people), etc. A higher Christian population is a characteristic of South Korea.

5.1.1.2 Life-Sustaining Treatment for Patients in Hospice and Palliative Care at the End of Life

Two Incidents to Have Shifted Public Opinion

Following two incidents in South Korea, discussions on end-of-life care have intensified.[3] The initial case, which occurred in 1997, involved a patient experiencing respiratory distress (Seoul District Court, Decision 97Gahap11306, Borame Hospital Case). At the family's request, the patient was discharged and subsequently died immediately following the removal of the ventilator. On December 4, 1997, a man with a severe brain injury was discharged from Borame Hospital in Seoul after his spouse cited an inability to afford the costs associated with his continued hospitalization. Following the removal of the artificial respirator, the patient died. Two physicians were convicted of aiding and abetting murder and received suspended sentences.

The second incident, which occurred in 2007, involved the Kim Hal-Mon-Ni Case, which gave rise to a debate on the subject of dying with dignity. Mr. Kim Hal-Mon-Ni, aged 78, had been in a vegetative state since February 18, 2008. His family initiated legal proceedings against Sebrance Hospital, seeking the discontinuation of life-sustaining treatment. On May 21, 2009, the Supreme Court granted Korea's first recognition of dying with dignity, ordering the hospital to remove the artificial respirator in accordance with the family's request (Seoul Western District Court, Decision 2007Gahap3959 / Supreme Court Decision 2009Da17417, Kim Hal-Mon-Ni Case).

The preceding two events have resulted in a shift in public opinion in favor of the legalization of the withdrawal of life-sustaining treatment in cases where it is deemed to be inhumane. The government assumed the role of convener and facilitator, establishing a special commission to deliberate and summarize the consensus of the people on end-of-life care.[4] The deliberation of legislation

---

[3.] Fuchigami, Kyoko (2023) "End-of-Life Care and Dignified Death in South Korea: Examining Self-Determination in Death and Meaning in Death" [in Japanese]. Conference materials presented at the Otani University Pure Land Buddhism Research Institute Tokyo Branch Open Symposium: "Religion and Life: Reflecting on 'A Good Death' from the Current State of End-of-Life Care in Japan, South Korea, and Taiwan" on February 12, 2023.

[4.] South Korea, Ministry of Health and Welfare's Council on the Institutionalization of Forgoing Life-Sustaining Treatments (2009–2010) and National Bioethics Review Committee's Task Force for Decision-Making about Futile Life Sustaining Treatment and Recommendations of the National Bioethics Advisory Committee (2012).

pertaining to advance medical directives for end-of-life care was prolonged due to opposition, particularly from the Catholic Church in South Korea.[5]

In January 2016, the Act on Decisions on Life-Sustaining Treatment for Patients in Hospice and Palliative Care at the End of Life of 2016 (ELDA) was submitted to the National Assembly and passed on the same day. The ELDA came into force on August 4, 2017, with the key provisions relating to the withdrawal of life-sustaining treatment coming into force on February 4, 2018.[6]

Provisions of the ELDA

The ELDA comprises 43 articles distributed across six chapters, in addition to a number of supplementary provisions. Article 1 sets out the objective of ensuring that the interests of patients are served in the best possible way, while respecting their right to self-determination and protecting their dignity. The document addresses the subject of hospice care, as well as decisions pertaining to life-sustaining treatment and their implementation.

Article 5 delineates the responsibilities of national and local governments and establishes the National Agency for Management of Life-Sustaining Treatment (Article 8). The implementation of the law is the responsibility of the National Agency for Management of life-sustaining Treatment (Article 9), and patients are permitted to alter or revoke their treatment plans at any time (Article 10). Regional healthcare institutions are designated as registration institutions for ADs, with support from national and local governments (Article 11). In accordance with Article 33, patient families may request records on life-sustaining treatment from relevant institutions, which are obliged to comply unless there is a legitimate reason. The penalties for violations are set out in Articles 39 to 43.

The ELDA initially focused on end-of-life care, with ADs pertaining to life-sustaining treatment documents prepared by older adults at any time. ACP involves a physician preparing a treatment plan for the patient, typically at the end of life. The ELDA authorizes the termination of four medical acts: ventilators, cardiopulmonary resuscitation (CPR), anti-cancer drugs, and dialysis. It is of the utmost importance to ascertain whether the patient's wishes are aligned with the proposed course of action before proceeding with the withdrawal.

If the patient's wishes can be confirmed, either directly or indirectly through the input of family members or physicians, the withdrawal of treatment may be

---

[5.] The Catholic Church argued that good hospice care should precede end-of-life decision legislation, and the scope of ADs should be limited to terminals. From comments of Park, In-Hwan (Professor of Civil Law, Inha University College of Law) to the questionnaires on March 26, 2024.

[6.] Fujiwara, Natsuto (2016) "Establishment of the 'Dying with Dignity' Law in South Korea: Legal Measures for End-of-Life Care" [in Japanese] *Foreign Legislation, The National Diet Library* 2016.4. https://dl.ndl.go.jp/view/download/digidepo_9929060_po_02670108.pdf?contentNo=1.

based on either (i) the patient's request, as outlined in a life-sustaining treatment plan prepared by the physician, or (ii) a DNAR document, which is available for individuals aged 19 and above.

As an alternative, confirmation may be provided by at least two family members (one if only one is available) that the patient has consistently expressed a desire to withdraw life-sustaining treatment. If the patient's wishes cannot be confirmed, the withdrawal of treatment requires the unanimous consent of the patient's family members (see Table 5.1).

Table 5.1: Overview of Criteria for Discontinuation of Life-Sustaining Treatment for Patients in the Dying Process (Article 17 to Article 18)

Patient's Intent Is	Criteria for Discontinuation of Life-Sustaining Treatment
Confirmable (direct confirmation by the patient themselves or from family members or physicians in an indirect manner)	1. The confirmation is based on the life-sustaining treatment plan created by the physician in accordance with the patient's request. 2. Confirmation is based on the advance directive for life-sustaining treatment, which is available for individuals aged 19 and above. 3. A confirmation that the patient (aged 19 and above) has consistently expressed a desire to discontinue life-sustaining treatment, affirmed by two or more patient family members (or one if only one is available).
Unconfirmable (for individuals below the age of 19)	4. The expression of the intention to discontinue life-sustaining treatment by the legal representative (limited to the parents).
Unconfirmable (for individuals aged 19 and above)	5. The expression of the intention to discontinue life-sustaining treatment is contingent upon the unanimous consent of the patient's family members. In the absence of patient family members, the discontinuation of life-sustaining treatment is not permitted.[7]

Source: The author made based on the provisions of the ELDA.

---

[7] It should be noted that the term "patient family" encompasses the patient's spouse, direct descendants, and direct ascendants aged 19 and above. In the event of their absence, it also includes siblings.

A significant concern in South Korea is the apparent lack of respect for the wishes of minors, particularly in the context of life-prolonging treatments. The ELDA permits physicians to make such decisions and requires that parents confirm them. However, minors are not permitted to make ADs. Similarly, decisions to suspend life-prolonging treatment are reserved exclusively for those with parental authority, assuming that minors are unlikely to prepare ADs. This reflects a perception that parents are solely responsible for these decisions, potentially overlooking conflicts between the parents' and the minors' wishes. Further consideration is required in accordance with the UN Convention on the Rights of the Child.

The law also details the creation and registration of DNAR documents, which are regulated by the Ministry of Health and Welfare of Korea. The National Agency for Management of Life-Sustaining Treatment collects and stores this data, making it available to hospitals upon request. Designated institutions conduct ACP and support DNAR document preparation. ACP facilitators are recommended to attend training programs offered by the National Agency.[8]

5.1.1.3 Significance and Challenge of the ELDA

The ELDA is a significant and appreciated legal instrument that allows patients with no prospect of recovery to decide to withdraw life-sustaining treatment. Furthermore, it provides attending physicians with legal grounds for such action. The number of registered participants in the law has exceeded initial expectations, suggesting that South Koreans are reconsidering their attitudes toward discussing human mortality, which has traditionally been considered taboo.[9] The ELDA is confronted with considerable challenges.

First, there is considerable ambiguity surrounding the extent to which the law upholds patients' rights to self-determination. As of September 26, 2025, there were 781 organizations that were registered as life-sustaining treatment registries, and 505 medical institutions that had established clinical ethics committees to carry out decisions on life-sustaining treatment. About 3,079,280 individuals had registered for ADs on life-sustaining treatment with 178,001 having registered life-sustaining treatment plans.[10] The implementation status included decisions under the Act to withdraw treatment for 455,142 individuals.

[8.] Shimizu, Katsuhiko (2016) "Hospice Life-Sustaining Medical Care Law Legalized in South Korea" [in Japanese] *Living Will* 2016.07, 11–13. http://www.drnagao.com/img/media/related_article2/livwill201607.pdf.

[9.] From comments of Park, In-Hwan (Professor of Civil Law, Inha University College of Law) to the questionnaires on March 26, 2024; Lee, Ye Jin, S. Ahn, J. Y. Cho, et al. (2022) "Change in Perception of the Quality of Death in the Intensive Care Unit by Healthcare Workers Associated with the Implementation of the 'Well-Dying Law' " *Intensive Care Medicine* Volume 48, 281–289. https://doi.org/10.1007/s00134-021-06597-7.

[10.] These figures are based on data provided by the National Agency for Management of Life-sustaining Treatment [in Korean]. https://www.lst.go.kr/main/main.do.

Of these patients, 42% had ADs or life-sustaining treatment plans in place. However, the decision to withdraw life-sustaining medical treatment was made in 33% of cases by the unanimous consent of two or more family members of the patient, and in 31% of cases by the consent of all family members.[11] Decisions by family surrogates outnumber those by patients themselves. The objective of Director Chung is to increase the proportion of cases where older adults make directives or request treatment plans to 50% from an administrative standpoint.[12]

Article 12(8) of the ELDA renders patient directives invalid in the event of a subsequent physician's plan, thereby impinging upon patient autonomy.[13] Nevertheless, there are instances where patient-created plans may be medically unsuitable, thereby justifying physician discretion. As the number of deaths in hospitals continues to increase, there is a growing concern that older adults admitted to hospital in the terminal stages of life may be subjected to significant financial burdens because of the costs associated with life-sustaining treatment before they die. Consequently, approximately 42% of older adults are observed to take the initiative in making ADs or life-sustaining treatment plans, demonstrating consideration for their families to avoid inconvenience.

While this may be perceived as an act of individual autonomy, it could be construed as an act of self-sacrifice driven by relational autonomy.[14] The findings of this study indicate that the enactment of the ELDA has had a limited impact on the provision of end-of-life care.[15] This study therefore urges a thorough analysis of the effects of the ELDA and its role in the autonomy of individuals and in the dynamics of relationships. The methodology employed to capture these sensitive outcomes, such as autonomy or self-sacrifice, is of paramount importance in assessing the outcomes of the ELDA.

Other findings of the research conducted by healthcare professionals indicate that approximately one-third of patients in the end-of-life process made decisions regarding their life-sustaining treatment following the implementation of the

---

[11.] Fuchigami (n 3).

[12.] This view represents the National Agency for Management of Life-Sustaining Treatment. Tsuji, Tokiko (2023) "South Korea's Life-Sustaining Treatment Decision Act, 290,000 Deaths Aiming for Direct Reflection of Individual Wishes at 50%" [in Japanese] *Asahi Shimbun Digital*, October 8, 2023. https://www.asahi.com/articles/ASRB4563ZR9HUTFL015.html.

[13.] Wu, Hong Min (2021) "Consideration of the Death with Dignity Act in South Korea" [in Japanese] *Weekly Social Security* Volume 75 Issue 3117, 48–53, 51–52.

[14.] Fuchigami (n 3).

[15.] Kim, Jeong-A., K. Do-kyung, M. S. Kyung, et al. (2023) "Current Status of Implementation of the Decision to Forgo Life-Sustaining Treatment through Big Data of the National Health Insurance Service" [in Korean] *Biomedical Ethics and Public Policy* Volume 7 Issue 1, 1–24. https://www.riss.kr/link?id=A108578270.

ELDA.[16] However, in the remaining cases, family members continue to exert a significant influence on decisions regarding life-sustaining treatment when death is imminent. This article proposes the enhancement of awareness of end-of-life decision-making processes among healthcare professionals and the public. In the case of ICU treatments in hospitals, the end-of-life decision is still made through subjective judgment by individual doctors after consultation with their families and further research is required.[17]

The second challenge is the inadequate preparation of various social resources necessary for the proper implementation of the ELDA. Numerous shortcomings have been identified in the social resources available to support the implementation of the ELDA. These include the lack of registration facilities for ADs, the absence of clinical ethics committees in medical institutions, the absence of support systems for the psychological burden of physicians making life-sustaining treatment decisions, and the lack of hospice facilities.[18] In urban areas, medical facilities are established, ensuring an adequate supply of the social resources required by the ELDA. However, in rural and depopulated areas, such resources are lacking, which has led to regional disparities in the social resources.

The third challenge involves criticisms of the provisions in the ELDA. Concerns have been raised regarding the lack of family involvement, restrictions on interruptible actions, the presence of punitive measures, and the inability to withdraw treatment without a prior directive or family consent.[19] It is essential to carefully consider removing punitive provisions, allowing for the withdrawal of life-sustaining treatments such as oxygen or intravenous nutrition, and providing opportunities for patients without ADs or family members to express their wishes in end-of-life situations.

ACP, as defined by the ELDA, is a specialized form of end-of-life care designed by physicians for terminal patients, which limits patients' ability to plan through ongoing discussions with doctors. This reflects a typical POLST-style ACP model that outlines circumstances surrounding the end of life. In 2018, the ELDA was partially amended to expand its scope, allowing patients to engage

[16.] Park, S. Y., B. Lee, J. Yeon, et al. (2021) "A National Study of Life-Sustaining Treatments in South Korea: What Factors Affect Decision-Making?" *Cancer Research and Treatment* Volume 53 Issue 2, 593–600. https://doi.org/10.4143/crt.2020.803.

[17.] Yong, H. J., and D. Kim (2024) "End-of-Life Care in the Intensive Care Unit: The Optimal Process of Decision to Withdrawing Life-Sustaining Treatment Based on the Korean Medical Environment and Culture" *Acute and Critical Care* Volume 39 Issue 2, 321–322. https://doi.org/10.4266/acc.2024.00675.

[18.] Wu (n 13) 52.

[19.] Kim, Do Kyong (2017) "Hospice-Palliative Care and Law" *Korean Journal of Internal Medicine* Volume 92 Issue 6, 489–493. https://doi.org/10.3904/kjm.2017.92.6.489.

in these conversations and establish ADs earlier in their illness trajectory, rather than only after being formally recognized as terminal.[20]

5.1.1.4 Commentary

Despite the widespread use of South Korea's ELDA by older adults, concerns remain about whether their preferences are fully respected. In some cases, older adults may prioritize their family's financial well-being over their own, avoiding healthcare costs that could burden their loved ones. Given South Korea's rapid population aging and declining birth rate, these demographic shifts will significantly affect social and familial relationships. Additionally, increasing poverty among the older population, driven by early retirement trends, has become a growing social issue. It is crucial to examine how end-of-life care decisions are made, especially as traditional values and family structures evolve.

Although South Korea's official stance is that end-of-life care decisions should align with the patient's wishes, families often make decisions on life-sustaining treatments on their behalf, with ACP guided by healthcare professionals. To more effectively reflect patients' preferences in end-of-life care through technical research, the current legal framework, including the limited scope of ADs for terminals, may need to be reconsidered and redesigned step-by-step. One potential solution could be to gradually adjust practices to better protect the individual autonomy of older adults while respecting traditional values.

5.1.2 Observation of Taiwan

5.1.2.1 Taiwan's Aging Population and Society

The key points concerning Taiwan's aging population and society are outlined as follows[21]: The policy goals for older adults in Taiwan, as outlined in the "White Paper on Ageing Society 2021" by the Ministry of Health and Welfare of Taiwan, include the promotion of the health and independence of older adults, the facilitation of their social participation, the fostering of intergenerational

---

[20.] From comments of Park, In-Hwan to the questionnaires on March 26, 2024; Park, H. Y., M. S. Kim, S. H. Yoo, et al. (2024) "For the Universal Right to Access Quality End-of-Life Care in Korea: Broadening Our Perspective after the 2018 Life-Sustaining Treatment Decisions Act" *Journal of Korean Medical Science* Volume 39 Issue 12, e123. https://doi.org/10.3346/jkms.2024.39.e123.

[21.] The national population in Taiwan is approximately 23.42 million (January 2024). The author had a lecture on Taiwan's social changes and testamentary law delivered by Sieh-Chuen Huang, Professor of Law and Vice Dean at the College of Law, National Taiwan University, via Zoom on February 9, 2024.

integration, the creation of an environment that is conducive to the well-being of older adults, and the ensuring of sustainable social development.

Like Japan, Taiwan experienced a post-war baby boom, and by 2025 individuals aged 75 and above constitute approximately 20% of the population. The post-war generation in Japan exhibited a high degree of self-awareness, innovative thinking, and contributed to societal changes. A comparable trend can be observed in Taiwan, which suggests the potential for changes in the behavioral patterns of older adults.

In Taiwan, there has been a notable shift in the contractual mindset of older adults, which has led to an increase in ADs for medical care and the pre-selection of asset management. Nevertheless, the current system exhibits certain deficiencies that necessitate improvement. The topic of death has traditionally been considered a taboo subject. However, influenced by American culture and other factors, there has been a shift in awareness regarding advance preparation for death. The coexistence of traditional and contemporary perspectives has led to the exploration of novel approaches to the management of death.

In the context of an aging society, a variety of property disposition techniques are being employed with the objective of meeting the practical needs of older adults. Some forms of disposition even extend to include disposition during one's lifetime.[22] Moreover, due to shifts in industrial structure and family dynamics, a significant proportion of inheritances are no longer confined to family estates but have become purely personal assets. Consequently, the disposition of property to third parties other than family members or the distribution of assets in a manner that differs from the statutory inheritance proportions is generally accepted.

The practice of family guardianship remains prevalent, and there has been no widespread adoption of third-party adult guardianship, as seen in Japan.[23] This is not due to the efficacy of family structures, but rather to the reluctance of the competent authority to be assigned as guardians and the lack of appropriate third-party guardians (such as social welfare organizations or professional guardians). As a result, courts frequently find themselves compelled to appoint family members as guardians.[24]

[22.] Huang, Sieh-Chuen (2012) "Social Changes and Testamentary Law in Taiwan" [in Japanese] *Ryukei Law Journal* Volume 12 Issue 1, 71–104.

[23.] Huang, Sieh-Chuen (2024) "Discussion and Progress on Adult Guardianship System and Decision-Making Support in Taiwan" [in Japanese] *Adult Guardianship Law Research* Issue 21, 82–92.

[24.] Remarks by Judge Chao-Chieh Chan at the Roundtable Discussion on "Practices and Challenges of Guardianship Declarations" held at the College of Law, National Taiwan University on November 9, 2012. Recorded in "Minutes of the Roundtable Discussion on Practices and Challenges of Guardianship Declarations" in Huang, Sieh-Chuen and Tzu-Chiang Chen (2019) (eds), *New Challenges in Legal Issues in an Aging Society: Focusing on Property Management.* 2nd ed. Taipei: New Sharing. 448–449.

5.1.2.2 Hospice Palliative Care Act (HPCA) and Patient Right to Autonomy Act (PRAA)

In Taiwan, the tradition of providing care for seriously ill family members at home until their demise is informed by the Confucian concept of "filial piety."[25] This is regarded as a "good death." Nevertheless, with the advent of medical advances and societal shifts, there has been a growing questioning of this practice.[26] In response to this, the concept of a natural death, or death without life-sustaining treatment in a hospital, has been proposed.

The Hospice Palliative Care Act (HPCA), enacted in 2000, established the legal framework for end-of-life care based on natural death under DNAR orders.[27] The Act comprises 15 articles in total, with the stated objective of "respecting the will of terminal illness patients regarding medical treatment and protecting their rights" (Article 1). In 2002, an amendment was enacted that permitted the withholding and withdrawal of life-sustaining treatment based on the patient's AD.

In 2012, another amendment was introduced, which permitted the withdrawal of life-prolonging treatment for terminally ill patients if a family member decided so and the patient did not express his/her wishes beforehand. Article 7 of the Act stipulates that the withholding or withdrawal of treatment requires two or more specialists to determine that the patient is terminally ill and that the patient's ADs are in place. In the absence of a close relative or an AD,[28] the attending physician consults with a specialist in palliative care and decides.[29]

In Taiwan, the practice of "end-of-life discharge" has become a common occurrence, whereby terminally ill patients are discharged from the hospital and brought home to die, surrounded by family members.[30] In Taiwanese

---

[25.] Morikawa, Takehiro (2020) "International Comparison of Institutional Frameworks for End-of-Life Medical Care and Aged Care" [in Japanese] *Annual Report on Public Policy Studies* Volume 14, 137–150; Tsai, Daniel Fu-Chang (2023) "The Law and Practice of Advance Directives in Taiwan" in D. Cheung and M. Dunn (eds), *Advance Directives across Asia: A Comparative Socio-Legal Analysis.* Cambridge: Cambridge University Press. 75–89; Tsai, Daniel Fu-Chang (1999) "Ancient Chinese Medical Ethics and the Four Principles of Biomedical Ethics" *Journal of Medical Ethics* Volume 25 Issue 4, 315–321. https://doi.org/10.1136/jme.25.4.315.

[26.] Zhong, Yicheng (2016) "Transformation and Practice of the Concept of 'Good End' in Taiwan—Focusing on the Legalization of End-of-Life Care" [in Japanese] Doctoral Dissertation, Ritsumeikan University. 80.

[27.] Ibid., 105.

[28.] "Close relative" refers to a person with age 20 or over and within the second degree of kinship.

[29.] Zhong (n 26) 112–118.

[30.] Yicheng, Chung (2015) "The Law and Ethics of End-of-Life Care in Taiwan: On the Practice of Terminal Discharge and a Criminal Court Case Concerning the Hospice and Palliative Care Act" [in Japanese] *Core Ethics* Volume 11, 123–134.

death culture, dying in a setting other than one's own home is perceived as a form of "dying as a stranger in a foreign land" (客死他鄉) , and is regarded as an undesirable outcome.[31] The practice of end-of-life discharge has existed in healthcare settings even before it was legalized. The enactment of the HPCA in 2000 is believed to have sanctioned this practice of end-of-life discharge, thereby rendering it legally possible to withhold or withdraw life-sustaining treatment in hospitals.

In 2016, the Patient Right to Autonomy Act (PRAA) was enacted to complement the HPCA and came into effect in 2019 after a three-year preparation period.[32] The Act comprises 19 articles, with the stated objective of "respecting patient autonomy in healthcare, safeguarding their rights to a good death, and promoting a harmonious physician–patient relationship" (Article 1). The PRAA requires hospitals to provide information to patients to enable them to create AD documents. Efforts to promote ACP have also commenced.[33] Since 2017, for example, Taipei City Hospital has been implementing ACP for patients within its facilities. All healthcare providers engaged in ACP must receive training programs.[34]

The "Management Method for Medical Institutions Providing Consultation Services for Advance Directive Documents" in Taiwan stipulates that hospitals providing ACP must have over 200 general beds and pass a municipal government evaluation. Additionally, they must have a dedicated area for the implementation of ACP. The ACP team must comprise a medical doctor and a nurse, psychologist, or social worker with at least two years of experience. It is also required that the personnel complete the training programs provided by the Ministry of Health and Welfare of Taiwan and maintain records until the completion of the ACP process. The fees for ACP services are determined by each hospital in collaboration with the municipal government.[35]

[31.] Ibid. In Taiwan, where Taoism is a prominent religion, it is believed that if a person dies outside of their home, their soul is unable to return to that residence. In such cases, a ritual called "summoning the soul" (招魂, "tamayobai") must be performed by a Taoist priest.

[32.] Taiwan, Ministry of Health and Welfare (2024) "Patient Autonomy Law to Take Effect Next Year: Ministry of Health and Welfare Announces Supporting Measures—Enforcement Rules of the Patient Autonomy Law" [in Chinese]. https://www.mohw.gov.tw/cp-3801-44221-1.html.

[33.] Wang, Shu-Chen, C.-J. Chang, S.-Y. Fan, et al. (2015) "Development of an Advance Care Planning Booklet in Taiwan" *Tzu Chi Medical Journal* Volume 27, 170–174, 174. https://doi.org/10.1016/j.tcmj.2015.07.003.

[34.] Chu, Dachen, Y.-F. Yen, H.-Y. Hu, et al. (2018) "Factors Associated with Advance Directives Completion among Patients with Advance Care Planning Communication in Taipei, Taiwan" *PLoS ONE* Volume 13 Issue 7, e0197552. https://doi.org/10.1371/journal.pone.0197552.

[35.] ACP clinics are provided by hospitals and charge approximately 3,500 NT (equivalent to US$107) for an initial consultation with patients, a fee that is perceived by many to be somewhat costly. Taiwan, Ministry of Health and Welfare (2024) "Patient Autonomy Law to Take Effect Next Year—Ministry of Health and Welfare Announces Supporting Measures—Regulations Governing the Management of Healthcare Institutions Providing Advance Care Planning Consultation" [in Chinese]. https://www.mohw.gov.tw/cp-3801-44221-1.html.

5.1.2.3 Discussion on the HPCA/PRAA

One distinctive aspect of ACP in Taiwan is the requirement that at least one family member or relative be invited to participate in the process. This demonstrates the influence of family collectivism based on relational autonomy. This differs from the approach taken in the U.K. and the U.S., where ADs can be made based on individual autonomy. In this regard, Taiwanese ACP encompasses not only individual autonomy but also relational autonomy in accordance with the law.

Furthermore, Taiwan incorporates religious rituals into end-of-life care and places a premium on spiritual care.[36] As Daniel F-C Tsai points out, current legislation strongly emphasizes the ethical principle of respecting patient autonomy. However, it also seeks to allow family members to maintain a key role in medical decision-making, which can create practical tensions.[37] He notes in his response to questionnaire that legally recognized ADs can reduce ambiguity and prevent violations of individual rights and autonomy. Moreover, legal ADs can help doctors avoid unethical practices that may be requested by families or influenced by misguided beliefs.

The legislators included provisions for family involvement in Article 9 of the PRAA, on the grounds that reliance solely on individual autonomy might not be sufficient to adapt to Taiwanese society. The Taiwanese PRAA places a high value on family involvement and stimulation in the subject of end-of-life care.[38] In this context, the concept of "Autonomy in Asia" entails family intervention, whereas the concept of "Autonomy in the West" is predicated on the primacy of individual autonomy.[39] It can be reasonably assumed that the provisions regarding family involvement in Article 9 were drafted by legislators with the intention of addressing situations where the individual's decision-making capacity is often diminished or lost.[40] It would appear prudent to adapt this implicit premise setting to a number of distinct categories in order to enhance its applicability to future users.

It is unclear whether this framework aligns with the desires of Taiwanese individuals in practice. Firstly, there is likely to remain considerable uncertainty

---

[36.] Zhong (n 26) 142–143.

[37.] Tsai (n 25) [2023] 89.

[38.] Kouy, BunRong (2019) "On Taiwan Patient Right to Autonomy Act: How Family Stimulates Autonomy" *Applied Ethics Review* Volume 67, 187–212.

[39.] Ibid.

[40.] Ibid., 206.

in practice as to how the basic legal provisions should be implemented and managed in professional healthcare settings. Practitioners' associations have demonstrated support for the HPCA and PRAA,[41] yet they have established their own guidelines and do not share a unified perspective in practice. Healthcare professionals' support is important to promote ADs and ACP. Secondly, in the event of conflicting interests between older adults and their family members, the older adults may opt to refrain from involving their family members. It may be preferable to regulate family involvement on a case-by-case basis, rather than as a mandatory requirement, to facilitate flexible treatment.

The legislative process has resulted in the enactment of pertinent laws, which have subsequently undergone gradual amendments. These amendments have been implemented with the objective of aligning the laws with traditional local customs pertaining to end-of-life treatment. It is notable that the prevalence of ADs remains relatively low, despite Taiwan's AD law being regarded as the most advanced in East Asia. In fact, between 2000 and 2022, 3.4% of the total population in Taiwan (0.8 million) signed HPCA forms,[42] which was less than the average in the U.S. and Europe.[43] As of March 2022, only 0.14% (33,000) of the population had completed an AD under the PRAA.[44]

There are several reasons why the utilization rates of ADs and ACP are low in Taiwan. These include limited awareness among citizens regarding the necessity of signing an AD, the provision of ACP clinics exclusively by hospitals, which charge approximately 3,500 NT (US$107) for the consultation, and that is considered by many to be expensive.[45] To address the financial constraints faced by ACP applicants, the Taiwanese government could consider providing economic subsidies to enhance the public's willingness to seek ACP discussions independently.[46]

In fact, starting July 1, 2024, ACP has been covered by the National Health Insurance (NHI) for hospitalized patients with full decision-making capacity who

---

[41.] Co-Shi Chantal Chao is a well-known palliative care practitioner in Taiwan who promoted legislations in the Parliament. Hospice Foundation in Taiwan (2024) "Prof. Co-Shi Chantal Chao Taiwan" https://www.hospice.org.tw/content/3480.

[42.] Tsai (n 25).

[43.] Tsai, Hsiao Ying (2022) "The Influence of Familism on Taiwan's Advance Care Planning (ACP) for End-of-Life" *Journal of the Japanese Society of Nursing Ethics* Volume 14 Issue 1, 48–51. https://www.jstage.jst.go.jp/article/jjne/14/1/14_20211011/_pdf.

[44.] Ibid.

[45.] From Daniel F-C Tsai's comments to the questionnaire in March 2024.

[46.] He, Yi-Jhen, M.-H. Lin, J.-L. Hsu, et al. (2021) "Overview of the Motivation of Advance Care Planning: A Study from a Medical Center in Taiwan" *International Journal of Environmental Research and Public Health* Volume 18 Issue 2, 417. https://doi.org/10.3390/ijerph18020417.

meet the following criteria: Patients aged over 65 years with catastrophic illnesses and diseases listed in the palliative care program; patients with mild dementia (scoring 0.5–1 on the Clinical Dementia Rating); patients with diseases listed in Subparagraph 5, Paragraph 1, Article 14 of the Patient Right to Autonomy Act; patients qualified for the integrated home-based health care program.[47]

5.1.2.4 Commentary

Taiwan's legislative approach to end-of-life care, exemplified by the HPCA and the PRAA, is commendable for prioritizing the preferences of older adults. Taiwan's legislation on ADs is the most progressive in East Asia, and its palliative care system ranks sixth globally in the 2015 Quality of Death Index.[48] However, two significant challenges remain: discrepancies with traditional values that emphasize family involvement and strains in the physician–patient relationship.

The future effectiveness of these laws will depend on how the Taiwanese government and parliament address these challenges. Given the evolving social context—marked by declining birth rates, an aging population, and more elderly individuals living alone—a pragmatic approach would be to gradually adjust legislative frameworks to better protect the autonomy of older adults while respecting traditional values. This strategy would help foster a harmonious evolution in the relationship between medical professionals and patients/families, making Taiwan's policies a model for legal frameworks in East Asia.

5.1.3 Observation of Singapore

5.1.3.1 Aging Society and National Policy in Singapore

The Republic of Singapore celebrates its 60th anniversary of independence in 2025, following its separation from Malaysia in 1965. The population of Singapore is 5.92 million (2023), comprising 4.15 million residents (citizens and permanent residents) and 1.77 million temporary residents, the majority of whom are foreign nationals.[49]

[47.] Taiwan, National Health Insurance Administration, Ministry of Health and Welfare (2024) "Advance Care Planning (ACP) to Be Covered by the NHI Starting July 2024" (July 23, 2024). https://www.nhi.gov.tw/en/cp-15374-f7edd-8-2.html.

[48.] The Economist Intelligence Unit (2015) *The 2015 Quality of Death Index Ranking Palliative Care across the World*. chrome-extension://efaidnbmnnnibpcajpcglclefindmkaj/https://impact.economist.com/perspectives/sites/default/files/2015%20EIU%20Quality%20of%20Death%20Index%20Oct%2029%20FINAL.pdf.

[49.] Singapore, Statistics Singapore (2024) "Population and Population Structure" https://www.singstat.gov.sg/find-data/search-by-theme/population/population-and-population-structure/latest-data.

Singapore's population is diverse, comprising ethnic Chinese (74% in 2022), Malays (14%), Indians (8%), and other ethnicities (4%). This reflects the country's multicultural ethos. Its legal system is based on English law from the colonial period, shaped by the challenges of a multicultural society. Despite rapid economic development, Singapore faces an aging population, with many older adults suffering from dementia.

Singapore's historical context emphasizes the family as the fundamental unit of society, as evidenced by the saying "where there is a family, there is a country" (有家有国).[50] The Maintenance of Parents Act of 1955 exemplifies this family-centric ideology, legally obligating children to support parents who are unable to support themselves at age 60 or due to illness, if the children can assist. In the event of noncompliance, the court may issue orders requiring financial support to be provided in the form of monthly payments or a lump sum. Failure to comply may result in imprisonment for up to six months or a fine of up to S$5,000.

As Singapore's economy developed, nuclear families became the norm, with both parents engaged in paid employment. This phenomenon gave rise to the "sandwich generation," comprising individuals who are responsible for the care of both older parents and children. The erosion of traditional familial support structures has led to a growing number of older adults residing alone, which raises concerns about their financial security. In 2022, the population aged 65 and above constituted 18.4% of the total population. The number of older adults in Singapore is projected to increase from 420,000 in 2014 to 900,000 by 2030, with an aging ratio of 25%. By 2050, the number is estimated to reach 1.14 million, exceeding a 27% aging ratio.

Singapore's demographic will undergo a significant transformation due to its aging population. Singapore is experiencing a faster rate of aging than Japan and South Korea, which will make it the world's fastest-aging nation by the 2050s. The total fertility rate is 1.14 (2019, World Bank), which is lower than Japan's, indicating a steady progression of aging and a declining birth rate.

Given these changes, the family remains the primary unit of society. Singaporeans are encouraged to prioritize self-reliance while promoting a caring community that supports vulnerable individuals. The government has implemented a social safety net, enacted legislation such as the Mental Capacity Act (MCA) of 2008 and Vulnerable Adults Act of 2016 and developed social systems.[51]

[50.] Sakurai, Yukio (2018) "Ageing in Singapore and Mental Capacity Act" [in Japanese] *Quarterly Comparative Guardianship Law* Volume 8, 53–67.

[51.] Tang, Hang Wu, Yukio Sakurai, and Yue-En Chong (2023) "Aging and the Law in Singapore and Japan: Adult Guardianship and Other Alternatives" *Journal of Ageing and Social Policy* Volume 37, 1–20. https://doi.org/10.1080/08959420.2023.2255484.

Singapore's welfare system is founded on self-reliance, aiming to facilitate autonomy through assistance, including pensions and housing policies, when necessary. The Singaporean welfare system is relatively lightweight, based on self-help and mutual assistance, and not aimed at becoming a welfare state. The growing need for government assistance due to an aging population challenges traditional welfare policies, compelling restructuring.

In this context, discussions on ADs and ACP must be situated within broader social and welfare policy frameworks. While tensions may emerge between individual autonomy and familial involvement, the government and Parliament continue to prioritize self-reliance, incorporating ADs and ACPs as part of this agenda. The key objective, therefore, is to identify effective strategies for promoting ADs and ACPs and to assess the appropriate level of governmental or institutional support required.[52]

5.1.3.2 Advance Medical Directive Act (AMDA) of 1996

The Advance Medical Directive Act (AMDA) was enacted in 1996 with the objective of regulating ADs in medical decision-making.[53] The MCA was enacted in 2008, largely following English law, MCA 2005. Therefore, the legal framework is established, and the issue is how to implement the law in Singaporean society. The MCA was the subject of parliamentary debate, during which it was suggested that the legal system be modified to make it more suitable for Singaporean citizens. The Act was amended twice, in 2016 and 2021, to achieve this goal.

The Ministry of Health of Singapore is responsible for conducting the campaign of advanced medical directive (AMD) and ACP for the public. For instance, the Ministry approved a S$18.1 million initiative in 2011 to develop and promote ACP on a national scale. This has led to the gradual implementation of ACP across public acute care hospitals, community hospitals, nursing homes, and eldercare providers. To date, nearly 5,000 plans have been lodged electronically, with 2,000 ACP conversation facilitators trained and over 1,000 community ACP advocates activated.[54]

---

[52] Chan, Tracey (2019) "Advance Care Planning: A Communitarian Approach?" NUS Centre for Asian Legal Studies Working Paper 2019.06.

[53] Singapore, Ministry of Health (2024) "Advance Medical Directive". https://www.moh.gov.sg/policies-and-legislation/advance-medical-directive; Singapore Statute Online (2024) "Advance Medical Directive Act 1996". https://sso.agc.gov.sg/Act/AMDA1996.

[54] Clement, Irwin, Alphonsus Wai, and Hoong Chung (2018) "Advance Care Planning in an Asian Country" in Keri Thomas, Ben Lobo, and Karen Detering (eds), *Advance Care Planning in End-of-Life Care*, 2nd ed. Oxford: Oxford online ed, Oxford Academic. https://doi.org/10.1093/oso/9780198802136.003.0023.

In 2020, the Ministry of Health of Singapore implemented the "My Legacy" portal, which serves as a comprehensive online resource for the public on end-of-life issues, including AMD.[55] However, the number of AMD and ACP users remains relatively low. As of July 19, 2025, the Parliament of Singapore debate revealed that over the past five years, 31,700 Singaporeans have signed their AMDs and 77,000 have made their ACP.[56]

In his analysis, Evans Chan identifies several factors that have contributed to the AMD initiative's shortcomings in promoting patient autonomy at the end of life. These include the social and policy context at the time of the initiative's inception, prevailing traditional values and familial approaches to healthcare decision-making, and limitations on anticipatory decision-making in human psychology.[57] Menon comments to the questionnaire, "ACP as it is currently conceived in Singapore may be beneficial to some people. It is more important that there is good communication, understanding of the patient's beliefs, values and preferences between the healthcare professionals, patient's loved ones and patients."

5.1.3.3 Discussion on the ADMA

The 2021 research on ACP implementation in Asia conducted by healthcare professionals concluded that, despite acknowledging its importance, Asian healthcare professionals perceived engaging in ACP as challenging. It is recommended that capacity building for ACP in Asia should focus on culturally adapting ACP models concerning the essential role of the family in Asia, education for healthcare professionals and the public, and providing institutional support for ACP.[58] The two analyses cited above demonstrate that the relationship with family members is an important factor that influences individual decision-making for healthcare, particularly in end-of-life care.

[55.] My Legacy (2024) "Live for Today, Plan for Tomorrow". https://mylegacy.life.gov.sg/.

[56.] Singapore, Ministry of Health (2023) "Number of Sign-Ups for Advanced Medical Directive and Advanced Care Plan" May 8, 2023. https://www.moh.gov.sg/news-highlights/details/number-of-sign-ups-for-advanced-medical-directive-and-advanced-care-plan.

[57.] Chan, Tracey (2023) "Advance Medical Directives in Singapore: A Faltering Policy for End-of-Life Care" in Daisy Cheung and Michael Dunn (eds), *Advance Directives across Asia: A Comparative Socio-Legal Analysis.* Cambridge: Cambridge University Press. 40.

[58.] Martina, Diah, Cheng-Pei Lin, Martina S. Kristanti, et al. (2021) "Advance Care Planning in Asia: A Systematic Narrative Review of Healthcare Professionals' Knowledge, Attitude, and Experience" *Journal of the American Medical Directors Association* Volume 22, P349.E1–P349.E28. https://doi.org/10.1016/j.jamda.2020.12.018.

As Evans Chan notes, Singapore has inherited the English common law system, but it operates within a multicultural Asian context where the family plays a central and often dominant role in the long-term care of older adults and terminally ill patients.[59] In this context, the legislation of English-origin laws, such as the AMDA and the MCA, presents a challenge to the local traditions and local customs in Singapore.[60]

Hang Wu Tang states that the tension between promoting individual autonomy and accommodating the family in the decision-making process plays out even more acutely in the Singapore context.[61] He suggests two reasons why the family plays a central role in the medical decision-making process. Firstly, the Asian family shoulders much of the burden of care, which in Western countries is performed by the state or state agencies. Secondly, this is a cultural issue. He highlighted these comments in the context of the Mental Capacity Act, but they are also relevant to AMDA.

As Tang proposes, healthcare professionals should be provided with a code of practice to follow before involving a patient's family members in the decision-making process.[62] This may seek to achieve a balance between furthering the patient's autonomy and recognizing the centrality of the family in certain contexts.

In their study, Sumytra Menon and her colleagues highlight the importance of ensuring that healthcare professionals and relevant family members adopt an autonomy-supportive approach, rather than an autonomy-undermining one, when interacting with patients.[63] This approach ensures that healthcare practices align with relevant laws and professional codes. Relational accounts of autonomy can inform assessments of the suitability of different forms of family involvement and health professionals' facilitation of treatment decision-making.

[59] Chan, Tracey, Nicola S. Peart, and Jacqueline Chin (2014) "Evolving Legal Responses to Dependence on Families in New Zealand and Singapore Healthcare" *Journal of Medical Ethics* Volume 40 Issue 12, 861–865, 863. https://doi.org/10.1136/medethics-2012-101225.

[60] Menon, Sundaresh (2013) "Euthanasia: A Matter of Life or Death?" *Singapore Medical Journal*. Volume 54 Issue 3, 116–128. https://doi.org/10.11622/smedj.2013043. PMID: 23546022.

[61] Tang, Hang Wu (2022) "Singapore's Adult Guardianship Law and the Role of the Family in Medical Decision-Making" *International Journal of Law, Policy and the Family* Volume 36, 1–12. ebac002. https://doi.org/10.1093/lawfam/ebac002.

[62] Ibid.

[63] Menon, Sumytra, V. A. Entwistle, A. V. Cambell, et al. (2020) "Some Unresolved Ethical Challenges in Healthcare Decision-Making: Navigating Family Involvement" *Asian Bioethics Review* Volume 12 Issue 1, 27–36. https://doi.org/10.1007/s41649-020-00111-9.

Furthermore, as Menon notes,[64] AMD only applies at the very end of someone's life by which time the family will have limited input on the patient's medical decisions. While the ACP as currently implemented in Singapore may be beneficial to some individuals, it is of greater importance that there is effective communication, understanding of the patient's beliefs, values, and preferences between healthcare professionals, the patient's loved ones, and the patient.

5.1.3.4 Commentary

The Singaporean government and Parliament enacted the AMD legislation earlier than other East Asian countries. However, there is a lack of clarity between policy-makers and citizens regarding views on end-of-life issues, evidenced by a discrepancy between the focus on individual autonomy and the role of family involvement.

A practical solution would be to adjust legislative frameworks and practices to better support the autonomy of older adults while respecting the traditional values of a multicultural society. This approach mirrors Taiwan's direction, making a comparative study of both countries valuable. Singapore is also leading in the digitalization of administrative data, including LPA and AMD, positioning it as an IT model state in East Asia.

5.2 A Comparative Analysis of ADs and ACP between East Asian Countries and Area

The following section presents a comparative analysis of the methods and performance of ADs and ACP in East Asia, which identifies common characteristics across the region.

5.2.1 Comparison of ADs and ACP in East Asia

5.2.1.1 Observations

It is challenging to conduct a direct comparison of the legal frameworks governing ADs in South Korea, Taiwan, and Singapore, as each country's laws and policies are shaped by a distinct historical and cultural context. Nevertheless, it is feasible to evaluate the stipulations of AD statutes in each nation, as illustrated

---

[64.] From the response of Sumytra Menon to the questionnaires in March 2024.

in Table 5.1.[65] The systems of ADs and ACP in end-of-life medical care in East Asia reflect different structures and levels of prevalence in the various countries.

In Japan, the utilization of an ending note as a method of advance preparation for end-of-life care is relatively limited in its diffusion. According to a survey conducted in 2021, approximately 8% of individuals aged between 50 and 80 and 13% of those aged 70 and above have an ending note, while 60% of its holders have completed the contents. Furthermore, more than 70% of holders aged 30–59 have already completed the form.[66] In Japan, ACP is not widely implemented due to several legal, cultural, and social challenges. The absence of formal legislation—limited to the 2018 guidelines for healthcare practitioners—along with a lack of public awareness and cultural taboos surrounding death, has hindered its adoption.

The government has initiated a pilot project to promote ACP in select regions, accompanied by a public campaign called the "life conference," which encourages older adults to discuss their end-of-life medical care with their relatives. Nevertheless, these initiatives have yet to gain widespread acceptance. The concept of "relational autonomy" has been proposed as a means of respecting both individual and family preferences in decision-making. As the number of single-living older adults without family caregivers continues to rise, local governments are legally obligated to provide care, funded through taxation, which imposes an additional financial burden on citizens.

In South Korea, ACP is legally supported by the ELDA. This legislation allows patients to make ADs concerning life-sustaining treatments. According to government data from September 26, 2025, 3.08 million citizens have completed ADs for life-sustaining treatment, 455,000 of whom have discontinued life-sustaining treatment. Additionally, 178,000 individuals possess an ACP issued by a medical practitioner. The expansion of ACP within clinical settings is ongoing, though challenges remain, particularly regarding social acceptance, education, and ensuring quality standards.

In Taiwan, palliative care directives and AMDs are utilized. ACP is mandated by the PRAA and must be completed prior to signing an AMD.[67] The Act requires

---

[65.] It is noteworthy that the highlighted sections in Table 5.1 indicate provisions for family involvement. The minimum age at which an individual can create an AD is the age of majority. In England and Wales, the age of majority is 16, while in most countries, it is 18. In South Korea, the age of majority is 19, and in Japan, it is 20.

[66.] Refers to the 2022 survey conducted by Mobile Marketing Data Labo and the 2021 End-of-Life Awareness Survey conducted by NPO Ra-Shi-Sa (2021) "Nationwide Survey on End-of-Life Awareness" [in Japanese]. https://www.ra-shi-sa.jp/_rashisa/wp-content/themes/rashisa/pdf/20210903_shukatsu-ishiki-survey.pdf.

[67.] The statement concerning Taiwan is based on an email dated February 2, 2024 from Chao-Tien Chang, Associate Professor in the Faculty of Law at National Taiwan University.

that ACP be facilitated by a multidisciplinary team within certified medical institutions. Additionally, a close relative and the designated health proxy must participate in the ACP process, though exceptions are made for individuals without close relatives.

In Taiwan, ACP places significant emphasis on relational autonomy, whereby close relatives are involved in the safeguarding of the patient's interests. Nevertheless, this emphasis on family involvement may potentially impinge upon individual autonomy. Financial constraints have also been identified, as the fee for ACP, set at NTD 3,500 (US$107), has been found to influence individuals' decisions to sign advance AMDs. Since July 2024, the ACP fee has been covered through the NHI for vulnerable individuals presenting with specific symptoms.

In Singapore, the AMDA 1996 and the MCA 2008 establish the Ministry of Health and Integrated Care Agency as the regulatory authority for ACP.[68] The AMDA permits patients to stipulate their preferences regarding the continuation of life-prolonging treatments in advance, whereas the MCA pertains to healthcare decision-making for patients who have lost the capacity to make decisions.

The ACP is commonly employed for patients with progressive diseases, dementia, and frailty, and is a collaborative decision-making process between patients, their families, and healthcare professionals. Healthcare professionals who facilitate ACP are required to undergo professional training, and their role is explicitly emphasized in the relevant literature.[69] The number of AMD and ACP users remains relatively low. The Parliament of Singapore debate revealed that over the past six years, 31,700 Singaporeans have signed their AMDs and 77,000 have made their ACP as of July 19, 2025.

5.2.1.2 Commentary

The evidence presented above demonstrates that the implementation of ADs and ACP in East Asia exhibits varying degrees of prevalence contingent on the legal framework and cultural context. It is noteworthy that, while the completion of end-of-life notes has reached a certain level of uptake in Japan, there is a paucity of statistical data on ACP. Conversely, the utilization of legal ADs is becoming increasingly prevalent in South Korea, with Taiwan and Singapore

---

[68.] The description for Singapore is derived from an email dated February 7, 2024 from Tracey Chan, Associate Professor, National University of Singapore.

[69.] In Hong Kong, ACP is promoted by the government and professional bodies, yet uptake remains low. Common obstacles include a lack of time, training and communication skills among health professionals, and a lack of awareness and preparedness among patients and families. A multi-pronged approach is required to promote ACP practice.

following suit. It is noteworthy that specific data on the discontinuation of life-sustaining treatment is available for South Korea. The comparison of ADs between three countries/area is summarizes in Table 5.2.

Table 5.2: Comparison of Advance Directives between South Korea, Taiwan, and Singapore

	South Korea	*Taiwan*	*Singapore*
Relevant Laws on ADs	Act on Decisions on Life-Sustaining Treatment for Patients in Hospice and Palliative Care or at the End of Life of 2016/2020[70]	Patient Right to Autonomy Act (PRAA) of 2015/2021 (major related law)[71] Hospice Palliative Care Act (HPCA) of 2000/2021(only limited for terminally ill patients)[72]	Advance Medical Directive Act of 1996/2020[73]

[70.] South Korea, Korean Law Information Center (2024). "Act on Decisions on Life-Sustaining Treatment for Patients in Hospice and Palliative Care or at the End of Life of 2016/2020." https://law.moj.gov.tw/ENG/LawClass/LawAll.aspx?pcode=L0020189. The enactment of legislation granting patients or their families the right to refuse life-sustaining treatment at the end of life was driven by public demand. In response, the government convened two advisory bodies to deliberate on the issue, which ultimately led to the passage of the law. The following sources were consulted for this study: the Council on the Institutionalization of Forgoing Life-Sustaining Treatments, established by the South Korean Ministry of Health and Welfare (2009–2010); and the Task Force for Decision-Making about Futile Life-Sustaining Treatment, as well as the Recommendations of the National Bioethics Advisory Committee, under the National Bioethics Review Committee (2012).

[71.] Taiwan, Laws & Regulations Database of the Republic of China (2024). "Patient Right to Autonomy Act of 2015/2021." https://law.moj.gov.tw/ENG/LawClass/LawAll.aspx?pcode=L0020066 or, Taiwan, Hospice Foundation of Taiwan. https://www.hospice.org.tw/content/2468. Zhong, Yicheng. 2016. "Transformation and Practice of the Concept of 'Good End' in Taiwan—Focusing on the Legalization of End-of-Life Care" [in Japanese]. Doctoral Dissertation, Ritsumeikan University 80.

[72.] Taiwan, Laws & Regulations Database of the Republic of China (2024). "Hospice Palliative Care Act of 2000/2021." https://law.moj.gov.tw/ENG/LawClass/LawAll.aspx?pcode=L0020066. Taiwan, Ministry of Health and Welfare (2023) "Patient Autonomy Law to Take Effect Next Year: Ministry of Health and Welfare Announces Supporting Measures—Enforcement Rules of the Patient Autonomy Law" [in Chinese]. https://www.mohw.gov.tw/cp-3801-44221-1.html.

[73.] Singapore, Singapore Statutes Online (2024) "Advance Medical Directive Act 1996". https://sso.agc.gov.sg/Act/AMDA1996. Singapore, Ministry of Health. 2024. "Advance Medical Directives." https://www.moh.gov.sg/policies-and-legislation/advance-medical-directive.

	South Korea	Taiwan	Singapore
Content of ADs[74]	Refraining or discontinuing life-sustaining treatment (withholding oxygen supply or discontinuing nutrition and hydration through intravenous drip is not allowed)	Withholding or withdrawal of life-sustaining treatment, artificial nutrition and hydration Palliative Care	The legislation provides for a standard template regarding the patient's treatment preferences and refusal options of withholding/withdrawal of extraordinary life-sustaining treatment.[75] While common law directives are possible, this provides more flexibility for individuals, the lack of a formal registry to ensure access when the AD is needed
Designation of Proxy	No provisions for the designation of a proxy	Not mandatory	The Advance Medical Directive Act 1996 does not cover enduring powers of attorney. This is covered by the Mental Capacity Act 2008

[74.] To assess the decision-making capacity of the person responsible for creating the AD, it is essential to refer to relevant legislation or capacity guidelines, such as the capacity toolkit or code of conduct. In Japan, a legal practice exists where a notary public issues a notarized document containing ADs, confirming that the individual has mental capacity.

[75.] In the AMDA, "extraordinary life-sustaining treatment" means any medical procedure or measure which, when administered to a terminally ill patient, will only prolong the process of dying when death is imminent, but excludes palliative care (Section 5.2).

	South Korea	Taiwan	Singapore
Criteria for Proxy	Same as above	An adult who demonstrates legal capacity and provides written consent to the designation. Those with conflicts of interest cannot act as a proxy: 1. The declarant's legatees. 2. Legatees of the declarant's remains or organs. 3. Other persons who shall benefit from the death of the declarant	The person must be at least 21 years old, mentally capable, not a healthcare provider, not bankrupt, and specified by the person. Professional proxies may be used for people without trusted family members
Criteria for Withholding Treatment in the Absence of ADs	For an agreement or cessation to be reached, it is necessary that the attending physician and at least one specialist in the relevant field be present, as well as *two or more family members who are in unanimous agreement regarding the discontinuation. Family members are defined as*	A diagnosis of terminal illness must be provided by two qualified healthcare professionals. If the patient is unable to express their will, consent may be provided by *a close relative:* *1. Spouse.* *2. Adult children and grandchildren.*	In making decisions on behalf of a person who lacks capacity, the following principles should be observed: the person's best interests, *consultation with their family (if feasible and appropriate to do so)*, and respect for any previously expressed wishes and values

	South Korea	Taiwan	Singapore
	follows: (a) the spouse; (b) lineal ascendants and descendants in the first degree; (c) lineal ascendants and descendants within the second degree, in the absence of any individuals falling under items (a) and (b); (d) siblings, in the absence of any individuals falling under items (a) through (c)	*3. Parents.* *4. Siblings* *5. Grandparents.* *6. Great grandparents, great grandchildren or third-degree collateral relative by blood.* *7. First-degree direct relation by marriage*	
Criteria for Discontinuation in Cases of Incapacity, Lack of ADs, and No Family Presence	Treatment cannot be discontinued	In the absence of a designated AD or close relatives, a medical recommendation for the best interests of the patient with a terminal illness would be provided following an examination by the hospice palliative care team	The written opinion of three healthcare practitioners, including a specialist, that the treatment is futile and prolongs the dying process[76]

[76.] Evans Chan states that this is a matter for professional medical judgment and institutional guidelines. There is no legal requirement for three opinions in cases of disagreement regarding the diagnosis of AMD. Menon notes that a written opinion from three doctors is required to carry out an AD under the AMDA. If the diagnosis is not AD under the AMDA, the doctor can decide.

	South Korea	*Taiwan*	*Singapore*
Supported Decision-Making	Can be implemented in the designated hospital	Not specifically mentioned. *ACP requires the involvement of one close relative*	While not explicitly provided for in the AMD Act 1996, it is possible to seek advice and support from others to do so. The appropriate statute is the Mental Capacity Act 2008, rather than the AMD Act. However, the AMD Act does require a medical practitioner to act as a witness, who is also required to explain the nature and effect of completing an AMD
Information-Sharing System for ADs[77]	Registered and stored in hospitals or nonprofit organizations designated by the Ministry of Health and Welfare, centralized in the National Life-Sustaining Medical Management Institution	After registration in the database of the Ministry of Health and Welfare, you will be registered on the health insurance card	A confidential registry of Advance Medical Directives maintained by the Registrar of Advance Medical Directives and accessible to authorized persons. There is an electronic system for storing and accessing ACPs in Singapore

Source: The author's summary of local researchers' responses

[77.] The duration of ADs depends on the specific circumstances of each case. To obtain accurate data regarding the duration of ADs, it is crucial to implement a system for registering ADs with the relevant authority through electronic data for statistical purposes.

5.2.2 Family Involvement in End-of-Life Medical Care

This section provides an overview of the role of the family in end-of-life medical care decision-making processes in East Asia, which represents a key feature of the East Asian model. Some research indicates that family communication among family members in end-of-life medical care in the context of the U.S.[78] The subsequent section focuses on the East Asian context, where family involvement is more profound and pervasive than in the U.S. In some cases, the family may assume the role of decision-maker on behalf of the individual. It is notable that relational autonomy, which is centered on the family as a basic unit of society, has an impact on decision-making in East Asia.

In Japan, the 2018 guidelines for healthcare professionals outline a framework for end-of-life medical and care decision-making. The 2018 guidelines are designed to facilitate communication between healthcare providers, patients, and their families. The MHLW encourages the implementation of "life conference," which are ACP discussions regarding end-of-life care. However, a high proportion of family members do not adhere to these recommendations, often substituting their own decisions for those of the patient. Recent research indicates that most of the population opposes the introduction of legislation governing end-of-life decisions. Furthermore, the number of individuals living alone without relatives is rising, underscoring the need for Japan to consider legislation or detailed guidelines to support the elderly in end-of-life situations.

A recent survey of Japanese healthcare practitioners revealed a growing recognition of the necessity for a legal framework, such as ADs, to guide decision-making in medical circumstances. However, there is a trend in medical institutions to prioritize institutional convenience over individual preferences, exemplified by the routine confirmation of DNAR orders from patients or families upon hospital admission.[79] This highlights the lack of established patient rights, and there has been little public response due to a lack of viable alternatives.

In South Korea, since the enactment of the ELDA, a significant number of older adults have created ADs, they refuse life-sustaining treatments or participating in end-of-life ACP to a greater extent than expected. This may be attributed to concerns about not wanting to burden their families financially with end-of-life

---

[78.] Trees, A. R., J. E. Ohs, and M. C. Murray (2017) "Family Communication about End-of-Life Decisions and the Enactment of the Decision-Maker Role" *Behavioral Sciences (Basel)* Volume 7 Issue 2, 36. PMID: 28590407; PMCID: PMC5485466. https://doi.org/10.3390/bs7020036.

[79.] Niigata University General Hospital (2022) "Guidelines in End-of-Life Care" [in Japanese]. https://www.nuh.niigata-u.ac.jp/wp-content/uploads/2022/03/tmc_guideline.pdf.

care, illustrating the strong influence of relational autonomy, often leading to self-sacrifice framed as self-determination.

In contrast, ADs and ACPs are not commonly used in Taiwan and Singapore. Nevertheless, family support often serves as an alternative to legal frameworks in such contexts. While family involvement is a notable feature of East Asian societies, its application varies between countries and is case-specific. It has been observed that families with robust relationships tend to achieve more favorable outcomes with ACP. Conversely, those with less robust family functioning may encounter difficulties in decision-making and communication, which could potentially limit the viability of ACP.[80]

In East Asia, family members are typically involved in end-of-life decision-making for older adults. However, legislation in South Korea and Taiwan provides clear guidelines regarding the family members who are involved in such decisions.

In South Korea, Article 18 of the ELDA stipulates that in the absence of an AD, treatment can be withheld if the attending physician and a specialist agree, and if two or more family members unanimously request the discontinuation of treatment. Family members include: (a) the spouse; (b) first-degree ascendants and descendants; (c) second-degree ascendants and descendants, in the absence of (a) and (b); and (d) siblings, if no other family members are available. It is imperative that the decision be unanimous among the designated family members, which resembles a quasi-family council. However, it should be noted that no formal family council system exists in South Korea.

In Taiwan, a terminally ill patient must be certified by two physicians, and if the patient is unable to express their wishes, a close relative may provide consent. According to Article 7 of the HPCA, close relatives include: 1. Spouse, 2. Adult children and grandchildren, 3. Parents, 4. Siblings, 5. Grandparents, 6. Great grandparents or third-degree collateral relatives, and 7. First-degree relatives by marriage. Although unanimous agreement is not required in Taiwan, the law specifies the hierarchy of decision-makers among relatives. Notably, Taiwan's Civil Code includes provisions for a family council system (Articles 1129–1137), but this system applies only to inheritance matters and does not extend to medical decision-making.[81]

[80.] Boerner, K., D. Carr, and S. Moorman (2013) "Family Relationships and Advance Care Planning: Do Supportive and Critical Relations Encourage or Hinder Planning?" *Journals of Gerontology, Series B: Psychological Sciences and Social Sciences* Volume 68 Issue 2, 246–256, 254. Advance Access publication January 3, 2013. https://doi.org/10.1093/geronb/gbs161.

[81.] The comments on family council were provided by Sieh-Chuen Huang via email to the author on July 24, 2024; Hsieh, Tian-Huai (2024) "An Empirical Legal Study on the Function of Family Council in Modern Society" Master Thesis at Taiwan National University. chrome-extension://efaidnbmnnnibpcajpcglclefindmkaj/https://tdr.lib.ntu.edu.tw/jspui/retrieve/53f3e14b-6262-4fa3-b484-9b2bfae9451e/ntu-112-1.pdf.

In South Korea and Taiwan, legal fictions are employed to ascertain the collective opinion of the patient's family members, thereby justifying decisions on the patient's behalf. However, this approach does not address the potential for conflict within families, which may be effectively suppressed by one or more dominant individuals. Conversely, in Japan and Singapore, there is no legislation nor guidelines specifying which family members should be involved. Consequently, family involvement in these decisions generally follows the local practices of medical institutions, nursing homes, or home care settings.

5.2.3 Traditional Values behind Family Involvement

5.2.3.1 Observations

In East Asia, the involvement of the family in end-of-life medical care decision-making process is rooted in the region's cultural and social values, which place the family at the center of care and responsibility.[82] In East Asia, traditional beliefs—largely shaped by Confucianism, Taoism, and Buddhism—place a significant emphasis on filial piety, which refers to the obligation of children to respect and care for their parents, particularly in older age or during periods of illness.[83] This cultural expectation situates family members at the center of decision-making processes concerning medical treatment, including end-of-life care.

The concept of collectivism, a key cultural feature in East Asia, is of particular significance in this context. In contrast to Western societies, which tend to emphasize individual autonomy and personal rights, East Asian culture places a greater emphasis on group harmony and familial obligations, which coincide with the notion of relational autonomy. In matters pertaining to health and life-or-death decisions, it is often deemed inappropriate for the individual to make decisions in isolation. In contrast, families are regarded as having a duty to safeguard the

---

[82] Bullock, K. (2011) "The Influence of Culture on End-of-Life Decision Making" *Journal of Social Work and End-of-Life Palliative Care* Volume 7 Issue 1, 83–98. PMID: 21391079. http://doi.org/10.1080/15524256.2011.5 48048; Blank, R. H. (2011) "End-of-Life Decision Making across Cultures" *Journal of Law, Medicine & Ethics* Volume 39 Issue 2, 201–214. https://doi.org/10.1111/j.1748-720X.2011.00589.x; Dzeng, E., T. Bein, and J. R. Curtis (2022) "The Role of Policy and Law in Shaping the Ethics and Quality of End-of-Life Care in Intensive Care" *Intensive Care Medicine* Volume 48, 352–354. https://doi.org/10.1007/s00134-022-06623-2.

[83] Ho, Zheng Jie Marc, L. K. Radha Krishnan, C. P. A. Yee (2010) "Chinese Familial Tradition and Western Influence: A Case Study in Singapore on Decision Making at the End of Life" *Journal of Pain and Symptom Management* Volume 40, Issue 6, 932–937. https://doi.org/10.1016/j.jpainsymman.2010.06.010; Cheng, S. Y., C.-P. Lin, H. Y.-L. Chan, et al. (2020) "Advance Care Planning in Asian Culture" *Japanese Journal of Clinical Oncology* Volume 50 Issue 9, 976–989; Li, W. W., S. Singh, and C. Keerthigha (2021) "A Cross-Cultural Study of Filial Piety and Palliative Care Knowledge: Moderating Effect of Culture and Universality of Filial Piety" *Frontiers in Psychology* Volume 12, 787724. PMID: 34925189; PMCID: PMC8678124. https://doi.org/10.3389/fpsyg.2021.787724.

well-being and dignity of their relatives, which frequently entails making medical decisions on their behalf.

In addition, the involvement of family in end-of-life medical care decisions is further reinforced by cultural taboos surrounding death, which prevent many individuals from openly discussing or preparing for their own end-of-life care. This reluctance leaves families to intervene and make pivotal decisions in a manner they deem to be optimal for the patient, frequently prioritizing the collective interest of the family over the explicit wishes of the patient. This is particularly evident in East Asia, where familial interdependence is an ingrained aspect of societal norms.

In Japan, despite the absence of a formal legal obligation to involve family members, customary practice favors a family-centered approach to decision-making. The process is guided by nonlegal norms, with families frequently making decisions on behalf of patients who lack the capacity to make decisions for themselves. This reflects the values of collective responsibility and interdependence. Notwithstanding the increasing promotion of individual autonomy in medical decision-making, traditional beliefs regarding family unity and collective care continue to exert a significant influence.

Moreover, a high proportion of healthcare professionals demonstrate respect for family involvement in medical decision-making, particularly in end-of-life medical care, despite their limited understanding of legal theory. Therefore, family involvement remains unchanged and serves to perpetuate the status quo. In Japan, there is no specific legislation regulating medical decision-making and informed consent. Instead, medical practices tend to respect family involvement.

In South Korea and Taiwan, the role of the family in end-of-life decision-making is explicitly recognized and even codified in law. In South Korea, for instance, the ELDA bestows upon families the authority to consent to or refuse life-sustaining treatments for incapacitated patients. This legal recognition reflects the broader cultural belief that decisions pertaining to death should be collectively made, with deference to familial hierarchies.[84] The study in South Korea reveals that family members often play a significant role in decision-making, even when advance care plans exist, reflecting the strong familial involvement based on traditional familial norms.[85]

---

[84] Choi, Kyungsuk (2016) "Legal and Ethical Issues Regarding End-of-Life Care in Korea" *Development and Society* Volume 45 Issue 1, 151–164. https://doi.org/10.21588/dns.2016.45.1.006.

[85] Kang, E. K., B. Keam, N.-R. Lee, et al. (2021) "Impact of Family Caregivers' Awareness of the Prognosis on Their Quality of Life; Depression and Those of Patients with Advanced Cancer: A Prospective Cohort Study" *Supportive Care in Cancer* Volume 29 Issue 1, 397–407. https://doi.org/10.1007/s00520-020-05489-8.

Similarly, Taiwan's PRAA aims to promote patient autonomy, but families often play a dominant role due to cultural obstacles such as taboos surrounding discussions of death.[86] The divergent interpretations of the "filial piety" between the HPCA and the PRAA may prove to be a complicating factor.[87] The "filial piety" posits that it is the family's responsibility and a means of demonstrating respect to older parents to make end-of-life medical decisions on their behalf. Consequently, the HPCA permits the justified withholding or withdrawing of life-prolonging treatment through surrogate decision-making by family members.

In contrast, the PRAA debate emphasizes the importance of "filial piety" in the context of individual autonomy. With this evolving interpretation, it is crucial to consider both the individual's wishes and family relationships in end-of-life medical care. Legislation often lags behind societal customs, but the PRAA is proactive in anticipating shifts in advance. However, it may intensify value conflicts between individual autonomy and "filial piety," potentially leading to underuse of ADs.[88]

It is imperative that they enhance their capabilities to address deficiencies in the PRAA, including the absence of penalties, inadequacies in medical institutions' scope of duty of disclosure, and the lack of a settlement mechanism for individuals who have not yet established ADs.[89] Furthermore, the HPCA and PRAA have divergent policies regarding physician liability.[90]

While the HPCA includes provisions for penalties against physicians who violate end-of-life procedures, the PRAA does not have penalty provisions for physicians. In contrast, Article 14 of the PRAA permits physicians to exercise professional autonomy in declining to implement a patient's AD based on their

---

[86] Tang, S. T., T.-W. Liu, M.-S. Lai, et al. (2005) "Concordance of Preferences for End-of-Life Care between Terminally Ill Cancer Patients and Their Family Caregivers in Taiwan" *Journal of Pain and Symptom Management* Volume 30 Issue 6, 510–518. PMID: 16376737. https://doi.org/10.1016/j.jpainsymman.2005.05.019. Hu, W. Y., T. Y. Chiu, R. B. Chuang, and C. Y. Chen (2002) "Solving Family-Related Barriers to Truthfulness in Cases of Terminal Cancer in Taiwan: A Professional Perspective" *Cancer Nursing* Volume 25 Issue 6, 486–492. PMID: 12464841. https://doi.org/10.1097/00002820-200212000-00014.

[87] Zhong, Yi-chun (2022) "Consideration of End-of-Life Medical Decision-Making Based on 'Filial Piety' and the Role of the Family: Using the Analysis of the 'Double Filial Piety Model' as a Clue" [in Japanese] *Otani University Shinshu Research Institute Research Bulletin* Volume 39, 163–180.

[88] Liang, Y. W., Y.-H. Lin, S.-T. Chen, et al. (2021) "Differential Acceptance of Advance Directives between Millennials and Baby Boomer Generations: A Cross-Sectional Survey Study among College Students and Their Relatives" *Journal of Palliative Care* Volume 37 Issue 3, 280–288. https://doi.org/10.1177/08258597211062757.

[89] Chen, Chih-Hsiung (2019) "Legislating the Right-to-Die with Dignity in a Confucian Society: Taiwan's Patient Right to Autonomy Act" *Hastings International and Comparative Law Review* Volume 42 Issue 2, 485–508. https://repository.uchastings.edu/hastings_international_comparative_law_review/vol42/iss2/4.

[90] Tsai (n 25).

"professional expertise or wishes." The divergence in policies regarding physician liability as set forth in both laws may give rise to confusion among patients.

It is notable that Singapore has established legal frameworks, such as the AMDA, with the objective of advancing patient autonomy. Nevertheless, even in Singapore, the influence of Asian family values—respect for elders and deference to authority—frequently results in families assuming the decision-making role, particularly when confronted with sensitive matters such as terminal illness. The extent to which patients in Singapore can exert autonomy in end-of-life care decision-making is influenced by five themes, as identified by healthcare professionals. These are: (i) collusion over truth-telling to the patient, (ii) deferment of autonomy by patients, (iii) negotiating patient self-determination, (iv) relational autonomy as the gold standard, and (v) obstacles to the realization of patient choices.[91]

5.2.3.2 Commentary

East Asian countries face the challenge of balancing traditional family-based decision-making with evolving legal frameworks that prioritize individual autonomy. This issue involves adapting both legislation and individual behaviors.[92] Family involvement in critical decisions is influenced not only by legal requirements but also by cultural norms rather than just traditional values.[93]

To promote individual autonomy, a possible solution for older adults is to encourage proactive planning, such as completing ADs or ACP, to express their wishes regarding end-of-life care.[94] Family involvement can support aligning the older adult's wishes with healthcare professionals' decisions.

It is essential to find the most effective way to encourage older adults to adopt this approach, a challenge that impacts not only older adults but also their families, healthcare professionals, and community. Public campaigns, including webinars,

---

[91.] Dutta, O., P. Lall, P. V. Patinadan, et al. (2020) "Patient Autonomy and Participation in End-of-Life Decision-Making: An Interpretive-Systemic Focus Group Study on Perspectives of Asian Healthcare Professionals" *Palliative & Supportive Care* Volume 18 Issue 4, 425–430. PMID: 31699170. https://doi.org/10.1017/S1478951519000865.

[92.] Sakurai, Yukio (2023) "Adaptation of Law and Policy in an Aged Society: Guardianship Law and People's Behavioral Pattern" *The Rest: The Journal of Politics and Development* Volume 13 Issue 2, 144–154. http://hdl.handle.net/10131/0002000015; Kawashima, Takeyoshi (1967) *Legal Consciousness in Law in Japan* [in Japanese]. Tokyo: Iwanami Shoten, Publishers; Seki, Hiroshi (2024) *Legal Consciousness of Modern Japanese People* [in Japanese]. Tokyo: Kodansha.

[93.] Mori, Masanori, and Morita Tatsuya (2020) "End-of-Life Decision-Making in Asia: A Need for In-Depth Cultural Consideration" *Palliative Medicine* Volume 34 Issue 2, NP4–NP5. https://doi.org/10.1177/0269216319896932.

[94.] Lin, Cheng-Pei, Shao-Yi Cheng, and Ping-Jen Chen (2018) "Advance Care Planning for Older People with Cancer and Its Implications in Asia: Highlighting the Mental Capacity and Relational Autonomy" *Geriatrics* Volume 3 Number 3, 43. https://doi.org/10.3390/geriatrics3030043.

workshops, TV dramas, and other media, could be effective tools for engaging the public in end-of-life decision-making.

5.3 Discussion on ADs and ACP in the East Asian Model

This section presents a discussion of the East Asian model, with particular emphasis on four apparently conflicting conceptual directions in relation to ADs and ACP. Through a process of deliberations, it is proposed that these conflicting directions could be reconciled and harmonized to complement one another.

5.3.1 Healthcare versus Asset Management

Healthcare professionals play a pivotal role in such processes to educate individuals that the initiatives for ADs and ACP are practically designed for the benefit of individuals and their family members. Healthcare professionals' understanding and support of ADs and ACP will significantly influence its acceptance and implementation.[95]

For example, a Japanese physician discusses two types of ACP in his lecture.[96] The first is for healthy people, who do not need to plan for specific end-of-life treatments. The second is for those with a life expectancy of less than a year, who should do ACP as soon as possible. He suggests that careful communication between the healthcare professionals and the patient is important to foster hope and trust. Clear disparities exist between the perspectives and positions of healthcare professionals and patients, and merely increasing opportunities for communication may still be insufficient to alter the practices of healthcare professionals. This is a common observation across various countries, indicating shared societal challenges. He therefore promotes early ACP with a surrogate who can respect the patient's wishes, values, and family members.

He also emphasizes the need to balance hope and readiness, using the phrase, "Hope for the best, prepare for the worst." This is vital because everyone needs hope until the final moment, otherwise they might feel hopeless and resist ACP.

[95.] Shimizu, Yukihiro (2021) "Practice and Challenges of POLST (Physician Orders for Life-Sustaining Treatment) and Advance Care Planning at Nanto Municipal Hospital" [in Japanese] *The Journal of the Japan Medical Association* Volume 149 Issue 11, 2007–2011.

[96.] This refers to an online lecture delivered by Yoshiyuki Kizawa, Professor of the Institute of Medicine at the University of Tsukuba, Japan and President of the Japanese Society for Palliative Medicine. The lecture was hosted by the Institute of Science Tokyo on February 26, 2024. Kizawa, Yoshiyuki (2020) "Advance Care Planning (ACP): To Practice Medical Care at the Final Stage of Life in accordance with the Individual's Wishes" [in Japanese] *Pharmacia* Volume 56 Issue 2, 105–109.

He has learned this lesson from his years of palliative care practice. To facilitate patients' engagement ACP, healthcare professionals must promptly assess and advocate for patients' concerns or attitudes regarding ACP.[97] Furthermore, the current study identified factors or concerns that might influence patients' responses to ACP. These findings must be considered when initiating the dialogue regarding ACP with patients with advanced cancer.

The ACP for cancer patients with dementia requires special attention. It should start early when the patient can still make decisions. Long-term outlooks are important, but they are hard to predict because each patient has a different diagnosis. Many dementia patients die before experiencing severe cognitive decline.

This highlights the need for ACP to cover more than just medical and care issues and ADs; it must also include mid- to long-term care plans, the patient's values, and financial matters for the patient to be taken care of over an extended period. Older cancer patients diagnosed with dementia often require assistance from others in both medical care and financial management over an extended period.[98] Currently, it is typically the patient's family providing this support.

However, with the increasing proportion of older adults living alone, there is a growing challenge where seeking assistance from family members or relatives may not always be feasible. It is considered necessary to establish legal and/or welfare frameworks that can support individuals in managing both medical care and financial matters. Otherwise, it takes time for healthcare practitioners to take care of these patients one by one.

At least, healthcare professionals may lack the capacity for financial management support, and even hospital-based medical social workers may not be able to address each individual request within the limited working time. Comparative law studies can provide insights into the legal frameworks used in foreign countries. Frameworks should be designed to meet the requirements and realities of hospitals to achieve effective and stable medical administration within the limited medical resources.

In Japan, as well as in any country or area, there has traditionally been a clear distinction between clinical medicine, responsible for medical care, and private law, responsible for asset management, in the systems of laws and policies. In the

---

[97.] Chen, Y. C., H. P. Huang, T. H. Tung, et al. (2022) "The Decisional Balance, Attitudes, and Practice Behaviors, Its Predicting Factors, and Related Experiences of Advance Care Planning in Taiwanese Patients with Advanced Cancer" *BMC Palliative Care* Volume 21, 189. https://doi.org/10.1186/s12904-022-01073-5.

[98.] This paragraph refers to an online lecture delivered by Asao Ogawa, a psycho-oncology physician and Director of the Department of Psycho-Oncology at the National Cancer Center Hospital East, at an online seminar hosted by Yokohama National University, Japan on November 12, 2023.

past, this division did not pose significant problems. However, in societies with extended life expectancy and aged populations, the realms of asset management and medical care have become closely intertwined.

It is evident that there is a need for some role, such as an intermediary agencies or specialized profession, to connect both aspects.[99] For example, creating a program to cultivate legal professionals with expertise in the medical field nationwide and annually fostering a certain number of talents with the support of local government entities is one proposed idea. If these legal professionals are available in the community, they can contribute to the social demands to help the patients for their financial management.

Besides these emerging demands, continuous education and training for healthcare professionals for ADs and ACP, along with diagnosis of patients on various occasions, are essential. The introduction of ADs and ACP as well as shared decision-making in healthcare is a complex process that requires a comprehensive and traditionally sensitive approach and the role of healthcare practitioners in these functions is crucial.

5.3.2 One-Size-Fits-All versus Consumer Choices

The 2012 Issue Paper of the Council of Europe emphasizes that

> "the right to live in the community is intricately linked with fundamental rights such as personal liberty, private and family life, and freedom from ill-treatment or punishment.[100] This right is explicitly articulated in the United Nations CRPD, particularly in Article 19, which advocates for full inclusion and participation in society.
>
> Article 19 outlines three key elements: choice, individualized support promoting inclusion and preventing isolation, and accessibility of public services to people with disabilities."

The overarching objective of "full inclusion and participation in society" outlined in Article 19 of the CRPD, along with the significance of its three key elements, is directly relevant to older adults. Among these elements, "choice" holds particular importance. "One-size-fits-all" approaches are prevalent in contemporary society. Providing individuals with the opportunity to make decisions tailored to their own circumstances can significantly enhance their well-being.

---

[99] Ibid.

[100] Council of Europe, Commissioner for Human Rights (2012) *The Right of People with Disabilities to Live Independently and Be Included in the Community.* Council of Europe, Commissioner for Human Rights. https://book. coe.int/en/commissioner-for-human-rights/7329-pdf-the-right-of-people-with-disabilities-to-live-independently-and-be-included-in-the-community.html.

Conversely, situations where only one option is available, not aligned with individual preferences, may lead to dissatisfaction. Such instances, lacking choice, are often described as "one-size-fits-all," contrasting with situations where individual autonomy prevails, termed as "consumer choices." ADs, ACP, and Advance Decision-Making fall within the domain of consumer choices, representing predetermined decisions where individuals aspire for their preferences to be honored even after a delay.

For example, Japan's adult guardianship system operates under a Civil Code framework, reflecting a standardized approach. Similarly, many government-imposed public measures tend to adopt such uniform models. In healthcare, although the NHI system aims for equal medical treatment for all, it necessitates some degree of conformity to a one-size-fits-all approach, driven by the need for uniform service provision within communities.

Nevertheless, today, characterized by recognition of development and improved quality of life, it is assumed that individuals have the freedom to enjoy consumer choices. This necessitates individual autonomy as consumers, and in cases of deficiency, support should be provided to enable individuals to exercise their autonomy through decision-making.

While consulting with family members or physicians is vital to ensure the validity of decisions, reliance solely on them will not lead to consumer choices. Ultimately, consumer choices are realized when individuals express their individual autonomy through active participation in the community or social systems. This argument applies equally to ADs, ACP, and Advance Decision-Making.

The discourse surrounding consumer choices intersects with the criteria utilized to discern the intentions of the principal. Subsequently, we will partially review the discourse on Article 12 of the CRPD. General Comment No. 1 advocates for the elimination of substituted decision-making and advocates for the implementation of supported decision-making, which respects the "will and preferences" of the principal. The "best interests" principle, in relation to adults, fails to serve as a safeguard compliant with Article 12.

To ensure that individuals with disabilities enjoy the right to legal capacity on par with others, the "will and preferences" paradigm must supplant the "best interests" paradigm. Supported decision-making underscores the principal's capacity to make decisions, provided they receive the necessary support to formulate and articulate their decisions. It prioritizes the desires of the principal.[101]

[101.] To guarantee that individuals with disabilities are able to exercise their legal capacity on an equal footing with others, it is imperative that the "will and preferences" paradigm supersedes the "best interests" paradigm (General Comment No. 1 by UN CRPD Committee).

In Japan, the initiative to develop guidelines for supported decision-making represents a positive step. This initiative aims to equip nursing home managers, social workers, and adult guardians with the tools to facilitate supported decision-making in the realm of community support services for individuals with disabilities and/or dementia, thereby honoring the will and preferences of the principals.[102]

In certain developed countries with demographic characteristics akin to Japan's, such as an aging population and a growing number of older adults with dementia, legislative measures or amendments to civil codes or guardianship laws offer support and protection to vulnerable adults. This legal framework, known as adult support and protection legislation, centers on the vulnerability of the principal and provides the necessary support and protection.[103] Such legislation seeks to minimize the encroachment on the principal's human rights and encourages the adoption of the least restrictive measures to achieve its objectives.[104]

In a legislative trend, the concept of "adult support and protection legislation" holds significance in promoting the values of the CRPD, as well as consumer choices and advance decision-making, which contribute to the well-being of the principals. In this context, individual autonomy and self-determination emerge as paramount, although older adults may also consider relational autonomy to reconcile with family members and stakeholders, provided it does not compromise the value of individual autonomy.

5.3.3 Legal Approach versus Practical Approach

In response to medical disputes, patients' legal rights, framed within the context of civil rights movements, have been debated, litigated, and subsequently legislated in the US and countries influenced by it. In contrast, Japan resolves medical disputes without the enactment of legislation, even in instances of criminal or civil incidents. This is achieved by relying on nonlegally binding

---

[102.] Sakurai, Yukio (2022) "Value of Legislation Providing Support and Protection to Vulnerable Adults: Vulnerability Approach and Autonomy" Chapter 2. Doctoral Dissertation, Yokohama National University. http://doi.org/10.18880/00014834.

[103.] Sakurai, Yukio (2023) "Value of Legislation Providing Support and Protection to Vulnerable Adults: Consideration for a Core Agency and Supported Decision-Making" *Journal of Aging Law and Policy (Stetson Law School)* Volume 14, 43–96. https://www.stetson.edu/law/agingjournal/media/JALP%20Vol.%2014%20Final.pdf.

[104.] The "least restrictive alternative" is derived from the case of *Shelton v. Tucker*, in which the U.S. Supreme Court ruled on December 12, 1960 (5–4) that the Arkansas statute requiring all public-school educators to disclose every institution to which they were affiliated over a five-year period was unconstitutional. Johnston, J. M., and Robert A. Sherman (1993) "Applying the Least Restrictive Alternative Principle to Treatment Decisions: A Legal and Behavioral Analysis" *The Behavior Analyst* Volume 16 Issue 1, 103–115.

instruments such as guidelines for healthcare practitioners and ending notes or end-of-life planning notes.

These notes, promoted by municipalities to older adults, are nonlegally binding documents that allow them to express their wishes regarding end-of-life healthcare, asset management, and so on. This dichotomy in approaches to handling medical disputes is referred to in this book as the "legal approach" for the former and the "practical approach" for the latter. The legal approach seeks development based on deductive reasoning from case law and statutory law, while the practical approach seeks development through inductive reasoning, deriving social norms from commonalities among things and events.

The advantage of the legal approach lies in its ability to safeguard patient rights by uniformly specifying methods and procedures for ADs and ACP, thereby exerting a consistent legal influence on the population. However, without accompanying penalties, the legal approach cannot enforce its authority, and there are inherent limitations to the law's impact. The discussion on ADs and ACP in healthcare is closely tied to the traditions and local customs of the respective populations. Therefore, the legal approach, based on individual autonomy and the patients' rights, may not be directly applicable in other countries with different social environments and values.

In this sense, the practical approach involves attempts by those working in the field to find methods accepted by the local populations, rooted in the social environment and values of that country or area, representing a bottom-up approach. The practical approach, lacking a legal basis, allows for flexible guidance on ADs and ACP methods under general legal principles, providing tools for stakeholders to use.[105]

Yet, in the practical approach, addressing individual cases requires significant human resources and time. Therefore, improving the working methods of healthcare practitioners to fit within the bounds of legal regulations and enhancing the operational efficiency of medical institutions poses challenges. Striving excessively for efficiency may compromise the quality of practical approaches. Hence, it is essential to consider legal approaches and predefine the procedures for ADs and ACP to enhance the efficiency of healthcare practitioners' administrative processes. The adoption of a practical approach by

---

[105.] Mizuno, Noriko (2011) "Medical Decision-Making and the Role of the Family: A Civil Law Perspective on the Guardianship System for the Mentally Disabled" [in Japanese] *The Journal of Law and Political Science* Volume 74 Issue 6, 880–912.

medical institutions or local authorities may, at times, prioritize these entities' interests over patient rights.

Countries or areas that have adopted a legal approach are making efforts to enhance the laws and policies related to ADs and ACP. They encounter various operational challenges, and the anticipated results may not have been realized yet. It is deemed essential to judiciously incorporate practical approaches alongside efforts to improve the legal framework.

This includes fostering bottom-up initiatives in healthcare and nursing fields. For example, to leverage the benefits of both ADs and ACP while compensating for their respective weaknesses, it might be worthwhile to consider utilizing both ADs and ACP in tandem to the person.[106] By combining both approaches, there is an expectation that the patient's wishes and values will be more comprehensively understood and respected.

As Sumytra Menon and Shumin Eunice Chua state, the application of law is not straightforward and requires interpretation.[107] Furthermore, the law does not contain written solutions to ethical dilemmas. Therefore, practical ethical reasoning, alongside knowledge of the law, is required to evaluate ethical issues and value conflicts in ACP. Ethical reasoning largely comes through a practical approach.

The practical approach and the legal approach are not mutually exclusive or in conflict; rather, they can complement each other by exchanging information and leveraging their respective strengths and weaknesses. By doing so, a healthy balance between practical and legal approaches as equilibrium may be achieved between the practical and legal approaches.

The use of specific written instructions along with communication and planning for future medical care in conjunction is anticipated to enable more effective delivery of healthcare. This situation is influenced by the traditional tendency to avoid discussions on death and end-of-life care, even when prepared in advance.

Focusing on Japan, it is considered appropriate to promote practical approaches for the time being. As awareness of ADs and ACP becomes more widespread among the population, the country can then proceed to develop detailed guidelines for ADs and ACP. Subsequently, a phased transition to legalization within

---

[106.] This concept was initially proposed by Chao-Tien Chang (National Taiwan University) in an email exchange with the author in March 2024.

[107.] Menon, Sumytra, and Shumin Eunice Chua (2024) "Ethics & Law on Advance Care Planning: A Perspective from Singapore" in Raymond Han Lip Ng, D. Marina, C. Lin, et al. (eds), *Advance Care Planning in the Asia Pacific*. Singapore: World Scientific Publishing. 97–103.

reasonable limits can be pursued. It is crucial to leverage advancements in dig-italization and scientific technologies like artificial intelligence (AI) to enhance the adaptability of the system.[108]

5.3.4 Individual Autonomy versus Relational Autonomy

There is a view on two diverse types of principles of autonomy with di-verse traditional background: "the Western principle of autonomy demands self-determination, assumes a subjective conception of the good and promotes the value of individual independence, while the East Asian principle of autonomy requires family-determination, presupposes an objective conception of the good and upholds the value of harmonious dependence."[109]

Although this may be a stereo-type argument to contrast between the Western principle of autonomy and the East Asian principle of autonomy, such argument demonstrates part of the truth regarding different approaches to autonomy in two jurisdictions.[110] The foundation of the East Asian model is rooted in relational autonomy, where individuals' decisions are influenced by the opinions of others, such as family members and healthcare professionals. This leads to a tendency for individual autonomy to be contextualized.

Relational autonomy spans a spectrum, from complete dependence on the opinions of family members to using them as references while primarily making decisions independently. The nature of this relationship also varies depending on whether there is a conflict of interest between the individual and the family members. Therefore, it is challenging to make a generalized statement about relational autonomy in the context of ADs and ACP.[111]

The U.S. model AD system and ACP, which prioritizes individual autonomy and the right to self-determination, may not be readily accepted in East Asian

---

[108.] Ikka proposes the enactment of the Medical Basics Act (provisional), which would serve to explicitly delineate the rights and obligations of healthcare practitioners and patients (Ikka, Tsunakuni (2011) "The History and Current Status of Medical Basic Law" [in Japanese] *Annual Report of Medical Law* Volume 26, 16–38; Ikka, Tsunakuni (2023) "Medical Jurisprudence on End-of-Life Care and Terminal Sedation" [in Japanese] in Tatsuya Morita and Shimon Tashiro (eds), *Questioning the Grey Zone of Sedation and Euthanasia: Perspectives from Medicine, Nursing, Bioethics and Law*. Tokyo: Chugai Igaku-sha. 211–230).

[109.] Fan, Ruiping (1997) "Self-Determination vs. Family-Determination: Two Incommensurable Principles of Autonomy" *Bioethics* Volume 11 Issue 3/4, 309–322, 309.

[110.] Ochiai, Emiko (2015) "Why Does the 'Japanese-Style Welfare Regime' Remain Familial? 4. Comments on the Report" [in Japanese] *Japanese Journal of Family Sociology* Volume 27 Issue 1, 61–68.

[111.] Haley, William E., R. S. Allen, S. Reynolds, et al. (2002) "Family Issues in End-of-Life Decision Making and End-of-Life Care" *American Behavioral Scientist* Volume 46 Issue 2, 284–298. https://doi.org/10.1177/000276402236680.

legal systems due to the clash between relational autonomy and individual autonomy behind the systems. Given this, it becomes clear that merely improving the legal framework is not sufficient to promote the widespread adoption of ADs and ACP.

In essence, it is not just about individuals accepting ADs, but also about creating a conducive environment for their utilization across society.[112] This involves family members, healthcare professionals, caregivers, and government authorities. Active involvement of governments in various regions is important. Strategies such as public awareness campaigns and educational programs in schools are crucial.

For example, Singapore's government has undertaken notable initiatives, such as promoting the adoption of enduring powers of attorney for asset management and advancing the digitization of documentation procedures and registration. Other countries could potentially draw inspiration from Singapore's government efforts in their own policy campaigns.

In East Asia, diversity encompasses a variety of factors, such as politics, economics, social systems, religion, ethnicity, lifestyle, and legal systems. This is one of the reasons why there is no unified regional organization for Asia like the European Union (EU) or the Council of Europe. Curiously, a common aspect in East Asia is the traditional taboo associated with discussions about death. The taboo nature of death prevents carers and healthcare practitioners, as well as family members, from fulfilling the wishes of older adults to help them face the theme of how they live and die, to give cheer to those who are living toward death, and to let them die positively.[113]

In Japan, the belief in *kotodama*, the spiritual power of words, is a prominent aspect of this phenomenon.[114] This belief posits that language possesses a spiritual force, and that uttering specific words can facilitate the realization of their content. This is akin to a form of indigenous faith. In various regions of East

---

[112.] Suen, M. H. P., A. Y. M. Chow, R. K. W. Woo, et al. (2024) "What Makes Advance Care Planning Discussion So Difficult? A Systematic Review of the Factors of Advance Care Planning in Healthcare Settings" *Palliative & Supportive Care* Volume 22, 1–14. https://doi.org/10.1017/S1478951524000464.

[113.] Fuji, Kazuhiko (2019) "A Proposal for Industrial Promotion in a Multi-Death Society" [in Japanese] Research in Statute of Economy, Trade & Industry (RIETI) Policy Discussion Paper Series 19-P-036.

[114.] As of December 2020, the Agency for Cultural Affairs of Japan reports that 87.9 million Japanese citizens adhere to Shintoism (48.5% of the population), 83.9 million are Buddhists (46.3%), 1.9 million are Christians (1%), and 7.3 million follow other religions (4%). The statistics are based on the religious group's declaration and the total population in the statistics exceeds the national scale due to over-declaration and the inclusion of multiple religions for a single individual. For example, a person may adhere to Shintoism and Buddhism, which is a common practice in Japan; Hara, Kazuya (2001) "The Word 'Is' the Thing: The 'Kotodama' Belief in Japanese Communication" *ETC: A Review of General Semantics* Volume 58 Issue 3, 279–291.

Asia, the perception of death as a taboo is often attributed to the influence of Confucianism, a classical Chinese philosophy.[115]

Every region should strive to put in place ADs and ACP that meet societal needs, while respecting its unique traditions and local customs. A study has indicated that providing Chinese individuals with chronic illnesses with positive death education may be beneficial.[116] It is crucial to educate people that these educational initiatives are practically designed for the benefit of older adults and their family members. However, changing a society's behavior and thought patterns is a significant challenge. It requires joint efforts and shared knowledge, highlighted by the display of successful examples.

According to traditions and local customs in East Asia, it has been considered rude to express one's own intentions in front of someone of higher status, or to suddenly make a declaration without prior consultation and agreement, as it may cause confusion among those present. Adhering to these customs often makes it difficult for individuals to express their intentions, leading to a risk of suppressing one's own desires.

The most important thing is for each person to clearly express their own intentions, and for others to respect this expression as much as possible. Such expression of intent requires consistent practice and cannot be achieved suddenly one day. It is therefore important to note that the introduction of these ADs and ACP systems should not be hurried. A slow and steady approach, considering the population's readiness and acceptance, is more likely to bring about positive outcomes.

Public discussions can be useful for presenting these ideas and addressing any doubts or misunderstandings. It should be recalled that the East Asian project adheres to the guiding principles of "Respect for Human Rights, Celebration of Diversity and Mutual Benefit," which reflect the core values of East Asia: they collectively prioritize universal human rights and the rule of law, celebrate diversity in all its aspects, and provide a pragmatic basis for East Asian academic cooperation aimed at mutual progress in aging populations.

[115.] Ho (n 83).

[116.] Leung, P. P., A. H.-Y. Wan, C. L.-W. Chan, et al. (2015) "The Effects of a Positive Death Education Group on Psycho-Spiritual Outcomes for Chinese with Chronic Illness: A Quasi-Experimental Study" *Illness, Crisis and Loss* Volume 23 Issue 1, 5–19. https://doi.org/10.2190/IL.23.1.b.v

CHAPTER 6

Advance Decision-Making for Future Disability in East Asia

This chapter compares models from the U.S. and Europe to gain deeper insights into the distinctive characteristics of East Asia's approach to ADs and ACP. It analyzes the legal relationships among medical doctors, patients, and family members in end-of-life care, clarifying key legal issues and summarizing fundamental concepts of healthcare decision-making. Additionally, it examines potential obstacles that may hinder the effective implementation of advance decision-making within the region, considering both legal and cultural challenges. Based on these findings, the study proposes key concepts, criteria, and draft provisions for legislation tailored to East Asia, offering a structured framework for further discussion and policy development.

6.1 A Comparative Analysis of Models between the U.S., Europe, and East Asia

This section presents a comparative analysis of the models prevalent in the U.S. and Europe, with the objective of gaining a more nuanced understanding of the distinctive features of the East Asian model.

6.1.1 The U.S. Model

The characteristics of ADs and ACP in the U.S., as described in Section 3.1 of Chapter 3, represent a legal framework aimed at upholding individual autonomy and the patient's right to self-determination. These features involve conferring expectations of legal binding force to the will and preferences expressed through legal documents—a practice referred to as "the U.S. model."[1]

[1.] American Bar Association (ABA) (2018) "Advance Directives: Counseling Guide for Lawyers" June 10, 2018. https://www.americanbar.org/groups/law_aging/resources/health_care_decision_making/ad-counseling-guide/.

Nevertheless, it is important to note that ADs have inherent limitations of legal binding force as discussed in more detail in Section 3.2 of Chapter 3. The National Institute on Aging (U.S.) states that "An advance directive is legally recognized but not legally binding. It is important to note that while your healthcare provider and proxy will endeavor to respect your advance directives, there may be circumstances in which they are unable to adhere to your wishes in their entirety."[2]

It is therefore important to note that "the U.S. model" demonstrates a style of proactive planning for end-of-life medical care that aims to promote individual autonomy through the utilization of legal documents of ADs. Despite the inherent limitations of legal binding force associated with ADs, this approach provides a valuable framework for ensuring that individuals' will and preferences regarding their end-of-life medical care are respected, to the extent possible.

This section focuses on the role of the Uniform Law Commission (ULC) in developing end-of-life care legislation in the U.S. Following the creation of the Model Health-Care Consent Act of 1982 and the Uniform Rights of the Terminally Ill Act of 1985, the ULC published the Health Care Decisions Act of 1993. While this act establishes comprehensive regulations regarding medical decisions and ADs, only seven out of the 50 states legislated based on this uniform act as it was published after many states had already enacted their own laws.

At the annual meeting of the ULC in July 2023, the Health Care Decisions Act 2023 was approved as a modernized and expanded revision of the 1993 uniform act.[3] This bill was made available on the ULC's website in October 2023. Nina Kohn highlights these features of the updated uniform act:

> *Provisions are put in place to facilitate the role of ADs, including the option of remote witnessing for healthcare proxies.[4] The legislation delineates the circumstances under which a surrogate may make healthcare decisions and the criteria for determining incapacity. It also establishes a process for patients to contest incapacity determinations. The act permits the inclusion of instructions regarding mental healthcare preferences and the appointment of proxies. It also permits the*

---

[2] National Institute on Aging (2022) "Advance Care Planning: Advance Directives for Health Care" October 31, 2022. https://www.nia.nih.gov/health/advance-care-planning/advance-care-planning-advance-directives-health-care.

[3] Uniform Law Commission (ULC) (2023) "Health-Care Decisions Act." https://www.uniformlaws.org/committees/community-home/librarydocuments?communitykey=3df274d6-776b-4780-8e4e-018a850ef44e&LibraryFolderKey=&DefaultView=.

[4] Nina Kohn is a professor at Syracuse University and a member of the Uniform Law Commission. Kohn, Nina A., and David M. Levy (2023) "The New Uniform Health Care Decisions Act: An Overview" *Bifocal* Volume 45 Issue 1, 6–7. https://www.americanbar.org/groups/law_aging/publications/bifocal/vol45/vol45issue1/new-health-care-decisions-act/.

limitation of the revocation of directives during acute mental health events. The role of default surrogates is expanded to encompass various relationships and family structures. Proxies are granted listed powers and duties, including the application for medical insurance for patients who lack other representatives. It also includes formats for ADs, which are designed for individuals with diverse backgrounds and use plain language, as well as specifying care preferences, goals, and values for future decisions (Section 11, see Appendix 2).

The U.S. model of ADs has gradually become a global standard, with its acceptance significantly influenced by the healthcare systems, welfare policies, and legal frameworks of each country or area. Here, let us briefly review some cases from several countries.

England is the birthplace of the modern hospice movement. Hospice services in England have shifted from facility-based care to providing care at patients' homes. While there is a significant demand for palliative care in England, expected to increase in the future, the supply remains insufficient, with observed challenges such as disparities related to diseases. In recent years, various national strategies and plans have been formulated in each country of the United Kingdom to address challenges related to end-of-life and palliative care. However, the recommended framework for end-of-life care faced significant criticism, leading to adjustments toward an individual assessment and care planning approach rather than a uniform one.[5]

Currently in England and Wales, separate formats for LPA for asset management and healthcare have been established within the framework of support systems for individuals lacking decision-making capacity. The Mental Capacity Act 2005, sections 24-26, largely codifies common law on ADs in England and Wales, using the term "advance decision." "As long as it is valid and applies to your situation, an advance decision gives your health and social care team clinical and legal instructions about your treatment choices. An advance decision may only be considered valid if: you're aged 18 years old or over and had the capacity to make, understand and communicate your decision when you made it you specify clearly which treatments you wish to refuse; you explain the circumstances in which you wish to refuse them; it's signed by you; you have made the advance decision of your own accord, without any harassment by anyone else; you have not said or done anything that would contradict the advance decision since you

---

[5] Kotera, Shoichi (2021) "End-of-Life Care in the UK: Recent Policy Developments" [in Japanese] *The Reference, the National Diet Library* Volume 843, 27–56.

made it."[6] Section 25 states that an advance decision is invalid if it was with-drawn while the person had capacity, if an LPA was later created for the same treatment, or if the person acted inconsistently with it. It also doesn't apply to treatments not covered, if specified circumstances don't apply, or if unforeseen circumstances that would have influenced the decision arise.

Scotland, influenced by both English common law and the French Civil Code, has a legal system distinct from that of England and Wales. The only advance decision currently provided for in Scottish law is the advance statements, which requires documenting the intentions of individuals with mental disorders only.[7] Scotland is currently undergoing a comprehensive mental health law review process, focusing on mental health law, abuse prevention law, and guardianship law.[8]

This mental health law review includes the promotion of ADs systems for medical care, adopting the concept of "advance choices," which refers to instructions or wishes given regarding potential issues that may arise when an adult has lost mental capacity. The proposal from the Law Society of Scotland adopts two forms of ADs and advance statements, which are already implemented in the State of Victoria's law (Australia).[9] The Victorian Medical Treatment Planning and Decisions Act 2016 allows Victorians to create legally binding advance care directives to make instructional or legally non-binding advance statement for values directives about medical treatment.

In this manner, English-speaking countries, while exerting mutual influence, persist in their endeavors to develop legal systems that more effectively align with their distinct national requirements. The AD systems under discussion, founded upon respective legislation, collectively seek to advance individual autonomy. Consequently, the AD systems of the English-speaking countries can be categorized as a cohort of the U.S. model, which prioritizes individual autonomy.

[6.] NHS (2023) "Advance Decision to Refuse Treatment (Living Will)" September 19, 2023. https://www.nhs.uk/conditions/end-of-life-care/planning-ahead/advance-decision-to-refuse-treatment/.

[7.] Sections 275 and 276 of the Mental Health (Care and Treatment) (Scotland) Act 2003 permit patients to make advance statements regarding their desired treatment in the event of future illness. These statements are documented when the patient is well and are consistent with the Act's guiding principle of considering the patient's past and present wishes.

[8.] The pertinent legislation is the Mental Health (Care and Treatment) (Scotland) Act 2003, the Adult Support and Protection (Scotland) Act 2007, and the Adults with Incapacity (Scotland) Act 2000.

[9.] Law Society of Scotland (2022) "Human Rights Must Be at the Core of Proposals for Law Reform around Advance Choices and Medical Decision-Making." https://www.lawscot.org.uk/news-and-events/law-society-news/advance-choices-and-medical-decision-making/; Maylea, Chris (2022) "Victoria, Australia, Is Getting a New Mental Health and Wellbeing Bill" *Bioethical Inquiry* Volume 19, 527–532. https://doi.org/10.1007/s11673-022-10212-9; Del Villar, Katrine, and Christopher J. Ryan (2020) "Self-Binding Directives for Mental Health Treatment: When Advance Consent Is Not Effective Consent" *The Medical Journal of Australia* Volume 212 Issue 5, 208–211. https://doi.org/10.5694/mja2.50505.

This legislative policy emphasizing individual autonomy in the State of Victoria is explicitly addressed in the documents and legislation for not only advance medical directives but also guardianship and administration law, as the author's studies have revealed. In practice, citizens may consider the effects of multi-cultural society, but in policy, this position has remained unchanged. Table 6.1 presents a provision-based comparison of legislative frameworks in England, the State of Victoria (Australia), and the U.S. (uniform law).

Table 6.1: Comparison between England, State of Victoria, and the U.S.

Item	England	State of Victoria	The U.S.
Relevant Laws on ADs	Mental Capacity Act (MCA 2005)	The Medical Treatment Planning and Decisions Act 2016	Uniform Health-Care Decisions Act (2023)
Content of ADs	Withhold/withdrawal of life-sustaining treatment	ADs articulate an individual's preferences for medical treatment	Two types: power of attorney and instruction. Choose agent and express wishes
Designation of Proxy	Free choice	Individuals can appoint a medical treatment decision-maker under the act	Name one or more agents. Specify authority, effectiveness, duration
Criteria for Proxy	The act allows individuals to appoint an enduring or lasting power of attorney for health and welfare	The designated proxy must act in the individual's best interests	Follow wishes or best interest. Consider values, benefits, burdens, alternatives

Item	England	State of Victoria	The U.S.
Criteria for Withholding Treatment in the Absence of ADs	Healthcare professionals consider the individual's best interests and consult with relevant parties	Healthcare professionals consider the individual's best interests and consult relevant parties	Surrogates make decisions for those without AD. Follow same criteria as agent. Consult others and seek second opinion
Criteria for Discontinuation in Cases of Incapacity, Lack of ADs, and No Family Presence	Decisions involve assessing best interests and may require consultation with healthcare professionals and others	Decisions involve assessing best interests and may require consultation with healthcare professionals and others	Discontinue treatment for those in hopeless condition without AD. Consent by surrogate or approval by clinical ethics committee, court, or entity. Based on clear and convincing evidence of wishes or best interest
Supported Decision-Making in Healthcare	The act promotes supported decision-making to maximize individual autonomy.	The act supports individuals in making their own decisions to the greatest extent possible	Right to make and communicate decisions with supporters. Identify and involve supporters. Respect and facilitate right. Provide accommodation and assistance

Item	England	State of Victoria	The U.S.
Information-Sharing System for ADs	Utilizes electronic systems for storing and accessing AD information.	Employs electronic systems for storing and accessing AD information	Use electronic systems for ADs. Store, access, update, and share ADs. Make ADs more portable

Source: The author

6.1.2 The European Model

Compared to the U.S. model, a distinctive feature of "the European model," as referred to in this article, is the utilization of the broad concept of "advance choices," which include asset management, advance medical directives, and so on. This seeks to achieve legal effects that extend across borders within Europe. At its core, both models share a common goal of achieving individual autonomy and self-determination.

While the development of a European model law, which is to be presented by the European Law Institute (ELI, Vienna) in 2025, or at latest in 2026, is an important aspect, its adoption within the EU is of paramount importance. However, the decision to comply with this model law is ultimately at the discretion of each individual country. In this context, this European model is still in a conceptual stage, as previously addressed.

In Europe, each country has legislation pertaining to healthcare insurance systems, with most healthcare professionals employed in the public sector. In this regard, the healthcare system and associated policy are predominantly managed by governmental authorities. To illustrate, the case of Sweden is presented as an example.

In this country, primary care physicians engage in discussions about end-of-life plans with older patients yet exclude families from these discussions due to legal constraints.[10] No legislation exists that explicitly addresses this practice; however, it has been implemented in this manner. The individualistic trend that

---

[10.] In a Zoom conference held on March 2, 2024, Titti Mattsson, a legal researcher at the University of Lund in Sweden, presented her findings; Jones, K., G. Birchley, R. Huxtable, et al. (2019) "End of Life Care: A Scoping Review of Experiences of Advance Care Planning for People with Dementia" *Dementia* Volume 18 Issue 3, 825–845. https://doi.org/10.1177/1471301216676121.

has characterized Sweden since the 1940s is currently undergoing a period of reevaluation, driven by social changes resulting from the country's diverse immigrant population. The 300 municipalities exert influence over lifestyles, yet there is a growing disparity in financial resources among municipalities.

The provision of end-of-life medical care in Europe is characterized by a high degree of diversity, with each country adopting a distinctive approach. In this book, we will examine the healthcare legislation and policy with a particular focus on the European regional policy on end-of-life medical care.[11] The background to the establishment of the European model is described below.

In Europe, human rights occupy a central position, particularly in light of the European Convention on Human Rights and the European Court of Human Rights. Ministerial Recommendations from the Council of Europe also exert considerable influence. Collectively, these frameworks serve to unify approaches to human rights, thereby countering historical regional diversity.

In 1999, the Council of Europe recommended Rec (99)4 that states should consider providing for and regulating anticipatory arrangements for subsequent incapacity. A decade later, Rec (2009)11 (Principle 1) and Principle 14 of Rec (2014)2 urged member states to enact legislation. Despite progress, ADs remain underdeveloped. Advance choices, which allow individuals to record preferences and instructions in advance, present challenges due to the time lag until they become operable.[12]

The key issues that must be addressed are to ensure that the document accurately reflects the wishes of the grantor and determining when it would be appropriate to disregard these wishes due to changing circumstances. For example, Alzheimer Europe maintains the position that for an advance directive to be valid, certain generally accepted criteria must be fulfilled.[13] These include that the person has the necessary and relevant capacity, is free from undue pressure, has not made a more recent version, and has stated wishes that are applicable to the current situation or proposed treatment.

The focus of measures related to the exercise of legal capacity has shifted from incapacitation and protection to autonomy and self-determination (UN CRPD, Article 12.4). This has led to a surge in legislative provision for enduring powers

---

[11.] Kai, Katsunori (2018) "Trends and Issues in Legislating and Establishing Rules for End-of-Life Care from a Comparative Law Perspective" [in Japanese] *Hanrei Jiho* Volume 2379, 130–139.

[12.] Ward, A. D. (2022) "Enhancing Autonomy: Advance Choices as the Key to the Future" Keynote Speech Delivered at the World Congress on Adult Capacity 2022 on June 7–9, 2022 in Edinburgh, Scotland.

[13.] Alzheimer Europe (2005) "Advance Directives." https://www.alzheimer-europe.org/policy/positions/advance-directives#:~:text=Alzheimer%20Europe%20is%20of%20the,are%20applicable%20to%20the%20current.

of attorney across Europe. However, the legal term of advance choices, which are more effective and certain, are expected to follow a similar trajectory as they become more available.

The objective of the ELI project is to influence the direction of development in the field of advance choices through a comparative approach. The project aims to benefit European citizens by promoting the provision, dissemination and uptake of advance choices, and fostering cross-border understanding and operation. Adrian D. Ward, a Scottish lawyer who was involved in the 2022 Law Society of Scotland report, has been engaged in the 2018 Council of Europe project, entitled "Enabling Citizens to Plan for Incapacity," and is now engaged in new initiatives with ELI.[14]

The ELI project will provide guidance to European states on how to enable their citizens to make advance choices with certainty about their effect when relevant circumstances arise. This will be done in a way that promotes the realization of relevant human and disability rights principles and that maximizes cross-European compatibility and operability.

It is the intention of the ELI project to produce a draft model law for advance choices and supporting materials in 2025, or at latest in 2026. The model law will be designed to provide optimal provision for advance choices with as much consistency as possible across Europe. The supporting materials will assist states in legislating accordingly and will aid in educating citizens and professionals, encouraging uptake.

A comparison with the Health Care Decisions Act of 2023 in the U.S. has been deemed not particularly relevant in European terms. The Health Care Decisions Act adopts the appointment of agents to make healthcare decisions. In terms of relevant European definitions, this signifies a durable power of attorney-type agreement as a bilateral measure to establish a proxy agreement between the principal and the represented, as opposed to an advance choice as a unilateral measure to be effective for multiple stakeholders.

A significant debate surrounds the question of how to achieve a balance between accessibility and data protection in advance choices. To enhance individual convenience, it is vital to guarantee straightforward access to pre-registered ADs. Conversely, rigorous management of personal data is imperative to safeguard privacy. This presents a challenge: how to reconcile these ostensibly contradictory requirements. This encompasses technical considerations of the hierarchy

---

[14.] Law Society of Scotland (n 9); Ward, Adrian D. (2018) *Enabling Citizens to Plan for Incapacity.* Council of Europe. chrome-extension://efaidnbmnnnibpcajpcglclefindmkaj/https://rm.coe.int/cdcj-2017-2e-final-rapport-vs-21-06-2018/16808b64ae.

of disapplication and data protection. Insights into the ongoing development of a Europe-wide registration system for pertinent information are essential. This project is currently underway, with specific details yet to be finalized.

6.1.3 The East Asian Model

East Asian countries and areas can be categorized into those that have enacted legislation or established guidelines for ADs and those that have not. Among the former are countries such as South Korea, Taiwan, and Singapore, while Japan and China belong to the latter group. Nevertheless, even in countries and areas where ADs are legally permitted and guidelines have been published, the current low utilization rates of legal measures such as ADs or ACPs indicate that the intended objectives of the laws may not have been fully achieved.

In other words, in East Asia, the influence of traditional values and moral norms established by Confucianism, Taoism, and Buddhism is more significant than that of law and policy toward civil autonomy, particularly regarding end-of-life medical decision-making. It can be posited that in East Asia, where legislation or guidelines on ADs have been enacted, family involvement remains a prevalent phenomenon. This can be characterized as the "East Asian model," which respects relational autonomy, and differs from the prevailing laws and policies that respect individual autonomy in the U.S. and Europe.

Three key characteristics can be identified as being distinctive of East Asia. Firstly, the topic of human death is prohibited from discussion due to traditions and local customs. Secondly, family involvement in end-of-life medical care decisions is highly prevalent, both by law and in practice. Thirdly, the results of ADs and ACP legislation have not fulfilled their original purpose. These three key characteristics are inextricably linked and form a coherent whole, shaped by the shared cultural background of East Asia.

The extent and manner of family involvement vary among individual cases, but in Japan, there is a common practice, particularly in medical settings, where family involvement is sought for consent or surrogate decision-making for medical procedures. This family involvement is widely accepted in end-of-life care, raising concerns about the treatment of older adults without family support in medical institutions.

In South Korea and Taiwan, the explicit inclusion of family involvement in regulations is a distinctive feature. In South Korea, the criteria for withholding treatment in the absence of advanced ADs require agreement or cessation by the attending physician and at least one specialist in the relevant field, in addition to unanimous statements from two or more family members who desire discontinuation. In Taiwan, similar criteria entail diagnosis by two physicians for terminal illness patients, and if the patient is unable to express their will, consent must be obtained from a close relative.[15] In Singapore, although family involvement is not explicitly stated in regulations, the relationship between older adults and family members is consistently considered in practice.

In East Asia, family involvement, whether formalized by law or practiced informally, is a defining characteristic. Therefore, in promoting ADs and ACP, the nature of the relationship between the individual and the family is always a key consideration. While this relationship may potentially limit individual autonomy, it should not be automatically viewed negatively, as it allows individuals to prioritize maintaining positive relationships with their loved ones. However, some individuals may feel compelled to avoid burdening their families, leading them to sacrifice their own needs.[16]

Establishing specific criteria for assessing whether limitations on individual autonomy are natural and reasonably acceptable can be challenging. If individuals can strike a reasonable balance between their individual autonomy and familial obligations based on their personal beliefs, it may be deemed acceptable. However, if the inclination toward self-sacrifice becomes extreme, there is a risk of violating the individual's human rights or neglecting their own well-being.

Recognizing the diverse political, economic, lifestyle, and legal systems across East Asia, the East Asian project emphasizes the importance of mutual respect for the traditions and local customs of each country and area. It also advocates for universal values such as international human rights and the rights of persons with disabilities, as outlined in relevant international treaties. Further research is required to ascertain why legal measures are rarely used and how they can be improved to achieve a certain level of implementation.

Furthermore, the East Asian project upholds the guiding principles of "respect for human rights, appreciation for diversity, and mutual benefit" within aging societies. These guiding principles may reflect the foundational values of East Asia, which commonly prioritize universal human rights and the rule of law,

---

[15.] See "Table 6.1: Advance Directives Comparison between South Korea, Taiwan, and Singapore" for detail.

[16.] Tanaka, Miho (2024) *Awareness of " Becoming a Burden to Others' among Older Adults in the End of Life: An Overview of Data from Japan and Other Countries"* [in Japanese] Research Report of the Japan Medical Research Institute No. 137.

celebrate diversity in all aspects, and provide a practical basis for international collaboration aimed at mutual advancement within aging populations.

Despite the existence of significant discrepancies in the legislative frameworks governing end-of-life medical care decisions across East Asian countries and areas, there is a discernible convergence in the prominence particularly accorded to family involvement, irrespective of the specific legislation under consideration. In alignment with the overarching principles of "respect for human rights, appreciation for diversity, and mutual benefit," it is feasible to cultivate a collaborative approach that can effectively address the challenges posed by an aging population in East Asia.

Creating policies beneficial to the public under a democratic constitution and the rule of law is challenging. The approach should foster confidence that government policies will benefit all stakeholders, requiring thorough verification and continuous improvement. No East Asian government has yet achieved these goals, and collaborative efforts across the region are likely to yield faster and more assured outcomes than working independently within individual countries. This book focuses on East Asia to explore the potential for such collaboration.

6.2 Legal Relationship between Doctors, Patients, and Family Members

This section presents an analysis of the legal relationship between medical doctors, patients, and family members in the context of end-of-life medical care. The objective is twofold: firstly, to clarify legal issues by summarizing key concepts related to healthcare decision-making and secondly, to consider directions for countermeasures, with reference to relevant discussions in the present book.

6.2.1 The Conception of Healthcare Decision-Making

A healthcare decision-making framework constitutes a structured approach to guiding medical decisions, rooted in legal principles, such as informed consent regulations, ethical considerations like respect for person, and the protection of individual rights. It provides a systematic methodology for resolving complex situations where competing interests—such as patient autonomy, clinical judgment, and societal welfare—intersect. At its core, the framework upholds the principle of autonomy, ensuring that individuals retain the right to make informed healthcare choices to the greatest extent possible.[17] These principles are balanced by beneficence and non-maleficence, which obligate healthcare providers to prioritize patient well-being and minimize harm. Additionally, the principle of justice ensures that healthcare decisions remain equitable, preventing discrimination or unjust disparities, particularly in the allocation of medical resources and access to care.

From a jurisprudential perspective, a healthcare decision-making framework necessitates procedural mechanisms that uphold fairness, inclusiveness, and legal certainty. A key component of this process is capacity assessment, recognizing that an individual's decision-making ability fluctuates based on the complexity of the medical decision and their personal circumstances. For individuals with diminished capacity, supported decision-making mechanisms facilitate their involvement to the greatest extent possible, often incorporating the assistance of legally appointed representatives or family members. This approach aligns with the concept of relational autonomy, distinguishing it from the classical notion of individual autonomy. When substitute decision-making becomes necessary, it must adhere to established legal standards, prioritizing either the patient's previously expressed preferences or their best interests where such preferences are unknown. These processes are governed by principles of proportionality, transparency, and accountability, ensuring that all interventions are legally justified, decision-making procedures are properly documented, and fundamental human rights are preserved.

The theoretical foundation of a healthcare decision-making framework draws upon established legal and ethical doctrines. The principles model, emphasizing autonomy, beneficence, non-maleficence, and justice, serves as a normative guide while allowing flexibility to accommodate diverse cultural and legal contexts. The framework typically employs a two-stage process: first, evaluating medically appropriate options through clinical expertise; and second, subjecting these options to an ethics-legal analysis that incorporates patient values, statutory requirements, and broader societal considerations. By integrating legal rigor with procedural safeguards, a healthcare decision-making framework ensures that decisions are not only medically sound but also legally defensible and culturally sensitive. This approach facilitates adaptability across jurisdictions while reinforcing the primacy of patient dignity and the rule of law in medical decision-making.

[17.] Beauchamp, Tom, and James Childress (2019) *"Principles of Biomedical Ethics*: Marking Its Fortieth Anniversary" *The American Journal of Bioethics* Volume 19 Issue 11, 9–12. https://doi.org/10.1080/15265161.2019.1665402.

6.2.2 Doctors–Patients Relationship

6.2.2.1 Justification of Clinical Actions

The fundamental objective of clinical actions undertaken by medical doctors is to act in the best interests of the patients. However, this objective is constrained by the subjective wishes, preferences, and values of the patients themselves, which must be considered within the objective medical professionals' duties. These are defined as medical legitimacy.[18] The relationship between doctors and patients is fundamentally governed by the principles of medical legitimacy, which mainly compose both the medical justification and the patient's informed consent.

In the U.S., medical justification is made possible by the biomedical principles of autonomy, non-maleficence, beneficence, and justice. In Europe, it is founded upon the principles of autonomy, dignity, integrity, and vulnerability, as previously discussed.[19] In the context of medical law in the U.S., the principle of informed consent represents a fundamental tenet. Medical professionals are obliged to provide patients with comprehensive information regarding their diagnosis, available treatment options, associated risks, and potential outcomes.

In the court case of *Canterbury v. Spence* (D.C. Cir. 1972),[20] the courts emphasized that a failure to secure informed consent constitutes a breach of the medical doctor's fiduciary duty, which represents a unique concept within the American legal tradition.[21] In civil law jurisdictions, medical doctors' duties are legally categorized as those of quasi-agency contracts with patients, whereby they are obliged to provide appropriate medical treatments based on medical standards.[22] Consequently, the obtaining of informed consent is a mandatory requirement for medical doctors, regardless of whether the jurisdiction is common law or civil law.

Furthermore, the necessity of obtaining informed consent is reinforced in global human rights frameworks, such as the Universal Declaration on Bioethics

---

[18.] Nakayama, Shigeki (2024) "Consent and Intimate Relationships in Medical Care: From the Constitutional Perspective of 'Respect for the Individual' (1)" [in Japanese] *Sandai Law Review* Volume 58 Issue 3, 269–296. http://hdl.handle.net/10965/0002000266.

[19.] Refers to "2-4 Notes on Law and Bioethics in Healthcare" of Chapter 2.

[20.] *Canterbury v. Spence* (1972) established the doctrine of informed consent, requiring medical doctors to disclose risks that a reasonable person would consider significant when making decisions about their medical care. JUSTIA, US Law (n.d.) "Canterbury v. Spence, No. 22099 (D.C. Cir. 1972)". https://law.justia.com/cases/federal/appellate-courts/cadc/22099/22099.html.

[21.] Higuchi, Norio (2007) *Thinking about Medicine and Law* [in Japanese]. Tokyo: Yuhikaku Publishing.

[22.] Teshima, Yutaka (2022) *Introduction to Medical Law*. 6th ed. Tokyo: Yuhikaku Publishing. 48–49; Yonemura, Shigeto (2016) *Lectures on Medical Law*. Tokyo: Nippon Hyoron Sha.

and Human Rights of 2005,[23] which emphasizes the significance of respecting patient autonomy. The fundamental concepts of informed consent and patient autonomy have been disseminated globally, including in East Asia. However, the manner in which these concepts are legislated and operationalized within each country or area is contingent upon the specific legal and regulatory framework that has been established.[24]

6.2.2.2 Justification of Clinical Actions in End-of-Life Medical Care

In the context of end-of-life medical care, the legal relationship between doctors and patients becomes more complex than that in ordinary clinical treatments. This is due to the inherent uncertainties surrounding prognosis and treatment efficacy, for example, terminally ill patients may experience fluctuations in their capacity to make decisions, necessitating a careful balancing act between medical benef- icence and respect for individual autonomy on the part of the attending doctor.[25]

In Japan, the Medical Practitioners' Act of 1948 (Article 4-2 (1)), implemented in 2018, requires doctors to provide care that is aligned with the wishes of the patient, wherever possible. However, studies have revealed inconsistencies in how medical doctors interpret and implement these legal obligations.[26] For exam- ple, a survey conducted by the MHLW of Japan found that many physicians are reluctant to discuss ADs in practice, although they acknowledge the importance of patients' individual autonomy.[27]

Comparative research indicates that legal obligations pertaining to informed consent and communication exhibit considerable variation across international contexts. In the U.S., the Patient Self-Determination Act of 1990, a federal law, explicitly promotes patient rights to participate in healthcare decisions, includ- ing the use of ADs. Furthermore, all states have legislated to recognize patient

---

[23.] UNESCO (2005) "Universal Declaration on Bioethics and Human Rights of 2005". https://www.unesco.org/en/legal-affairs/universal-declaration-bioethics-and-human-rights?hub=66535.

[24.] For example, Japan lacks explicit legislation concerning patient autonomy.

[25.] Kolva, Elissa, Barry Rosenfeld, and Rebecca Saracino (2018) "Assessing the Decision-Making Capacity of Terminally Ill Patients with Cancer" *The American Journal of Geriatric Psychiatry* Volume 26 Issue 5, 523–531. https://doi.org/10.1016/j.jagp.2017.11.012.

[26.] Masaki, Sakiko, Hiroko Ishimoto, and Atsushi Asai (2014) "Contemporary Issues Concerning Informed Consent in Japan Based on a Review of Court Decisions and Characteristics of Japanese Culture" *BMC Medical Ethics* Volume 15, Article number 8. https://doi.org/10.1186/1472-6939-15-8.

[27.] Japan, Ministry of Health, Labour, and Welfare (MHLW) (2018) "61st Medical Division Meeting of the Social Security Council" [in Japanese] Minutes for the Meeting held on April 11, 2018. https://www.mhlw.go.jp/stf/shingi2/0000212218_00001.html.

rights in state laws. In contrast, in Japan, the legal issue of patients' rights in end-of-life medical care has not been legally recognized to the same extent, in part because there has been no court case that requires serious discussion, such as that concerning the withdrawal of life-sustaining treatment.[28]

As previously discussed,[29] in addition to the legal and non-legal materials, as well as ethics in the medical domain, traditional values such as *toku* (virtue) exert considerable influence in the social domain in East Asia. The term "traditional values" can be interpreted as the optimal moral conduct or the establishment of harmonious human relationships, even in the medical domain. In this context, the values of harmony and the obligations within the family and community are accorded primacy, superseding individual freedoms and rights in legal, non-legal, and ethical matters.

It is evident that a distinctive legal system must be devised to satisfy the specific requirements of East Asian populations, which are shaped by the values of relational autonomy rather than individual autonomy. Furthermore, such a system must align with the legal systems of the U.S. and Europe. While this system may present a challenge, once established, it will facilitate the implementation of practices and enable amendments to the legal system in response to the evolving needs of different generations in a long-term perspective.

6.2.3 Patients–Family Members Relationship

The relationship between patients and their family members is shaped by a complex interplay of cultural norms and societal values, which can vary significantly across different cultural contexts. In the legal domain, this area is categorized as a matter of private autonomy, whereby the power of the state or public institution cannot intervene without reasonable justification.

In East Asia, familial roles frequently entail decision-making responsibilities, particularly in instances where patients are unable to make decisions for themselves.[30] This familial dynamic may result in a dilemma between respecting the patient's autonomy and adhering to family preferences.[31] Such dilemmas

---

[28.] A lawsuit is currently pending in Japan concerning the murder of a woman from Kyoto City with the incurable disease ALS by a medical doctor. This case may be worthy of discussion. Asagumo, Anri (2022) "Relational Autonomy, the Right to Reject Treatment, and Advance Directives in Japan" *Asian Bioethics Review* Volume 14, 57–69. https://doi.org/10.1007/s41649-021-00191-1.

[29.] Refers to "2-4 Notes on Law and Bioethics in Healthcare" of Chapter 2.

[30.] Refers to "5-2 (3) Traditional Values behind Family Involvement" of Chapter 5.

[31.] Menon, Sumytra, V. A. Entwistle, A. V. Campbell, et al. (2020) "Some Unresolved Ethical Challenges in Healthcare Decision-Making: Navigating Family Involvement" *Asian Bioethics Review* Volume 12 Issue 1, 27–36. https://doi.org/10.1007/s41649-020-00111-9.

are especially prevalent in societies where family-oriented decision-making is regarded as a moral obligation.

The legal framework in countries such as South Korea and Taiwan acknowledges the role of the family in medical decision-making, yet strives to achieve a balance between this and the rights of patients in theory. In accordance with the Korean Act on Hospice and Palliative Care (ELDA), family members are permitted to consent to the withdrawal of life-sustaining treatment in the absence of documented patient wishes or where such wishes cannot be reasonably inferred.[32] Similarly, the PRAA of Taiwan permits family members to make decisions when advance directives are unavailable, provided that they act in good faith and prioritize the patient's welfare.[33]

Conversely, Japanese legislation and guidelines do not address specific provisions concerning the involvement of family members, resulting in a lack of uniformity in clinical practices.[34] For instance, hospital ethics committees frequently act as intermediaries in disputes between families and medical professionals. However, these mechanisms are informal and lack a clear legal foundation.[35] It can be assumed that more explicit guidelines to resolve such disputes and ensure that patient preferences are not unduly affected by family pressures would be beneficial.

The practice of family members acting as de facto proxies in medical decision-making is accepted on the basis of cultural and social norms, despite the absence of a legal foundation. This is in contrast to the legal concept of "ex lege representation."[36] The term "ex lege representation" denotes an adult protection measure that confers legal authority upon other individuals to act ex lege (by operation of law) on behalf of the adult, obviating the necessity for a decision by a competent authority or a voluntary measure by the adult.[37]

---

[32] Refers to "5-2 (2) Family Involvement in End-of-Life Medical Care" of Chapter 5.

[33] Ibid.

[34] Nakayama (n 18).

[35] Ikka, Tsunakuni (2013) "Reconsideration of Hospital Ethics Committee" [in Japanese] *Bioethics* Volume 23 No. 1, 23–30.

[36] The term "ex lege representation" was proposed by Adrian Ward in an email exchange. ELI (2022) "European Commission's Public Consultation on the Initiative on the Cross-Border Protection of Vulnerable Adults: C. Inclusion of a Conflicts Rule on Ex Lege Powers of Representation" 17–18. chrome-extension://efaidnbmnn-nibpcajpcglclefindmkaj/https://www.europeanlawinstitute.eu/fileadmin/user_upload/p_eli/Publications/ELI_Response_Protection_of_Adults.pdf.

[37] FL-EUR (n.d.) "Questionnaire: Legal Protection and Empowerment of Vulnerable Adults". https://fl-eur.eu/working_field_1__empowerment_and_protection/country-reports.

The shortcomings of the legal system for de facto proxies of family members are apparent. The establishment of a legal framework that incorporates the concept of ex lege representation would enhance the legitimacy and transparency of representation by family members while aligning it with the protection of individual rights. However, if family members are authorized to represent the patient, a number of issues may arise with regard to who represents all family members and how to resolve any disputes among family members. These issues cannot be simply solved.

6.2.4 Self-Decisions, Supported Decisions, or Shared Decisions of Patients

The spectrum of patient decision-making models in healthcare encompasses a range of approaches, varying from those based on individual autonomy to those based on relational autonomy. These approaches include autonomy-based self-decisions, supported decisions where a third party provides assistance to the patient, and shared decisions in collaborative approaches involving medical doctors and family members. The typical style of self-determination is self-decision, provided that the patient has sufficient decision-making capacity.

The concept of self-determination hinges on the notion of an independent decision-making process by the patient in question. However, it is important to recognize that this decision-making process is influenced by a multitude of factors, both conscious and unconscious. One such theoretical stipulation is the concept of a "nudge," which is a policy tool that guides people's behavior through non-coercive psychological influences.[38] A researcher has proposed that when a nudge has a significant impact on people's autonomy, it should be subjected to at least some safeguards.[39]

The concept of supported decision-making is a legal concept derived from a combination of the vulnerability approach and a rights-based approach.[40] In this context, a third party provides assistance to a patient who lacks the capacity to make decisions independently. In Japan, the concept of supported decision-making is less developed than in Western countries, with the adult guardianship system

---

[38] Zeilstra, Rebecca (2024) "Nudging and the Safeguards of the Rule of Law" *German Law Journal* Volume 25 Issue 5, 750–771. https://doi.org/10.1017/glj.2024.30.

[39] Ibid.

[40] Sakurai, Yukio (2023) "Supported Decision-Making in the Japanese Context: Developments and Challenges" *The Journal of Aging and Social Change* Volume 3 Issue 1, 151–169. https://doi.org/10.18848/2576-5310/CGP/v13i01/151-169.

primarily concerned with financial matters.[41] This situation results in a dearth of medical decision-making support.

Recently, initiatives by advocacy groups, nongovernmental organizations and even medical doctors have called for the expansion of supported decision-making frameworks to include healthcare contexts.[42] In the State of Victoria, Australia, models promote supported decision-making by training healthcare providers in pilot projects and offering legal safeguards to uphold patient autonomy.[43] They demonstrate how to promote supported decision-making in the community.

The concept of shared decision-making has emerged as a significant element in global health policy, with proponents advocating for its implementation as a means of advancing patient-centered care.[44] This approach is consistent with the principles of medical ethics, as it fosters mutual understanding and trust among stakeholders. The ACP has been developed based on this approach. In this sense, the legal concept of the medical doctor's fiduciary duty is more suitable to this approach than a quasi-agency contract.

Nevertheless, the implementation of shared decision-making is constrained by practical limitations, including time constraints, inadequate training for healthcare professionals, and cultural reluctance to challenge medical authority.[45] These challenges could be overcome through comprehensive policy reforms and educational initiatives that emphasize the value of collaborative decision-making. However, special consideration must be given to specific cases, such as those involving minor patients or individuals with disabilities,[46] to ensure their rights are protected. Further research and practice are essential to advance this field.

---

[41] Arai, Makoto (2019) "Japan Adult Guardianship Laws: Development and Reform Initiatives" in Lusina Ho and Rebecca Lee (eds), *Special Needs Financial Planning: A Comparative Perspective*. English Edition. Cambridge: Cambridge University Press. 61–86.

[42] Ogawa, Asao (2019) "End-of-Life Care for Dementia" [in Japanese] *Journal of Psychiatry* Volume 121, 289–297.

[43] Then, Shih-Ning, and C. Bigby (2024) "Supported Decision-Making and the Disability Royal Commission" *Research and Practice in Intellectual and Developmental Disabilities* Volume 11 Issue 1, 86–106. https://doi.org/10.1080/23297018.2024.2330961.

[44] Glyn, Elwyn, D. Frosch, R. Thomson, et al. (2012) "Shared Decision Making: A Model for Clinical Practice" *Journal of General Internal Medicine* Volume 27 Issue 10, 1361–1367. https://doi.org/10.1007/s11606-012-2077-6.

[45] Confucian familism weakens patient-clinician shared decision-making in end-of-life care of advanced cancer patients. Yang, Yuexi, T. Qu, J. Yang, et al. (2022) "Confucian Familism and Shared Decision Making in End-of-Life Care for Patients with Advanced Cancers" *International Journal of Environmental Research and Public Health* Volume 19, 10071. https://doi.org/10.3390/ijerph191610071.

[46] Sobode, Oluwaseun Rebecca, R. Jegan, J. Toelen, et al. (2024) "Shared Decision-Making in Adolescent Healthcare: A Literature Review of Ethical Considerations" *European Journal of Pediatrics* Volume 183, 4195–4203. https://doi.org/10.1007/s00431-024-05687-0.

The types of decisions are options for the patient, dependent on the patient's physical and mental needs as well as their will and preferences. The style of patient decision-making is contingent on the specific condition, but in any case, individual autonomy of the patient must be prioritized. In other words, an undue influence on the patient must be restricted. In this context, a patient-centered approach is important in the cases of supported decision-making and shared decision-making.

6.2.5 Advance Decisions of Patients, Substituted Decisions of Families, or Best Interests of Doctors

The spectrum of patient decision-making models in healthcare is further sub-divided into several categories, depending on the timing of decisions, whether reactive or proactive. Advance decisions, such as living will or ADs, constitute a legal instrument that enables patients to articulate their preferences with regard to prospective medical care. The objective of these instruments is to obviate potential disagreements by elucidating patients' preferences in advance. As discussed in Chapter 2,[47] proactive decisions are preferable to realize individual autonomy.

The implementation of these tools is confronted with considerable cultural challenges in a multitude of societies, most notably in East Asia.[48] The legal system in East Asia is based on Western ideology and social frameworks. However, local populations live in societies with traditions and local customs that have been established over generations. Consequently, a legal system based on Western ideology is not always recognized by local populations. For instance, studies conducted in Japan have revealed that only a small proportion of adults have completed ADs.[49] The primary barriers to AD completion have been identified as a lack of legal awareness and discomfort with discussing death.

In the absence of ADs, families frequently assume the role of substitute decision-makers, which can give rise to ethical challenges. For example, in cases involving life-sustaining treatments in Taiwan, families are confronted with a dilemma between perceived obligations within the social domain and

---

47. Refers to "2-3 (3) Policy Orientation in East Asia" of Chapter 2.

[48.] Refers to "5-2 (3) Traditional Values behind Family Involvement" of Chapter 5.

[49.] Sakurai, Yukio (2024) "The Role of Law and Bioethics in Human Life and Death: Japanese Medical Law in End-of-Life Care" *Australian Journal of Asian Law* Volume 25 No. 1, 89–105. https://ssrn.com/abstract=4964356. In Japan, there is a paucity of enduring powers of attorney for asset management, which bear resemblance to ADs for end-of-life medical care. Consequently, proactive preparations for end-of-life are not a prevalent phenomenon.

the patient's best interests.[50] The ethical tension between substituted decisions and patient autonomy is a recurring theme in the literature on medical ethics.[51]

In contrast, the MCA 2005 in England and Wales provides relatively clear provisions for substituted decision-making and emphasizes the patient's best interests.[52] The best interests standard, frequently invoked by medical professionals in Japan, often lacks explicit legal criteria. This ambiguity can result in reliance on institutional policies or individual judgment, which has the potential to raise concerns about the accountability of medical professionals.[53]

In order to address these issues, scholars have put forth the suggestion of implementing frameworks that integrate ACP into the fabric of routine medical practice. Such frameworks would not only advance patients' individual autonomy but also mitigate the emotional burden on relevant families and medical professionals. The feasibility and benefits of structured ACP initiatives are illustrated by international examples such as the Respecting Choices program in the U.S.[54]

This expanded analysis elucidates the intricate interrelationship between legal and ethical considerations in end-of-life medical decision-making. It is recommended that future reforms endeavor to harmonize these dimensions, ensuring an equitable, compassionate, and patient-centered approach to care. Another avenue for consideration is the legal concept of "advance decision-making" in the East Asian context, which will be discussed in the following section.

6.3 Proposals for Advance Decision-Making for Future Disability in East Asia

This section presents an analysis of the potential challenges that may impede the implementation of the legal term of advance decision-making in the context of East Asia. The study presents the principal concepts, criteria and draft main

[50.] Kouy, BunRong (2019) "On Taiwan Patient Right to Autonomy Act: How Family Stimulates Autonomy" *Applied Ethics Review* Volume 67, 187–212.

[51.] Beauchamp and Childress (n 17).

[52.] Carolyn, Johnston, and Jane Liddle (2007) "The Mental Capacity Act 2005: A New Framework for Healthcare Decision Making" *Journal of Medical Ethics* Volume 33 Issue 2, 94–97. https://doi.org/10.1136/jme.2006.016972.

[53.] Atsushi, Asai, Taketoshi Okita, and Seiji Bito (2022) "Discussions on Present Japanese Psychocultural-Social Tendencies as Obstacles to Clinical Shared Decision-Making in Japan" *Asian Bioethics Review* Volume 14 Issue 2, 133–150. https://doi.org/10.1007/s41649-021-00201-2.

[54.] Refers to "3-2 (2) The Advancement of ADs" of Chapter 3; Forlini, J., and L. Goldberg (2014) "*Respecting Choices*: A Case Study for Incorporating Advance Care Planning into Person and Family-Centered Health Care Delivery" *Health Policy Brief—National Academy of Social Insurance* Volume 9, 1–3. https://www.nasi.org/wp-content/uploads/2014/02/Health_Policy_Brief_09.pdf.

provisions of advance decision-making legislation tailored to East Asia and puts forward a proposal for an avenue for further consideration.

6.3.1 Challenges for Establishing Advance Decision-Making

In East Asia, traditional values rooted in Confucianism, Taoism, and Buddhism form the foundation of social norms, prioritizing virtues and harmony in human relationships.[55] These values emphasize family and community obligations over individual freedoms and rights, with a preference for customary moral guidelines rather than codified legal mandates, even in areas where legislation is absent. Consequently, in end-of-life medical care, traditional values often prevail over individual autonomy to preserve social cohesion and order.

The pre-1947 Civil Code of Japan formalized the governance of families by conferring significant authority upon the male "head of household" (*koshu*).[56] The family governance system was based on the stem family structure, whereby the eldest son inherited the family assets and assumed the role of family leader. This system has endured in varying degrees to the present day, particularly in matters governed by Taiwanese heritage. Comparable legal family governance systems previously existed in societies shaped by Roman law, such as Italy and Spain.[57]

In his analysis, Emmanuel Todd, a noted anthropologist, observes that Japan's stem family history fostered relational autonomy and a family-centric focus, while Anglo-American nuclear family systems—prevalent in the U.S. and U.K.—prioritize individual autonomy and legal principles.[58] Despite the official promotion of nuclear family systems, he argues that stem family traditions in Japan remain deeply ingrained in societal customs and cultural mentality.

This enduring influence is evidenced by the continued prevalence of inherited family enterprises in fields such as medicine, dentistry, and traditional arts, where private autonomy often supplants formal legal norms in decision-making. This

---

[55.] Refers to "2-3 (3) Policy Orientation in East Asia" of Chapter 2 for the paragraph.

[56.] Refers to "2-2 (3) Autonomy in the East Asian Context" of Chapter 2.

[57.] For example, in Italy, the family council system was abolished in 1975, following the amendment of the Family Code. In Spain, the establishment of the adult guardianship system in 1983 saw the abolition of the provision for family council in the Spanish Civil Code.

[58.] Todd, Emmanuel (1985) *The Explanation of Ideology: Family Structures and Social Systems*, translated by David Garrioch. Oxford [Oxfordshire]: B. Blackwell; Todd theory is criticized by the recent publication: Gutmann, Jerg, and Stefan Voigt (2022) "Testing Todd: Family Types and Development" *Journal of Institutional Economics* Volume 18, 101–118. https://doi.org/10.1017/S1744137421000175. In recent empirical studies, Todd's theory of social structure, which is based on family structure, has been the subject of criticism. However, the validity of its theoretical framework has not been completely negated.

dynamic is further reflected in healthcare contexts, where the stem family-based mentality may compel family members, either willingly or reluctantly, to conform to the opinion of the family leader de facto, fostering unified conduct despite conflicting perspectives within the family.

In contrast, Western societies prioritize individual autonomy and human rights, with decisions grounded in legal legitimacy rather than moral or familial judgments. In the West, the patient's autonomy is paramount, and documents such as living will and ADs are recognized as legally enforceable instruments. These cultural differences present significant challenges, as policies and legislation inspired by Western legal principles may not align with societal norms or public expectations in East Asia.

Additionally, a practical challenge arises from the unequal distribution of legal and procedural knowledge about ADs among patients, healthcare professionals, and families. Despite the introduction of AD systems, awareness and understanding remain insufficient, compounded by the dominance of conventional medical decision-making practices.[59] This knowledge gap and the divergence in perceptions between healthcare professionals and patients impede the successful implementation of ADs.[60] However, the adoption of shared decision-making frameworks through ACP—even when not legally binding—offers a viable alternative, fostering communication among patients, families, and healthcare providers to bridge these gaps.

Furthermore, administrative inefficiencies and legislative stagnation serve to compound these challenges. Effective governance under democratic principles is contingent upon the existence of robust public trust, transparent policy evaluation, and iterative reform. However, these prerequisites remain unmet in many parts of East Asia.[61] Japan, in particular, encounters notable difficulties, with minimal governmental action on ADs and ACP.[62] Legislative responsibility has been largely deferred to the public, while the influence of political actors, such as the JMA, has obstructed meaningful legislative progress.

---

[59] Refers to "3-2 (1) SUPPORT Study" of Chapter 3 for the paragraph; The field of medical law and ethics plays a pivotal role in determining the manner in which ADs are aligned with medical judgments. For instance, the legislation in the State of Queensland (Australia) permits health professionals to override valid ADs if they are deemed to be inconsistent with the tenets of good practice; see Section 103, Protection of health provider for non-compliance with advance health directive, Powers of Attorney Act 1998 (Queensland). https://www.legislation.qld.gov.au/view/html/inforce/current/act-1998-022#sec.103.

[60] Refers to "5-3-1 Healthcare versus Asset Management" of Chapter 5 for the paragraph.

[61] Refers to "2-3 (3) Policy Orientation in East Asia" of Chapter 2 for the paragraph.

[62] Refers to "4-4 (3) Necessity of Governmental Actions for Legislation" of Chapter 4.

Nevertheless, implementing evidence-based policy reforms, along with establishing mechanisms for public engagement and oversight, may offer a viable path forward to ensure that ADs and ACP become practical, accessible, and effective tools for end-of-life decision-making.

6.3.2 The Principal Concepts of Advance Decision-Making

This section examines the emerging legal concept of "advance decision-making" as it is proposed in East Asia. To avoid confusion between the frameworks in East Asia and Europe, the term "advance decision-making" is adopted to describe the practice in East Asia, while the term "advance choices" is studied in Europe. The goal of advance decision-making in East Asia is to foster a more comprehensive and supportive approach to ADs and ACP. It involves legally or ethically significant instructions given or preferences expressed by a competent adult regarding potential future scenarios in which they may lose capacity.

These scenarios may cover a range of areas, including health, welfare, personal affairs, asset management, and legal decisions, except where explicitly restricted by law. Legally binding instructions are referred to as "advance instructions," while preferences based on values, beliefs, or personal principles—intended to guide decisions without a legal obligation—are termed "advance statements."

It is of the utmost importance to address legal and practical challenges related to medical advance decision-making and mental health advance statements to facilitate their effective implementation. Although the legal terminology of advance decision-making in East Asia may not always correspond to that used in European legal frameworks, it is essential to ensure that it has clear legal effects within East Asia. In this context, advance decision-making may be supported by mutual agreements that appoint a representative to manage an older adult's affairs, including assets, healthcare, and life management.

This is because the current legal infrastructure for proactive measures remains underdeveloped in East Asia. Thus, it would be advantageous to expand opportunities for older adults to engage in proactive legal instruments, such as ADs, ACP, or advance decision-making. This is a markedly distinct legal feature from the European concept of advance choices, which has a predominantly unilateral nature in fulfilling legal requirements set forth by international entities.

The principles of advance decision-making encompass both individual and relational autonomy, provided that they are conducive to an individual's well-being and free from undue influence. The central legal issue in advance decision-making is how relational autonomy can be incorporated into legislation. In other words, it requires establishing criteria to determine the extent and boundaries of family members' and other stakeholders' involvement in decision-making processes.

For instance, in Singapore, it is notable that the legislation does not explicitly mention the involvement of family members, which may give rise to interpretive ambiguity. In contrast, South Korea and Taiwan have legal systems founded on the principle of respecting individual autonomy. Nevertheless, the explicit recognition of family involvement in legislation has resulted in *de facto* substituted decision-making by family members. This raises concerns that incorporating provisions that allow family members or other parties to assume an individual's will and preferences or decision-making authority may undermine the legal principle of individual autonomy.

From a legal–technical perspective, it is recommended that the law refrain from specifying detailed criteria for recognizing the involvement of family members and others. Instead, this issue should be delegated to subsidiary administrative regulations or guidelines, which would be subject to periodic review by an independent, neutral oversighted body.

The role of such a neutral body would be to monitor and ensure the implementation of the law and, if necessary, modify the criteria over time, thereby reducing potential inconsistencies between legislation and evolving societal norms. The precise legal framework and composition of this body would be determined at a later stage. This approach would theoretically uphold the principle of autonomy while ensuring practical flexibility and adaptability.

Once the legal concept of advance decision-making is established, it is necessary to consider its relationship to existing ADs and ACP. An AD represents one method of expressing an individual's legally binding decisions, which falls under the umbrella of advance decision-making. In contrast, ACP represents a collaborative approach, involving shared decision-making between the individual, healthcare professionals, and family members. While conceptually distinct, these mechanisms can complement and reinforce one another.

A key question arises regarding how to resolve discrepancies when the content expressed in these three methods—ADs, ACP, and advance decision-making—conflicts. From a legal standpoint, priority could be given to the most recent expression of intent, as this may reasonably be considered a revision of prior decisions. It becomes the responsibility of the healthcare team to ascertain whether the individual's intention has remained consistent or evolved through discussions with family members and healthcare professionals. This principle can be summarized as follows: "If your mind is changed, you have the right to change your mind."[63]

In cases where the individual's intention cannot be ascertained, it falls to the family to make a reasonable presumption regarding their will and preferences. If this, too, proves challenging, the decision must ultimately rest with the healthcare professionals, who bear the responsibility of determining what course of action aligns with the individual's best interests.

6.3.3 Criteria as Guiding Principles for Advance Decision-Making

The integration of the traditional values in East Asian systems, including family involvement, with Western-style legislation based on the protection of individual autonomy and human rights requires a delicate equilibrium between relational values and the safeguarding of individual rights. To achieve a harmonious integration of these two perspectives, the following criteria can be employed as guiding principles.

By establishing these criteria as guiding principles, a framework can be developed that respects traditional values while ensuring legal measures protect individual autonomy and human rights. This balanced approach promotes a more integrated system that recognizes the importance of both traditional values and legal standards.

1. **Respect for Cultural Context:**
   It is imperative that legal measures are informed by an understanding of cultural differences and, where appropriate, reflect the values of virtue and relational autonomy. In East Asia, the legal system could acknowledge the role of family and community in decision-making processes while upholding the principle of individual autonomy. In the context of end-of-life decisions, family involvement may be permitted, while ensuring that the patient's wishes and preferences are given paramount consideration.

2. **Prioritizing Individual Intent in Legal Context:**
   It is of the utmost importance to prioritize the wishes of the individual, particularly in the context of end-of-life care, even when traditional values are considered. It is imperative that legal measures explicitly

---

[63.] Alzheimer's Society (n.d.) "Reviewing and Changing Your Advance Decision." https://www.alzheimers.org.uk/get-support/legal-financial/reviewing-changing-advance-decision#content-start.

include mechanisms to protect the individual's right to make autonomous decisions. Furthermore, while family input can serve as a complementary consideration, it must not override the individual's right to make decisions.

3. **Flexibility in the Legal Framework:**
   It is essential that legislation is sufficiently flexible to accommodate the diverse cultural practices that exist without compromising the fundamental rights of individuals. Hybrid approaches could facilitate the integration of formal legal mechanisms, such as ADs, with informal, culturally sensitive practices, such as family discussions and flexible guidelines. This flexibility could help meet cultural expectations while providing legal safeguards.

4. **Mediating Institutions Be Incorporated:**
   The proposal of mediating institutions, such as clinical ethics committees or advisory boards, may assist in the resolution of conflicts between traditional values and legal rights. Such bodies can provide guidance informed by cultural considerations, facilitate the resolution of disputes, and ensure that decisions are made in accordance with both moral values and legal standards.

5. **Public Education and Advocacy:**
   To reconcile traditional values such as virtues with legal measures, it is essential that public education and advocacy efforts raise awareness of both the cultural importance of virtue-based practices and legal rights. This dual approach can assist individuals and families in comprehending the significance of integrating traditional values with legal safeguards, thereby facilitating the ability to make more informed and balanced decisions.

6.3.4 Draft Main Provisions for Advance Decision-Making Legislation

To facilitate the discussion on the legal framework of advance decision-making in East Asia, we will provide, by way of example, a number of key clauses that constitute advance decision-making as below. This proposal represents an alternative approach to the model legislation proposed in the context of the European project. It is important to note that advance decision-making is still under consideration. This test document has been drafted by the author personally with the intention of incorporating the characteristics of the East Asian model.

At the time of drafting this book, the draft model law of advance choices was not yet available. In order to provide context and ensure alignment with relevant legislation, the author has referenced the Medical Treatment Planning and

Decisions Act 2016 (Victoria) in Australia and the document titled "Respecting Patients' Will in End-of-Life Care Tentative Version 3," which was drafted by the Center for Applied Philosophy & Ethics at Kyoto University, Japan.[64]

Legislative Proposal

The Act is provisionally referred to as the "Act on Respecting Persons' Will and Preferences and Advance Decision-Making in End-of-Life Medical Care."[65] The objective of this legislative proposal is to establish a social framework that enables older adults to receive medical care that aligns with their expressed wishes and preferences, and to pass away peacefully. Despite advancements in medical technology that extend the lives of terminally ill patients, end-of-life medical care policies remain unclear, causing confusion among stakeholders. The legislation aims to guarantee that medical professionals furnish patients with transparent and comprehensive information regarding their illness and its probable progression. This would facilitate patients making well-informed decisions concerning their medical care and the drafting of ADs. In cases where patients are unable to make decisions, the law seeks to provide support to families, representatives, or medical teams in making the necessary decisions on their behalf.

Purposes

The purposes of this Act are as follows:

(1) to enable persons to execute in advance a choice containing binding instructions or expressing preferences and values regarding various future aspects, including health, welfare, personal matters, asset management, and legal decisions;

(2) to facilitate various aspects of decisions for individuals lacking decision-making capacity;

(3) to empower persons to appoint:

(a) another person to make various aspects of decisions on their behalf in the absence of decision-making capacity;

(b) another person to support and represent their interests in making various decisions.

[64.] Victorian Legislation (2024) "Medical Treatment Planning and Decisions Act 2016" Act Number 69/2016. https://www.legislation.vic.gov.au/in-force/acts/medical-treatment-planning-and-decisions-act-2016/011; Center for Applied Philosophy & Ethics, Kyoto University (2018) "Respecting Patients' Will in End-of-Life Care Tentative Version 3" [in Japanese]. http://www.cape.bun.kyoto-u.ac.jp/project/project02/eol/.

[65.] A legislative proposal is presented by the drafter at the Diet prior to the initial reading of the proposed legislation.

(4) Nevertheless, to respect a person's wishes and not to compel them to create advance decision-making if they believe it is appropriate not to do so.

End of Life
(1) The term "end of life" is used to describe an incurable and irreversible condition that is expected to result in death within a relatively short period of time, even with the administration of life-sustaining medical treatment.
(2) The determination of the end of life will be made based on the diversity of conditions, including:
    (a) acute end of life in emergency medical care, etc.;
    (b) subacute end of life for cancer, etc.; and
    (c) chronic end of life for elderly people, etc. The specifics of this determination will be outlined in a separate ordinance or guidelines of the Ministry of Health, Labour, and Welfare of Japan.

Decision-Making Capacity
(1) A person is deemed to possess decision-making capacity for decisions falling within the purview of this Act if the person is capable of:
    (a) comprehending the pertinent information and the implications of the decision;
    (b) retaining the information for the duration necessary for decision-making;
    (c) utilize or weigh the information as part of the decision-making process;
    (d) communicate the decision, views, and needs regarding the decision through speech, gestures, or other means.
(2) In accordance with the stipulations of subsection (1), an adult is presumed to possess the capacity to make decisions, unless evidence to the contrary is presented.
(3) With respect to the requirements of subsection (1)(a), a person is deemed to understand information pertinent to a decision if they are able to comprehend an explanation of the information, tailored to their circumstances, whether through modified language, visual aids, or any other means.

Types of Directives
(1) An advance instruction, for the purposes of this Act, is defined as follows:
    (a) is an explicit statement in an advance instruction that reflects a person's various aspects of decision;
    (b) takes effect as if the person giving it has consented to or refused the commencement or continuation of various aspects, as applicable.

(2) An advance statement, for the purposes of this Act, is defined as a statement in an advance care directive reflecting a person's preferences and values as the basis for various aspects of decisions on their behalf, including, but not limited to, acceptable outcomes.

Principles

(1) A person has the right to receive the same standard of medical care as others and has the right to make choices and decisions about his or her own medical care.

(2) A person exercising a power or performing a function or duty under this Act shall observe the following principles:

    (a) The term "person" is defined as follows:

        (i) an individual with the right to make informed decisions about their various aspects;

        (ii) an individual who should receive information about various aspects, including health, welfare, personal matters, asset management, and legal decisions, presented in a sensitively communicated and clear manner to enable informed decisions.

    (b) The informed decisions of a person made under paragraph (a) should be respected and implemented;

    (c) A person has the right to be treated with respect for their cultural identity, personal beliefs, values, and personal characteristics.

    (d) An individual is entitled to accept or decline the advice of their stakeholders, including family members, provided that it is deemed to be beneficial to their well-being without undue influence. The manner in which stakeholders interact with the individual and exercise their decision-making authority shall be subject to a distinct administrative regulation or guidelines, which would be subject to periodic review by a neutral body.

(3) All individuals, including healthcare professionals, are expected to adhere at all times to the guiding principles of human rights, respect for diversity and mutual benefit, and to comply with the law and medical ethics.

(4) The decision-making process regarding a patient's medical care, including the provision of life-sustaining care at the end of life, is conducted through a consultative approach involving the patient, their family members, or other stakeholders. In this process, the person's will and preferences are held as the primary consideration. In the event of a dispute between the aforementioned parties, healthcare professionals and the medical team

may determine the patient's best interests in accordance with the relevant regulatory and procedural frameworks.

Healthcare Professionals Cannot Be Compelled

(1) This Act does not authorize the creation of any legal instrument that would compel a healthcare professional to administer a specific decision to a patient. This includes, but is not limited to, the following:
  (a) a statement in an advance directive or an advance decision-making;
  (b) a decision made by a decision-maker appointed by the patient in advance.

(2) A healthcare professional may advise a person to engage in ACP with relevant stakeholders, including family members, if ACP is deemed beneficial to the person and occurs without undue influence.

Eligibility for Advance Decision-Making

Any person aged 18 or above is eligible to make an advance decision-making if:

(a) the person in question:
  (i) possesses the capacity to make decisions regarding each statement in the choice;
  (ii) demonstrates an understanding of the nature and effect of each statement in the choice.
(b) the requirements of this part and relevant regulatory are met.

Appointment of a Decision-Maker

(1) An adult with decision-making capacity may appoint another adult as their appointed decision-maker.

(2) An appointment as an appointed decision-maker may be made in the following manner:
  (a) At the same time as an advance decision is made;
  (b) At any other time.

Powers of the Appointed Decision-Maker

An appointed decision-maker is granted the powers set out in XXXX or in any other Act, unless otherwise specified in the document of appointment.

Appointment of Support Person

(1) Any person aged 18 or above, with a decision-making capacity may appoint another person, aged 18 or above, as their support person.

(2) Only one support person may be appointed for a person.

Role of Support Person
(1) The role of a support person for the person making the appointment is:
    (a) to support the person in making, communicating, and giving effect to their decisions;
    (b) to represent the interests of the person concerning their decision, even when the person lacks decision-making capacity for decisions.
(2) A support person acting in the capacity of a support person does not have the power to make a person's decisions.

Clinical Ethics Committee
(1) It is desirable for medical institutions to establish a clinical ethics committee, which may include a clinical ethics support department.
(2) The clinical ethics committee shall be constituted by the head of the medical institution, medical, nursing, and pharmaceutical managers, and individuals from outside the institution.
(3) The functions of the clinical ethics committee are as follows:
    (a) Deliberating on requests from healthcare professionals, patients, and patients' families regarding decisions on medical policy, particularly withholding or discontinuing life-sustaining medical treatment
    (b) Decisions about medical policy, especially regarding the withholding or discontinuation of life-sustaining medical treatment, and responding to consultations from healthcare professionals, patients, and patients' families
    (c) Creation and amendment of guidelines for medical institutions
    (d) Provision of medical ethics education for medical personnel at medical institutions.

6.3.5 A Possible Avenue for Advance Decision-Making in East Asia

A comprehensive approach to end-of-life medical care in Japan necessitates a synthesis of individual autonomy with communal responsibility, as provided under Article 13 of the Constitution of Japan. This article upholds the principle of individual autonomy "to the extent that it does not infringe upon the public welfare," as further reinforced by the general principles outlined in Article 4 of the Constitution.[66] While medical decision-making and ADs should align with the protection and promotion of individual autonomy, Japan's rapidly aging

---

[66.] Refers to "2-2 (1) Individual Autonomy" of Chapter 2 for the paragraph.

demographic structure and corresponding high mortality rate demonstrate that autonomy alone is insufficient.

Instead, a comprehensive socio-legal framework is required—one that integrates legal mechanisms with a supportive social environment to effectively implement and protect individual autonomy. A socio-legal approach constitutes a multidisciplinary method of studying law that incorporates non-legal dimensions, including societal norms and policy considerations, to produce holistic insights.[67] This approach links the analysis of law to the examination of its social context and explores the role of legal systems in the establishment, preservation, or transformation of societal practices.

In order to achieve this, legislative reforms, supplementary guidelines, and robust public education programs must be developed, alongside systematic training for medical professionals, social workers, and relevant stakeholders. These measures are critical to fostering the adoption and proper utilization of ADs and ACP within society based on principles of "respect for human rights, appreciation for diversity, and mutual benefit."

In the context of healthcare-related decision-making, it is of the utmost importance to adopt a legally sound and practically viable approach that safeguards the rights and responsibilities of patients, families, and healthcare professionals. Legal researchers must engage in active collaboration with healthcare practitioners to ensure the integration of legal principles into clinical practice. Such collaboration will bridge the gap between theoretical legal constructions and practical implementation, thereby enriching jurisprudence and promoting the formulation of responsive and effective healthcare policies.

As Shigeaki Tanaka suggests,[68] the development of multilayered, participatory platforms for consensus-building—including voluntary forums and bottom-up, community-driven decision-making mechanisms—may serve as an effective means of transitioning away from the current top-down, government-driven administrative models.

Further research is essential to clarify and refine the legal underpinnings of advance decision-making for older adults in East Asia. It is recommended that such research adopt a collaborative, interdisciplinary approach through the joint efforts of academic consortia spanning East Asia, Australia, and Europe. To

---

[67.] Schiff, David N. (1976) "Socio-Legal Theory: Social Structure and Law" *The Modern Law Review* Volume 39 Issue 3, 287–310. https://doi.org/10.1111/j.1468-2230.1976.tb01458.x.

[68.] Tanaka, Shigeaki (2004) "On the Legal Involvement in Bioethics" [in Japanese] in Shigeaki Tanaka (ed), *Perspectives on Modern Law: Aspects of Self-Determination*. Tokyo: Yuhikaku Publishing. 131–175.

facilitate this, the establishment of regional academic platforms for the exchange of data, case studies, and policy frameworks is crucial. These platforms would promote cross-regional cooperation, foster mutual understanding, and facilitate international discourse on these critical legal and ethical issues.

As Adrian D. Ward, a distinguished Scottish legal expert with over six decades of experience, underscores, citizens' initiatives are integral to influencing legislative outcomes and ensuring the effective execution and monitoring of laws.[69] Ward posits that the enactment of a well-designed law marks only the midpoint of the legislative process; its full success depends on robust citizen engagement. It is therefore imperative for citizens to strategically advocate within democratic frameworks to influence policymaking, particularly regarding advance decision-making and end-of-life care legislation as discussed herein. It is anticipated that increased reliance on citizens' initiatives will play an expanding role in shaping public policy and ensuring legislative responsiveness to societal needs in East Asia.

[69.] This remark is based on the closing speech delivered by Adrian D Ward at the World Congress of Adult Support and Care (Argentina 2024) at the Buenos Aires University on August 30, 2024.

CHAPTER 7

Conclusion

This study emphasizes human rights, diversity, and mutual benefit in East Asia, advocating a nuanced approach that respects each country's legal and cultural context while balancing individual and relational autonomy in decision-making. The conclusion calls for a socio-legal framework that fosters advance decision-making through legislation, policy, and public education, highlighting the role of government initiatives and regional collaboration in shifting societal attitudes toward end-of-life care.

7.1 Conclusion of the Study

This study addresses the growing issues of an aging population and rising dementia rates in East Asia, with a particular focus on Japan, South Korea, Taiwan, and Singapore. The necessity for action against cognitive decline and dementia risk is underscored by societal shifts, including higher death rates, declining births, and increasing single-living older adults occurring in East Asia. The central question is how law and policy frameworks can be employed to address these challenges and ensure meaningful end-of-life medical care for older adults. In response, the study puts forward a proposal for a "Project for Advance Decision-Making for Future Disability in East Asia," which draws inspiration from the ELI.

This study presents a comparative analysis based on two main analytical axes: (i) comparisons among East Asian countries and area, and (ii) comparisons of conceptual models between the U.S., Europe, and East Asia. An examination of ADs and ACP within East Asia reveals both similarities and differences, particularly regarding legislation and family involvement in end-of-life medical care decisions. An analysis of conceptual models offers insights into the characteristics of the

East Asian model. The study emphasizes the need to achieve a balance between individual autonomy and family involvement, considering the societal values.

The study is based on the principles of human rights, diversity, and mutual benefit, which are fundamental tenets in the context of East Asia. The study then examines the influence of legal and cultural factors on the uptake of ADs and ACP, advocating a nuanced approach that respects the distinctive attributes of each country and area. While individual autonomy remains a fundamental principle, relational autonomy can facilitate the reconciliation of family dynamics in decision-making.

The conclusion emphasizes a socio-legal approach, establishing legal systems for end-of-life medical care that reflect individual autonomy and creating a social environment that facilitates individual decisions, to foster the legal concept of advance decision-making. Five criteria are proposed as guiding principles, and draft provisions constituting advance decision-making are put forth for further consideration. This would entail the facilitation of relevant legislation, guidelines, or policies. It is emphasized that governmental initiatives such as public education and policy play an important role in transforming societal attitudes toward death, despite the presence of cultural taboos surrounding the topic. This highlights the importance of learning and collaboration within East Asia.

7.2 Limitations of the Study and Future Tasks

This study has made a significant contribution to the understanding of potential solutions to the issues of end-of-life medical care for older adults. However, the main limitation of this study is that it is a literature analysis and, therefore, does not include empirical research to investigate the distinctive end-of-life medical care cases in East Asia. In lieu of empirical research, the comparative analysis is based on the legislation of ADs and ACP between East Asia countries and areas, as well as conceptualized models in East Asia and others. Consequently, the study does not offer a comprehensive examination of the operational aspects of ADs and ACP.

The discourse surrounding the legal concept of advance decision-making in East Asia is still in its infancy, with numerous issues yet to be discussed and agreed upon. Further discussion is necessary to conceptualize the most appropriate form of advance decision-making for East Asian individuals, to identify potential issues that need to be considered in adopting this concept in each country and area, and to clarify the benefits that can be expected from adopting this concept.

Furthermore, the scope may be constrained to specific geographical regions, which could lead to the exclusion of nuances that exist in other parts of the world. Future research in this field prioritizes an expansion of the geographical scope to encompass greater Asia, Australia, Europe, and North America. This should include a more comprehensive examination of practices and a deeper exploration of the psychological intricacies that may shape the uptake of ADs, ACP, and advance decision-making. Such collaborative efforts should encompass multidisciplinary discussions.

These limitations do not negate the importance of the academic analysis of this study. These challenges represent future research tasks.

BIBLIOGRAPHY/LEGISLATION/
COURT CASE

BIBLIOGRAPHY

Chapter 1

1.1 Family Involvement or Proactive Preparations

All Japan Hospital Association (AJHA) (2011) "Assessment of the Actual Situation of Older Adults with Gastrostomy and Survey Research on Management in Nursing Homes and Residential Homes" [in Japanese] 11. https://www.ajha.or.jp/voice/pdf/other/110416_1.pdf.

Arai, Hidenori, Ouchi, Y., Toba, K., Endo, T., Shimokado, K., Tsubota, K., Matsuo, S., Mori, H., Yumura, W., Yokode, M., Rakugi, H. and Ohshima, S. (2015) "Front-runner of Super-aged Societies." *Geriatrics & Gerontology International* Volume 15, Issue 6: 673-687. https://doi.org/10.1111/ggi.12450.

Cabinet Office of Japan (2024) "Annual Report on the Ageing Society 2024: Trends in Persons Aged 65 and over Living Alone. (Figure 1-1-9)" [in Japanese] https://www8.cao.go.jp/kourei/whitepaper/w-2024/zenbun/06pdf_index.html.

Courts of Japan (2024) "Overview of Adult Guardianship Related Cases" [in Japanese] https://www.courts.go.jp/toukei_siryou/siryo/kouken/index.html.

Japan, MHLW (2020) "White Paper on the Health, Labour, and Welfare 2020" [in Japanese] 5. https://www.mhlw.go.jp/content/000735866.pdf.

Japan, Ministry of Health, Labour, and Welfare (MHLW) (2021) "Part 1 Population and Households Chapter 2 Population Dynamics: Table 1-25 Death Composition and Ratio" [in Japanese] https://www.mhlw.go.jp/toukei/youran/indexyk_1_2.html.

MHLW (2023) "Verification Research into Various Issues Related to Cemetery and Burial Laws, Including the Handling of Bodies Infected with COVID-19" [in Japanese] https://mhlw-grants.niph.go.jp/project/159849.

Saito, Tomoko, Tsuneo Konta, Sachiko Kudo, et al. (2024) "Factors Associated with Community Residents' Preference for Living at Home at the End of Life: The Yamagata Cohort Survey" *Global Health & Medicine* Volume 6 Issue 1, 70–76. https://doi.org/10.35772/ghm.2023.01072.

Sudore, R. L., H. D. Lum, J. J. You, et al. (2017) "Defining Advance Care Planning for Adults: A Consensus Definition from a Multidisciplinary Delphi Panel" *Journal of Pain Symptom Management* Volume 53 Issue 5, 821–832.

Takahashi, Yasushi (2024) "Reference 8: Necessity of Forecasting Future Demand for Medical and Welfare Facilities: Taking into Account the Rapid Change of the Elderly Population in the Later Stages of Life" [in Japanese] (A Survey Delivered at the 3rd Study Meeting on New Regional Medical Care Concept, etc. Held on May 22, 2024).

Takao, Yasuo (2024) "Understanding Fertility Policy through a Process-Oriented Approach: The Case of Japan's Decline in Births" *Journal of Population Research* Volume 41 Issue 12, 11–27. https://doi.org/10.1007/s12546-024-09333-2.

The Japan Research Institute (2024) "Regarding the Implementation of the Social Welfare Promotion Project in FY2024" [in Japanese] MHLW Delegated Research Project in FY2024. https://www.jri.co.jp/page.jsp?id=108519.

Uemura, Kazumasa (2015) "1. Advance Directives and Living Will (General Rules)" [in Japanese] *Geriatrics and Gerontology International* Volume 52 Issue 3, 207–210. https://www.jpn-geriat-soc.or.jp/publications/other/pdf/clinical_practice_52_3_207.pdf.

Yomiuri Online (2024) "Unclaimed Bodies up 30 per cent in Five Years, with an Increase in the Number of People Living Alone and the Refusal of Relatives to Take Them in... Yomiuri Survey" [in Japanese] (June 3, 2024).

1.2 Importance of the East Asian Project

Cheng, S. Y., S. Y. Suh, T. Morita, et al. (2015) "A Cross-Cultural Study on Behaviors When Death Is Approaching in East Asian Countries: What Are the Physician-Perceived Common Beliefs and Practices?" *Medicine (Baltimore)* Volume 94 Issue 39, e1573. PMID: 26426631; PMCID: PMC4616852. https://doi.org/10.1097/MD.0000000000001573.

Dementia Australia (2024) "Diagnostic Criteria for Dementia" https://www.dementia.org.au/information/for-health-professionals/clinical-resources/diagnostic-criteria-for-dementia.

European Law Institute (ELI) (2024) "Advance Choices for Future Disablement." https://www.europeanlawinstitute.eu/projects-publications/current-projects/current-projects/advance-choices/.

Japan, Cabinet Office (2018) "Annual Report on the Ageing Society 2018" https://www8.cao.go.jp/kourei/english/annualreport/index-wh.html.

Law Society of Scotland (2022) "Human Rights Must Be at the Core of Proposals for Law Reform around Advance Choices and Medical Decision-Making" https://www.lawscot.org.uk/news-and-events/law-society-news/advance-choices-and-medical-decision-making/.

Livingston, G., J. Huntley, A. Sommerlad, et al. (2020) "Dementia Prevention, Intervention, and Care: 2020 Report of the Lancet Commission." *The Lancet* Volume 396 Issue 10248, 413–446.

Our World in Data "Deaths per Year (Chart)" https://ourworldindata.org/grapher/number-of-deaths-per-year.

Sakurai, Yukio (2023a) "Adaptation of Law and Policy in an Aged Society: Guardianship Law and People's Behavioral Pattern" *The Rest: The Journal of Politics and Development* Volume 13 Issue 2, 144–154. http://hdl.handle.net/10131/0002000015.

Sakurai, Yukio (2023b) "Supported Decision-Making in the Japanese Context: Developments and Challenges" *The Journal of Aging and Social Change* Volume 3 Issue 1, 151–169. https://doi.org/10.18848/2576-5310/CGP/v13i01/151-169.

The World Factbook (2024a) "Death Rate" https://www.cia.gov/the-world-factbook/field/death-rate/country-comparison/.

The World Factbook (2024b) "Total Fertility Rate" https://www.cia.gov/the-world-factbook/field/total-fertility-rate/country-comparison/.

Voss, Steffen (1992) "These Factors Have a Profound Impact on Contemporary Social Dynamics—Japanese Legal Consciousness: Especially Traditional Legal Consciousness" [in Japanese] *Japanese Language and Culture Training Program Report Collection, Hiroshima University.* 77–81. https://ir.lib.hiroshima-u.ac.jp/00039306.

Yeung, Wei-Jun Jean (2016) "Living Alone: The Trend of One-Person Households in Asia" chrome-extension://efaidnbmnnnibpcajpcglclefindmkaj/https://fass.nus.edu.sg/cfpr/wp-content/uploads/sites/17/2020/09/Aug16E.pdf.

1.3 Objective and Prior Research of the Study

Akiba, Shunsuke (2021) "Self-Other Relationships and Relational Autonomy in Self-Determination regarding Medical Care" [in Japanese] *Bioethics* Volume 31 Issue 1, 46–54.

Carney, Terry (2019) "Adult Guardianship and Other Financial Planning Mechanisms for People with Cognitive Impairment in Australia" in Lusina Ho and Rebecca Lee (eds), *Special Needs Financial Planning: A Comparative Perspective*. Cambridge: Cambridge University Press. 3–29.

Chan, T. E. (2019) "Advance Care Planning: A Communitarian Approach?" *Journal of Law and Medicine* Volume 26 Issue 4, 896–921.

Cheung, D., and M. Dunn (eds) (2023) *Advance Directives across Asia: A Comparative Socio-Legal Analysis*. Cambridge: Cambridge University Press.

Donnelly, Mary (2010) *Healthcare Decision-Making and the Law: Autonomy, Capacity, and Limits of the Liberalism*. Cambridge: Cambridge University Press.

Donnelly, Mary (2017) "Developing a Legal Framework for Advance Healthcare Planning: Comparing England, Wales and Ireland" *European Journal of Health Law* Volume 24 Issue, 167–184. https://doi.org/10.1163/15718093-12341412.

Herring, Jonathan (2022) *Medical Law and the Ethics*. 9th ed. Oxford: Oxford University.

Higuchi, Norio (2007) *Thinking about Medicine and Law* [in Japanese]. Tokyo: Yuhikaku Publishing.

Higuchi, Norio (2008) *Continued: Thinking about Medicine and Law* [in Japanese]. Tokyo: Yuhikaku Publishing.

Higuchi, Norio (2015) "Legal Issues on Medical Interventions in Terminally Ill Patients" [in Japanese] *Medical Care and Society* Volume 25 Issue 1, 21–34. https://doi.org/10.4091/iken.25.21.

Higuchi, Norio (2020) "Current Status and Issues of End-of-Life Care Legal Issues" *Japanese Journal of Geriatrics* Volume 2 Issue 5, 579–584.

Higuchi, Norio, and Fusako Seki (eds) (2019) *Elder Law: Legal Basics for a Super-Aged Society* [in Japanese]. Tokyo: Tokyo University Press.

Ho, Luisa, and Rebecca Lee (eds), (2019) *Special Needs Financial Planning: A Comparative Perspective*. Cambridge: Cambridge University Press.

Kawakami, A., E. W. Y. Kwong, C. K. Y., Lai et al. (2021) "Advance Care Planning and Advance Directive Awareness among East Asian Older Adults: Japan, Hong Kong and South Korea" *Geriatrics and Gerontology International* Volume 21, 71–76. https://doi.org/10.1111/ggi.14086.

Kodama, Satoshi, and Miho Tanaka (2024) "International Collaborative Research on Ethical and Legal Issues in End-of-Life Medical Care in East Asia" [in Japanese] https://www.asian-eolc-ethics.com/.

Machino, Saku (1986) *Patient Self-Determination and Law* [in Japanese]. Tokyo: University of Tokyo Press.

Machino, Saku (1996) "Patient Self-Determination vs. Doctor's Paternalism" [in Japanese] *Bioethics* Volume 6 Issue 1, 32–34.

Machino, Saku (2000) "Self-Determination and Determination by Other" [in Japanese] *Journal of Medical Law* Volume 15, 44–52.

Machino, Saku (2007) "Patients' Right to Self-Determination and Doctors' Duty to Treat: In the Wake of the Kawasaki Kyodo Hospital Case Appeals Court Decision" [in Japanese] *Criminal Law Journal* Volume 8, 47–53.

Machino, Saku (2013) "Caring-From a Legal Point of View" *Sophia Bioethics* December 2013, 103–109.

Mackenzie, Catriona (2013) "The Importance of Relational Autonomy and Capabilities for an Ethics of Vulnerability" in Catriona Mackenzie, Wendy Rogers, and Susan Dodds (eds), *Vulnerability: New Essays in Ethics and Feminist Philosophy (Studies in Feminist Philosophy)*. Oxford: Oxford University Press. 33–59. https://doi.org/10.1093/acprof:oso/9780199316649.003.0002.

Martina, D., C. Lin, M. Kristanti, et al. (2021) "Advance Care Planning in Asia: A Systematic Narrative Review of Healthcare Professionals' Knowledge, Attitude, and Experience" *Journal of the American Medical Directors Association* Volume 22, P349.E1–P349.E28. https://doi.org/10.1016/j.jamda.2020.12.018.

MacKenzie, Catriona (2019) "Feminist Innovation in Philosophy: Relational Autonomy and Social Justice" *Women's Studies International Forum* Volume 72, 144–151. https://doi.org/10.1016/j.wsif.2018.05.003.

Morikawa, Takehiro (2020) "International Comparison of Institutional Frameworks for End-of-Life Medical Care and Aged Care" [in Japanese] *Annual Report on Public Policy Studies* Volume 14, 137–150.

NUS (National University of Singapore) Centre for Asian Legal Studies Working Paper 19.06. NUS Law Working Paper No. 2019/020. https://ssrn.com/abstract=3459382.

Pun, Jack K. H. (2022) "Communication about Advance Directives and Advance Care Planning in an East Asian Cultural Context: A Systematic Review" *Oncology Nursing Forum* Volume 49 Issue1, 58–70. https://doi.org/10.1188/22.ONF.58-70.

Tanaka, Miho, Satoshi Kodama, Ilhak Lee, et al. (2020) "Forgoing Life-Sustaining Treatment–A Comparative Analysis of Regulations in Japan, Korea, Taiwan, and England" *BMC Medical Ethics* Volume 12 Issue 1, 1–15.

Teshima, Yutaka (2022) *Introduction to Medical Law.* 6th ed. Tokyo: Yuhikaku Publishing. 48–49.

Tsai, Daniel Fu-Chang (1999) "Ancient Chinese Medical Ethics and the Four Principles of Biomedical Ethics" *Journal of Medical Ethics* Volume 25 Issue 4, 315–321. https://doi.org/10.1136/jme.25.4.315.

Tsai, Daniel Fu-Chang (2023) "The Law and Practice of Advance Directives in Taiwan" in D. Cheung and M. Dunn (eds), *Advance Directives across Asia: A Comparative Socio-Legal Analysis.* Cambridge: Cambridge University Press. 75–89.

Yonemura, Shigeto (2016) *Lectures on Medical Law.* Tokyo: Nippon Hyoron Sha.

1.4 Methodology

Dzeng, Elizabeth, Thomas Bein, and J. Randall Curtis, et al. (2022) "The Role of Policy and Law in Shaping the Ethics and Quality of End-of-Life Care in Intensive Care" *Intensive Care Medicine* Volume 48, 352–354. https://doi.org/10.1007/s00134-022-06623-2.

Sakurai, Yukio (2023) "A Study on the Use of Public Interest Corporations regarding Asset Management for Older Adults: Plans for Dealing with Issues in an Ageing Society" [in Japanese] Excellence Award in the First Thesis Contest of the Japan Association of Charitable Organization (JACO). http://doi.org/10.18880/00015170.

Chapter 2

2.1 Vulnerability Approach and Safeguarding Law

Arendt, Hannah (1958) *The Human Condition*. Chicago: Chicago University Press.

Donnelly, Sarah, Marita O'Brien, Judy Walsh, et al. (2017) *Adult Safeguarding Legislation and Policy Rapid Realist Literature Review* https://researchrepository.ucd.ie/handle/10197/9183.

Fineman, Martha Albertson (2012) "Elderly as Vulnerable: Rethinking the Nature of Individual and Societal Responsibility" *Elder Law Journal* Volume 20, 101–142. https://ssrn.com/abstract=2088159.

Herring, Jonathan (2012) "Elder Abuse: A Human Rights Agenda for the Future" in Israel Doron and Ann M. Soden (eds), *Beyond Elder Law: New Directions in Law and Aging*. London: Springer.

Herring, Jonathan, and Jesse Wall (2015) "Autonomy, Capacity and Vulnerable Adults: Filling the Gaps in the Mental Capacity Act" *Legal Studies* Volume 35 Issue 4, 698–719.

Honkasalo, Marja-Liisa (2018) "Guest Editor's Introduction: Vulnerability and Inquiring into Relationality" *Suomen Antropologi* [Journal of the Finnish Anthropological Society] Volume 43 Issue 3, 1–21. http://hdl.handle.net/10138/305956. https://doi.org/10.30676/jfas.v43i3.82725.

Kohn, Nina A. (2014) "Vulnerability Theory and the Role of Government" *Yale Journal of Law and Feminism* Volume 26, 1–27. https://digitalcommons.law.yale.edu/yjlf/vol26/iss1/2.

Levinas, Emmanuel (1961) *Totality and Infinity: An Essay on Exteriority*. Translated by Alphonso Lingis. Pittsburgh: Duquesne University Press.

Mandelstam, Michael (2008) *Safeguarding Vulnerable Adults and the Law*. London: Jessica Kingsley Publishers.

Montgomery, L., J. Anand, K. McKay, et al. (2016) "Implications of Divergences in Adult Protection Legislation" *Journal of Adult Protection* Volume 18 Issue 3, 1–16. https://doi.org/10.1108/JAP-10-2015-0032.

Sakurai, Yukio (2021) "Vulnerability Approach and Adult Support and Protection: Safeguarding Laws for Adults at Risk" *The Journal of Aging and Social Change* Volume 11 Issue 1, 19–34. https://doi.org/10.18848/2576-5310/CGP/v11i01/19-34.

Sakurai, Yukio (2022) "Value of Legislation Providing Support and Protection to Vulnerable Adults: Vulnerability Approach and Autonomy" Doctoral Dissertation, Yokohama National University. http://doi.org/10.18880/00014834.

Wayne, Michael Martin, Sabine Michalowski, Jill Stavert, et al. (2016) "The Essex Autonomy Project: Three Jurisdictions Report: Towards Compliance with CRPD Art. 12 in Capacity/Incapacity Legislation across the UK." https://doi.org/10.13140/RG.2.2.10734.72002.

2.2 Individual Autonomy and Relational Autonomy

Bedford, Daniel (2020) "Introduction: Vulnerability Refigured" in Daniel Bedford and Jonathan Herring (eds), *Embracing Vulnerability, the Challenges and Implications for Law.* London: Routledge.

Braun, Joan (2020) "Legal Interventions to Protect Vulnerable Adults: Can Relational Autonomy Provide a New Way Forward?" *Elder Law Review* Volume 12 Issue 2, 1–25. https://www.westernsydney.edu.au/__data/assets/pdf_file/0017/1714220/PEER_REVIEWED_BRAUN_Article.pdf.

Carney, Terry (2020) "People with Dementia and Other Cognitive Disabilities: Relationally Vulnerable or a Source of Agency and Care?" (Sydney Law School Research Paper No. 20/17) *Elder Law Review* Volume 12 Issue 1, 1–21. https://ssrn.com/abstract=3561294.

Dworkin, Gerald (1988) "The Nature of Autonomy" in Gerald Dworkin (ed), *The Theory and Practice of Autonomy.* Cambridge: Cambridge University Press. 3–20.

Dworkin, Gerald (2015) "The Nature of Autonomy" *Nordic Journal of Studies in Educational Policy* (An Unchanged Republishing) Volume 2 Article: 28479.

Fineman, Martha Albertson (2004) *The Autonomy Myth: A Theory of Dependency.* New York: The New Press.

Fineman, Martha Albertson (2017) "Introducing Vulnerability" in Martha Albertson Fineman and Jonathan W. Fineman (eds), *Vulnerability and the Legal Organization of Work*. New York: Routledge. 1–10. https://doi.org/10.4324/9781315518572.

Gómez-Vírseda, C., Y. de Maeseneer, and C. Gastmans, et al. (2019) "Relational Autonomy: What Does It Mean and How Is It Used in End-of-Life Care? A Systematic Review of Argument-Based Ethics Literature" *BMC Medical Ethics* Volume 20, Article No. 76, 1–15. https://doi.org/10.1186/s12910-019-0417-3.

Hasuo, Hiroyuki (2010) "The Structure of 'Autonomy' in Kant's Moral Philosophy: New Possibilities through Practice of Duty of Love" [in Japanese] *Civilization Structure Theory* Volume 6, 15–34.

Hayakawa, Seisuke (2014) "Caring and Vulnerable Agency" *Studies on Action Theory* Volume 3, 1–10.

Herring, Jonathan (2010) "Relational Autonomy and Rape" in S. Day Sclater, F. Ebtehaj, E. Jackson, and M. Richards (eds), *Regulating Autonomy*. Oxford: Oxford Legal Studies Research Paper No. 12.

Herring, Jonathan (2014a) "The Disability Critique of Care" *Elder Law Review* Volume 8 Article 2, 12.

Herring, Jonathan (2014b) *Relational Autonomy and Family Law*. London: Springer Science & Business Media.

Herring, Jonathan (2016) *Vulnerable Adults and the Law*. Oxford: Oxford University Press (Kindle) 1998.

Herring, Jonathan (2020) "Ethics of Care and Disability Rights: Complementary or Contradictory?" in Loraine Gelsthorpe, Perveez Mody, and Brian Sloan (eds), *Spaces of Care*. London: Hart Publishing. 180.

Ikeya, Hisao (2016) "Bioethics and Vulnerability" [in Japanese] *The Bulletin of Ryotokuji University* Volume 10, 105–128.

Inaba, Kazuo (2008) "Patient Decision-Making and the Role of the Family from a Legal Perspective (Patient Decision-Making and the Role of the Family)" [in Japanese] *Journal of Philosophy and Ethics in Health Care and Medicine* Volume 26, 87–90.

Jinno, Reisei (2016) "Medical Practice and Family Consent" [in Japanese] *Hiroshima Law Review* Volume 12, 223–245.

Lindsey, Jaime Tabitha (2018) "Protecting and Empowering Vulnerable Adults: Mental Capacity Law in Practice" Doctoral Dissertation. University of Birmingham. 1–341.

Mackenzie, Catriona (2008) "Relational Autonomy, Normative Authority and Perfectionism" *Journal of Social Philosophy,* Volume 39, 512–533.

Mackenzie, Catriona (2014) "Three Dimensions of Autonomy: A Relational Analysis" in Andrea Veltman and Mark Piper (eds), *Autonomy, Oppression, and Gender.* Oxford: Oxford University Press. 15–41.

Mackenzie, Catriona (2019) "Feminist Innovation in Philosophy: Relational Autonomy and Social Justice" *Women's Studies International Forum* Volume 72, 144–151. https://doi.org/10.1016/j.wsif.2018.05.003.

Menon, Sumytra, V. A. Entwistle, and A. V. Campbell, et al. (2020) "Some Unresolved Ethical Challenges in Healthcare Decision-Making: Navigating Family Involvement" *Asian Bioethics Review* Volume 12 Issue 1, 27–36. https://doi.org/10.1007/s41649-020-00111-9.

Morita, Tatsuya, Aya Enzo, Masanori Mori, et al. (2020) "Relational Autonomy in Advance Care Planning" [in Japanese] *Palliative Care* Volume 30 Issue 5, 399–402.

Nishimura, Jun (2021) "Ethics of Care and Social Security Law: For the Conversion from the Benefit-Centered Law to the Support-Centered Law" [in Japanese] *Journal of Kanagawa University of Human Services* Volume 18 Issue 1, 9–18.

Obayashi, Keigo (2022) "What Is Public Welfare: Public Welfare as the Standard" [in Japanese] *Hougaku Seminar* Volume 807, 39–44.

Odaka, Tomoo (1965) *The Ultimate in Law* [in Japanese]. 2nd ed. Tokyo: Yuhikaku Publishing.

Ohe, Hiroshi (1999) "Rights and Relationships" [in Japanese] *St. Paul's Review of Law and Politics* Volume 53, 149–178.

Oki, Masao (1983/2024) *Japanese Concept of Law: A Comparison with Western Concept of Law* [in Japanese]. Tokyo: University of Tokyo Press.

O'shea, Tom (2012) "Critics of Autonomy" Essex Autonomy Project: Green Paper Report 1-26.

Rawls, John (2010) *A Theory Justice* [in Japanese]. 2nd ed. Translated by Takashi Kawamoto, Yuuko Kamishima, and Satoshi Fukuma et al. Tokyo: Kinokuniya Bookstore.

Ryan, Richard M., and L. Edward (2006) "Self-Regulation and the Problem of Human Autonomy: Does Psychology Need Choice, Self-Determination, and Will?" *Journal of Personality* Volume 74 Issue 6, 1557–1585.

Sakurai, Yukio (2023) "International Cooperation of Asian Law Systems beyond Diversity" *Political Reflection Magazine* Volume 9 Issue 3, 27–31.

Sato, Koji (1990) "The Meaning of 'Self-Determination' in the Constitutional Studies" [in Japanese]. *Legal Philosophy Annual Report* [1989] 76–99.

Series, Lucy (2015) "Relationships, Autonomy and Legal Capacity: Mental Capacity and Support Paradigms" *International Journal of Law and Psychiatry* Volume 40, 80–91.

Straehle, Christine (2017) "Introduction: Vulnerability, Autonomy, and Applied Ethics" in Christine Straehle (ed), *Vulnerability, Autonomy and Applied Ethics.* London: Routledge.

Tahara, Shotarou (2017) "What Should Autonomous Agents Be Like? From the Individualistic to the Substantive Conception" [in Japanese] *Waseda Rilas Journal* Volume 5, 193–203.

Tahara, Shotaro (2022) "Substantive Conceptions of Autonomy: An Approach Based on Shared Characteristics" [in Japanese] *Bulletin of the Faculty of Humanities, Ibaraki University: Studies in Social Sciences* Volume 1, 55–76.

Takikawa, Hirohide (2001) "Between Self-Decision and Self-Responsibility: A Philosophy of Law Consideration" [in Japanese] *Law Seminar* September 2001, 32–35.

Todd, Emanuel (2022) *Où en sommes-nous? Une esquisse de l'histoire humaine* (Where Are We? A Sketch of Human History) [in Japanese]. Japanese edition. Tokyo: Bungeishunju.

Wright, Megan S. (2020) "Dementia, Autonomy, and Supported Healthcare Decision Making" (Pennsylvania State Law Research Paper No. 05-2019) *Maryland Law Review* Volume 79, 257–324.

Young, Robert (1986) *Personal Autonomy: Beyond Negative and Positive Liberty.* London: Routledge.

2.3 Value Model for the East Asian Project

Cambridge Dictionary. (n.d.-a) https://dictionary.cambridge.org/ja/dictionary/english/reactive.

Cambridge Dictionary. (n.d.-b) https://dictionary.cambridge.org/ja/dictionary/english/proactive.

Cambridge Dictionary. (n.d.-c) https://dictionary.cambridge.org/ja/dictionary/english/assistance.

Cocks, Errol, and Gordon Duffy (1993) *The Nature and Purposes of Advocacy for People with Disabilities.* Parth: Edith Cowan University Publications. 121. https://ro.ecu.edu.au/ecuworks/7172.

Doron, Israel (2003) "A Multi-Dimensional Model of Elder Law: An Israeli Example" *Ageing International* Volume 28 Issue 3, 242–259.

Doron, Israel (2009) "A Multi-Dimensional Model of Elder Law" in Doron, Israel (ed), *Theories on Law and Ageing: The Jurisprudence of the Elder Law.* Berlin, Heidelberg: Springer. 59–74.

Kim, M. (2024) "South Korea's Birthrate Is 0.72, Marking the Lowest Level for the Eighth Consecutive Year: Accurate Understanding of the Youth's Mindset and Effective Measures Implementation Needed" [in Japanese] NLI Research Institute, March 4, 2024. https://www.nli-research.co.jp/report/detail/id=77782?site=nli.

Mizuno, Noriko (2023) "Conditions for Making Civil Law Work (1) (2)" [in Japanese] *Lawyers Association Journal* Volume 75 Issue 7/8, 1285–1297/1515–1540.

Yamada, Masahiro (2020) *Why Did Japan's Measures to Counteract Declining Birthrates Fail? The True Reasons behind the Avoidance of Marriage and Childbirth* [in Japanese]. Tokyo: Kobunsha.

2.4 Notes on Law and Bioethics in Healthcare

Beauchamp, T. L., and J. F. Childress (2001) *Principles of Biomedical Ethics.* 5th ed. Oxford: Oxford University Press.

Fox, Renée C. (1990) *The Evolution of American Bioethics: A Sociological Perspective—Social Science Perspectives on Medical Ethics.* Dordrecht: Springer.

Higuchi, Norio (2005) "The Role of Legalization and Norms in Medicine: Under- and Over-Law" [in Japanese] in H. Shiroyama and T. Yamamoto (eds), *Environment and Life: Melting Boundaries Transcending Law.* Volume 5. Tokyo: University of Tokyo Press. 139–180.

Higuchi, Norio (2022) "Reading the World Medical Association's Code of Ethics (Latest 2022 Edition)" *Law Association Journal* Volume 140 Issue 8, 1013–1040.

Inoue, Shigeru (1981) *Philosophy of Law* [in Japanese]. Tokyo: Iwanami Shoten Publishers.

Nakano, Toshio (2002) "Law and Ethics" [in Japanese] *Sociology of Law* Volume 56, 1–15.

Oishi, Makoto (2006) "The Cabinet Legislation Bureau's Function in Forming National Order" [in Japanese] *Public Policy Studies* Volume 6, 7–16.

Okinaga, Takako (2022) "Bioethics Theory" [in Japanese] in Takayoshi Tsukada and Kazuhiko Maeda (eds), *Bioethics and Medical Law*. 3rd ed. Tokyo: Iryokagakusha. 39–40.

Shimizu, Tetsuro (2013) "Origin and Essence of Caring in Healthcare: A Logical Investigation" [in Japanese] *Journal of Japan Academy of Nursing Science* Volume 33 Issue 2, 101–103.

Tanaka, Shigeaki (2004) "On the Legal Involvement in Bioethics" [in Japanese] in Shigeaki Tanaka (ed), *Perspectives on Modern Law: Aspects of Self-Determination*. Tokyo: Yuhikaku Publishing. 131–175.

Yonemura, Shigeto (n.d.) "For the Cooperation of Medical Science, Ethics and the Law" [in Japanese] *The Graduate School of Law, Tohoku University* chrome-extension://efaidnbmnnnibpcajpcglclefindmkaj/https://web.tohoku.ac.jp/hondou/files/psj-4.pdf.

Chapter 3

3.1 Origins and Types of Advance Directives

Casetext "Cruzan, by Cruzan v. Harmon" https://casetext.com/case/cruzan-by-cruzan-v-harmon.

Ishida, Hitomi (2020) "Legal Aspects of ACP" [in Japanese] *Takaoka Law Review* Volume 38, 123–157. https://doi.org/10.24703/takahogaku.38.0_123.

JUSTIA US LAW, In Re Quinlan 70 NJ 10 (1976) 355 A.2d 647 N The Matter of Karen Quinlan, an Alleged Incompetent. The Supreme Court of New Jersey. Decided March 31, 1976. https://law.justia.com/cases/new-jersey/supreme-court/1976/70-n-j-10-0.html.

Kamei, Ryuta (2015) "Patient Advance Directives: Focusing on the Relationship with Civil Law" *Chiba University Law Review* Volume 30 Issue 1–2, 370 (277)–324 (323).

Kutner, Louis (1969) "Due Process of Euthanasia: The Living Will, a Proposal" *Indiana Law Review* Volume 44 Issue 4, 539–554, 551. https://www.repository.law.indiana.edu/ilj/vol44/iss4/2/.

National Library of Medicine (2023) "Informed Consent" https://www.ncbi.nlm.nih.gov/books/NBK430827/.

UPI (1985) "Chronology of Karen Ann Quinlan's Life" (UPI Archives, June 12, 1985) https://www.upi.com/Archives/1985/06/12/Chronology-of-Karen-Ann-Quinlans-life/2454487396800/.

Weinmeyer, Richard (2013) "Legal Constraints on Pursuit of a 'Good Death'" *Virtual Mentor* Volume 13 Issue 12, 1056–1061. https://doi.org/10.1001/virtualmentor.2013.15.12.hlaw1-1312.

3.2 Limitations and Criticisms of ADs and ACP

Buck, Kimberly, L. Nolte, M. Sellars, et al. (2021) "Advance Care Directive Prevalence among Older Australians and Associations with Person-Level Predictors and Quality Indicators" *Health Expectations* Volume 24, 1312–1325. https://doi.org/10.1111/hex.13264.

Connors, Alfred F., Jr., N. V. Dawson, N. A. Desbiens, et al. (1995) "A Controlled Trial to Improve Care for Seriously Ill Hospitalized Patients: The Study to Understand Prognoses and Preferences for Outcomes and Risks of Treatments (SUPPORT)" *JAMA* Volume 274 Issue 20, 1591–1598. Erratum in: *JAMA* Volume 275 Issue 16, 1232. PMID: 7474243.

Forlini, J., and L. Goldberg (2014) "Respecting Choices: A Case Study for Incorporating Advance Care Planning into Person and Family-Centered Health Care Delivery" *National Academy of Social Insurance* Volume 9, 1–3. https://www.nasi.org/wp-content/uploads/2014/02/Health_Policy_Brief_09.pdf.

Masuda, Yuichiro, and Akihisa Iguchi (1998) "The Current Status of the 'Patient's Right to Die' in the US: With a Focus on the Advance Directive" [in Japanese] *Overseas Social Security News* Spring 1998 Issue 118, 29–44.

Morrison, R., D. E. Meier, R. M. Arnold, et al. (2021) "What's Wrong with Advance Care Planning?" *JAMA* Volume 326 Issue 16, 1575–1576. https://doi.org/10.1001/jama.2021.16430.

National Institute on Aging (2022) "Advance Care Planning: Advance Directives for Health Care" https://www.nia.nih.gov/health/advance-care-planning/advance-care-planning-advance-directives-health-care.

Rietjens, J. A. C., R. L. Sudore, M. Connolly, et al. (2017) "Definition and Recommendations for Advance Care Planning: An International Consensus Supported by the European Association for Palliative Care" *Lancet Oncology* Volume 18 Issue 9, 543–551. PMID: 28884703. https://doi.org/10.1016/S1470-2045(17)30582-X.

Sabatino, Charles (2015) "Myths and Facts about Health Care Advance Directives" *Bifocal* Volume 37 Issue 1, American Bar Association. https://www.americanbar.org/groups/law_aging/publications/bifocal/vol_37/issue_1_october2015/myths_and_facts_advance_directives/.

Seki, Fusako (2018) "End-of-Life Care in the United States: Decision-Making Support Seen in Hospice Care" [in Japanese] *Comparative Law Research* Volume 80, 7–25.

Tsai, Hsiao Ying (2022) "The Influence of Familism on Taiwan's Advance Care Planning (ACP) for End-of-Life" *Journal of the Japanese Society of Nursing Ethics* Volume 14 Issue 1, 48–51. https://www.jstage.jst.go.jp/article/jjne/14/1/14_20211011/_pdf.

Yadav, Kuldeep N., N. B. Gabler, E. Cooney, et al. (2017) "Approximately One in Three US Adults Completes Any Type of Advance Directive for End-of-Life Care." *Health Affairs* Volume 36 Issue 7, 1244–1251.

3.3 Comparison and Evaluation of ADs across Asia

Sinclair, Craig, M. Sellars, K. Buck, et al. (2021) "Association between Region of Birth and Advance Care Planning Documentation among Older Australian Migrant Communities: A Multicenter Audit Study" *The Journals of Gerontology: Series B* Volume 76 Issue 1, 109. https://doi.org/10.1093/geronb/gbaa127.

Yokosuka City (2023) "Yokosuka City Ending Plan Support Business" [in Japanese] https://www.city.yokosuka.kanagawa.jp/2610/syuukatusien/ending-plan-support.html.

3.4 International Response to Voluntary Assisted Dying

Asai, A., T. Okita, Y. Shimakura, et al. (2023) "Japan Should Initiate the Discussion on Voluntary Assisted Dying Legislation Now" *BMC Medical Ethics* Volume 24 Issue 1, 5. PMID: 36726120; PMCID: PMC9890417. https://doi.org/10.1186/s12910-023-00886-0.

Australia, Department of Health Victoria (2024) "Assisted Voluntary Dying" (April 30, 2024) https://www.health.vic.gov.au/voluntary-assisted-dying/about.

Australia, Victorian Voluntary Assisted Dying Review Board (2023) "Annual Report: July 2022 to June 2023" chrome-extension://efaidnbmnnnibp-cajpcglclefindmkaj/https://www.safercare.vic.gov.au/sites/default/files/2023-08/VADRB%20Annual%20Report%202022-23.pdf.

Buletsa, S. B. (2019) "Features of Euthanasia in Eastern Asia Countries" in collective monograph / Reviewers: Sabina Grabowska, Joanna Marszałek-Kawa, and Tetiana Kolomoiets, *Jurisprudence Issues in the Development of Legal Literacy and Legal Awareness of Citizens*, Chapter 2, 17–37. Liha-Pres. http://catalog.liha-pres.eu/index.php/liha-pres/catalog/view/59/660/3554-1.

Delogu, G., D. Morena, V. Tortorella, et al. (2024) "First Case of Medically Assisted Suicide in Italy Set New Legal Perspectives" *Clinical Therapeutics* Volume 175 Issue 1, 7–10. PMID: 38358470. https://doi.org/10.7417/CT.2024.5026.

Herring, Jonathan (2022) *Medical Law and Ethics*. 9th ed. Oxford: Oxford University Press.

Japan, National Diet Library, "Short Message [Portuguese] Legalization of Euthanasia" [in Japanese] *Reference to Foreign Legislation* No. 297-1.]

Jeanneret, R., and S. Prince (2024) "Nurses and Voluntary Assisted Dying: How the Australian Capital Territory's Law Could Change the Australian Regulatory Landscape" *Journal of Bioethical Inquiry* Volume 21, 393–399. https://doi.org/10.1007/s11673-024-10370-y.

Kennedys Law (2024) "Lessons from Victoria's Voluntary Assisted Dying Laws" September 13. https://kennedyslaw.com/en/thought-leadership/article/2024/lessons-from-victoria-s-voluntary-assisted-dying-laws/.

Law Council of Australia (2024) "Full Medical Not a Given When Deciding to End One's Life" October 25, *The Canberra Times*, January 19, 2024. https://lawcouncil.au/media/news/opinion-piece-full-medical-not-a-given-when-deciding-to-end-vones-life.

Minami, Takako (2022) "Progress of Voluntary Assisted Dying Legislation and the Characteristics of State Legal Systems in Australia" [in Japanese] *Journal of Kagawa Prefectural College of Health Sciences* Volume 13, 19–27. http://doi.org/10.50850/00000337.

Ries, Nola M., and Elise Mansfield (2022) "Supported Decision-Making: A Good Idea in Principle but We Need to Consider Supporting Decisions about Voluntary Assisted Dying" in Daniel J. Fleming and David J. Carter (eds), *Voluntary Assisted Dying: Law? Health? Justice?* Canberra: ANU Press. 49.

Suzuki, Carol M. (2019) "The Pursuit of Dignified Death for Competent Terminally Ill Persons in the United States" *Journal of Clinical Ethics* Volume 7, 60–73.

SWI Swissinfo.ch (2023) "Which Countries Adopt Euthanasia?" Issued on January 31, 2023 [in Japanese] https://www.swissinfo.ch/eng/topic/life-aging/.

Tanaka, Miho, and Satoshi Kodama (2021) "Outline of Legal Systems and Data regarding Euthanasia in Foreign Countries Version 1" [in Japanese] Japan Medical Association Research Institute Working Paper. https://www.jmari.med.or.jp/result/report/post-3303/.

Tayama, Teruaki (2024) "Judgement of the Federal Constitutional Court on 26 February 2020" [in Japanese] *Quarterly Comparative Guardianship Law* Volume 21, 3–71.

The Guardian (2024) "What Happens Next after MPs' Vote in Favor of Assisted Dying Bill?" November 29. https://www.theguardian.com/society/2024/nov/29/what-happens-next-assisted-dying-bill.

UK Parliament (2024) https://commonslibrary.parliament.uk/research-briefings/cbp-10123/.

White, Ben P., Ruthie Jeanneret, and Lindy Willmott (2023) "Barriers to Connecting with the Voluntary Assisted Dying System in Victoria, Australia: A Qualitative Mixed Method Study" *Health Expectations* Volume 26 Issue 6, 2695–2708. PMID: 37694553 PMCID: PMC10632633 DOI: 10.1111/hex.13867.

White, Ben P. (Ed.) (2025) *Research Handbook on Voluntary Assisted Dying Law, Regulation and Practice.* Edward Elgar Publishing.

Willmott, L., and B. P. White (2021) "The Challenging Path to Voluntary Assisted Dying Law Reform in Australia: Victoria as a Successful Case Study" in L. Willmott and B. P. White (eds), *International Perspectives on End-of-Life Law Reform*. Cambridge: Cambridge University Press.

Chapter 4

4.1 Laws Concerning Human Life and Death in Japan

Sakurai, Yukio (2024) "The Role of Law and Bioethics in Human Life and Death: Japanese Medical Law in End-of-Life Care" *Australian Journal of Asian Law* Volume 25 Issue 1, 89–105. https://ssrn.com/abstract=4964356.

Yoshida, Hisashi, and Kaida, Mamoru (1963) "Death under Civil Law (1)" [in Japanese] *The Chuo Law Review* (Hogaku Shimpo) Volume 70 Issue 9, 696.

4.2 Issues of Healthcare Policy in Japan

Aita, Kaoruko, M. Takahashi, H. Miyata, et al. (2007) "Physicians' Attitudes about Artificial Feeding in Older Patients with Severe Cognitive Impairment in Japan: A Qualitative Study" *BMC Geriatrics* Volume 7, 22. PMID: 17705852; PMCID: PMC1997114. https://doi.org/10.1186/1471-2318-7-22.

Baba, Hiroko, M. N. Aung, A. Miyagi, et al. (2024) "Exploring the Contribution of Japan's Experience in Addressing Rapid Aging in Asia: Focus on Dementia Care" *Global Health & Medicine* Volume 6, 19–32. 2023–01124. PMID: 38450119 PMCID: PMC10912802. https://doi.org/10.35772/ghm.2023.01124.

Boyle, Patrick (2022) "Threats against Health Care Workers Are Rising: Here's How Hospitals Are Protecting Their Staffs" (AAMC, August 18, 2022) https://www.aamc.org/news/threats-against-health-care-workers-are-rising-heres-how-hospitals-are-protecting-their-staffs.

Fukuoka Medical Association (2023) "Special Feature: Nuisance Behaviors in Healthcare Settings" (Medical Information Chamber Report No. 261, September 29, 2023) [in Japanese] https://www.city.fukuoka.med.or.jp/jouhousitsu/.

Goto, Yuri (2020) "Definition of the End of Life in Passive Euthanasia and the Justification and Grounds for Discontinuing Treatment: In the Wake of the Fussa Hospital Dialysis Discontinuation Incident" *Law Journal* Volume 98, 95–131.

II, Masako, Moriyama, Michiko, and Watanabe, Sachiko (2023) "Patient Behavior During the COVID-19 Pandemic and Impacts on Medical Institution Revenue" *Public Policy Review* Volume 19 Issue 1, 1–39.

Japan, Cabinet Office (2019a) "Estimating the Number of Older Adults with Dementia (Figure 1–2–11), Annual Report on the Ageing Society FY 2018" [in Japanese] https://www8.cao.go.jp/kourei/whitepaper/w-2017/html/gaiyou/s1_2_3.html.

Japan, Cabinet Office (2019b) "The Outline to Promote Dementia Policy Program" [in Japanese] (June 18, 2019) https://www.mhlw.go.jp/stf/seisakunitsuite/bunya/0000076236_00002.html.

Japan, MHLW (2023) "Overview of National Medical Expenses for Fiscal Year 2021" [in Japanese] chrome-extension://efaidnbmnnnibpcajpcglclefindmkaj/https://www.mhlw.go.jp/toukei/saikin/hw/k-iryohi/21/dl/data.pdf.

Japan, MHLW Grants System (2009) "Integrated Data Infrastructure Construction and Utilization for Continuous Examination and Planning of Municipalities and Insurers' Health, Medical, Long-Term Care, and Welfare Policies" [in Japanese] https://mhlw-grants.niph.go.jp/project/16067.

Japan Nursing Association (2024) "Measures against Violence in Medical Settings" [in Japanese] https://www.nurse.or.jp/nursing/shuroanzen/safety/violence/index.html.

Kimura, Mitsue (2004) "Trends and Legal Basis of Administrative Sanctions against Physicians" [in Japanese] *Tokyo Metropolitan University Law Journal* Volume 45 Issue1, 31–48.

Kotera, Shoichi (2019) "Dementia: Situation, Policies and Issues" [in Japanese] *The Reference, the National Diet Library* Volume 826, 29–58.

m3.com (2024) "Survey on End-of-Life Care for Older Adults" [in Japanese] (January 13, 2024) https://www.m3.com/news/series/iryoishin/12962.

Naoki, Ikegami, and J. C. Campbell (1996) *Medical Care in Japan: Control and a Sense of Balance* [in Japanese]. Tokyo: Chuokoron-Shinsha.

Sado, Mitsuhiro, et al. (2014) "Study on the Economic Impact of Dementia in Japan: Summary of FY 2014 and Collaborative Research Reports" [in Japanese]

Comprehensive Research Project on Dementia Measures. https://mhlw-grants. niph.go.jp/niph/search/NIDD00.do?resrchNum=201418007A.

Shimazaki, Kenji (2013) "The Path to Universal Health Coverage: Experiences and Lessons from Japan for Policy Actions" Japan International Cooperation Agency (JICA).

Shimazaki, Kenji (2020) *Japan's Healthcare: Systems and Policies: Revised and Expanded Edition* [in Japanese]. Tokyo: University of Tokyo Press.

Suzuki, Wataru (2015) "Statistical Considerations on the Potential Reduction of End-of-Life Medical Expenses Using Receipt Data" [in Japanese] Doctoral Dissertation, Gakushuin University.

The Japan Geriatrics Society (2019) "Proposals for Promoting ACP" [in Japanese] chrome-extension://efaidnbmnnnibpcajpcglclefindmkaj/https://www. jstage.jst.go.jp/article/geriatrics/56/4/56_56.411/_pdf.

Umeda, Sayuri (2023) "Japan: Diet Passes Dementia Basic Act" Law Library of Congress https://www.loc.gov/item/global-legal-monitor/2023-09-07/ japan-diet-passes-dementia-basic-act/.

WHO (2021) "Dementia" (January 27, 2021) https://www.who.int/news-room/ fact-sheets/detail/dementia.

Yukawa, Keiko, and Takuya Matsushige (2023) "Issues in End-of-Life Care and Organizing and Prospecting Ethical and Legal Issues of Voluntary Stopping of Eating and Drinking (VSED) in Japan" *Journal of the National Institute of Public Health* Volume 72 Issue 1, 22–30. https://www.niph.go.jp/en/journal-en/ data-72-1-e72-1-en/.

4.3 Legal and Ethical Framework for ADs and ACP

Higuchi, Norio (2024) "5. Understanding the Laws and Guidelines Surrounding End-of-Life Care" in Kaoru Aida (ed), *ACP Concepts and Practice.* Tokyo: University of Tokyo Press.

Hoshi, Takako (2019) "The Urgent Need to Establish a Legal System for Medical Consent" [in Japanese] Japan Research Institute, Research Focus No. 2019-028. November 5, 2019.

Inaba, Kazuo (2007) "Chapter 10 Laws and Precedents at the End of Life" in Takao Takahashi and Atsushi Asai (eds), *Japanese Bioethics: Retrospective and Prospects Kumamoto University Bioethics Collection 1* [in Japanese]. Fukuoka: Kyushu University Press. 209–239.

Inada, Akiko (2012) "Supreme Court Decision on the Kawasaki Kyodo Hospital Case: Third (3rd) Decision December 7, 2009" [in Japanese] *Criminal Case* Volume 63, Issue 11, 1899 et seq." *Kochi University Review of Social Science* Volume 105, 47–69.

Japan, MHLW (2006) "Terminal Medical Care" 5th Social Security Council Special Subcommittee on Medical Care for the Elderly Held on December 12, 2006 [in Japanese] https://www.wam.go.jp/wamappl/bb11GS20. nsf/0/23ce16303db-c18bb4925724300097c6b/$FILE/shiryou1.pdf.

Japan, MHLW (2018a) "61st Medical Division Meeting of the Social Security Council" [in Japanese] Minutes for the Meeting held on April 11, 2018 https://www.mhlw.go.jp/stf/shingi2/0000212218_00001.html.

Japan, MHLW (2018b) "Revision of Guidelines for the Medical Care Decision-Making Process in End-of-Life" [in Japanese] (March 14, 2018) https://www.mhlw.go.jp/stf/houdou/0000197665.html.

Japan, Ministry of Justice (2024) "Guidelines for Lifelong Support Businesses for the Elderly, etc." [in Japanese] https://www.moj.go.jp/MINJI/minji07_00358.html.

Kai, Katsunori (2009) "Rulemaking and Legal Issues in End-of-Life Medical Care" [in Japanese] *Journal of Medical Law* Volume 24, 81–87.

Kai, Katsunori (2010) "Chapter 10: Euthanasia and Death with Dignity in Japanese Law" *Journal International de Bioéthique* Volume 21 Issue 4, 135–147.

Tanaka, Akashi (2023) "Rulemaking and Consensus of Bioethical Problems: Historical Analysis of Japanese End-of-Life Care Policies" [in Japanese] *Bulletin of the Department of General Education* Volume 53, 71–82.

Tanaka, Miho, and Kodama Satoshi (2020) "Ethical Issues around the Withdrawal of Dialysis Treatment in Japan" *Asian Bioethics Review* Volume 12 Issue 1, 51–57. January 16. PMID:33717330; PMCID: PMC7747336. https://doi.org/10.1007/s41649-020-00109-3.

Tasaka, Akira (2013) "Permissibility of Discontinuing Treatment" [in Japanese] *Shimane Law Review* Volume 56 Issue 4, 101–119.

Tatsui, Satoko (2013) "Norms Surrounding End-of-Life Care" in Katsunori Kai (ed), *End-of-Life Care and Medical Law, Medical Law Course*. Volume 4. Tokyo: Shinzansha Publisher. 216–233.

Tsutsumi, Tsubasa (2018) "Revision of the Guidelines for Medical and Care Decision-Making Process in the Final Stage of Life" [in Japanese] *Aging and Health* Volume 87, 10–13. https://www.tyojyu.or.jp/kankoubutsu/pdf/Aging%26Health_No.87_light.pdf.

Uchida, Hirofumi (2021) *Medical Law and the Rights of Patients and Medical Workers* [in Japanese]. Tokyo: Misuzu Shobo.

4.4 Relational Autonomy-Based Approach to ADs

Asagumo, Anri (2022) "Relational Autonomy, the Right to Reject Treatment, and Advance Directives in Japan" *Asian Bioethics Review* Volume 14 Issue 1, 57–69.

General Incorporated Association Shukatsu Council (2021) "Survey on 'Ending Note'" [in Japanese] https://prtimes.jp/main/html/rd/p/000000019.000074510.html.

Handa City (2023) "Handa City Version of 'My Advance Directive about Medical Care'" [in Japanese] https://www.city.handa.lg.jp/hoken-c/kenko/iryo/hoken/jizensijisho.html.

Herring, Jonathan (2022) *Medical Law and the Ethics*. 9th ed. Oxford: Oxford University Press.

Ikka, Tsunakuni (2011) "The History and Current Status of Medical Basic Law" [in Japanese] *Annual Report of Medical Law* Volume 26, 16–38.

Ikka, Tsusnakuni (2013) "Reconsideration of Hospital Ethics Committee" [in Japanese] *Bioethics* Volume 23 Issue 1, 23–30.

Ikka, Tsunakuni (2019) "Law and Ethics of End-of-Life Care: What Is Permissible, What Is Not Permissible, and Its Basis" [in Japanese] *Hospital* Volume 78 Issue 7, 508–513.

Ikka, Tsunakuni (2023) "Medical Jurisprudence on End-of-Life Care and Terminal Sedation" [in Japanese] in Tatsuya Morita and Shimon Tashiro (eds),

Questioning the Grey Zone of Sedation and Euthanasia: Perspectives from Medicine, Nursing, Bioethics and Law. Tokyo: Chugai Igaku-sha. 211–230.

Japan, Diet Proceedings Search System. https://kokkai.ndl.go.jp/#/.

Japan, MHLW (2018) "Survey Report on Awareness regarding Medical Care in End of Life" [in Japanese] (March 2018) https://www.mhlw.go.jp/toukei/list/dl/saisyuiryo_a_h29.pdf.

Japan, MHLW (2023) "Opinion Exchange Meeting for Simultaneous Remuneration Revision in 2024 (3rd Session)" [in Japanese] (May 18, 2023) https://www.youtube.com/watch?v=NPMJ7YbDojk.

Japan, MHLW "Policy on Medical and Care at the End of Life" [in Japanese] https://www.mhlw.go.jp/stf/seisakunitsuite/bunya/0000161103.html.

Japan, the Supreme Court (2009) "Decision for the Kawasaki Kyodo Hospital Case on December 7, 2009" [in Japanese] https://www.courts.go.jp/app/hanrei_jp/detail2?id=38241.

Japan, Tokyo Fire Department (2019) "Responding to Victims Who Do Not Want Cardiopulmonary Resuscitation" [in Japanese] https://www.tfd.metro.tokyo.lg.jp/lfe/kyuu-adv/acp.html.

Japan, Tokyo High Court (2007) "Decision for the Kawasaki Kyodo Hospital Case on February 28, 2007" [in Japanese] https://www.courts.go.jp/app/hanrei_jp/detail3?id=35145.

Kai, Katsunori (2021) "The Scope of Patients' Advance Directives and Self-Determination (Rights)" [in Japanese] in Makoto Tadaki and Gunnar Dutge (eds), *Comprehensive Research on End-of-Life Care, Euthanasia, and Death with Dignity*. Tokyo: Chuo University Press. 111–127.

McKenzie, Catriona (2019) "Feminist Innovation in Philosophy: Relational Autonomy and Social Justice" *Women's Studies International Forum* Volume 72, 144–151. https://doi.org/10.1016/j.wsif.2018.05.003.

Mobile Marketing Data Labo (2022) "Parent-Child Comparison Survey on End-of-Life Planning and Asset Management for Seniors" [in Japanese] https://mmdlabo.jp/investigation/detail_2134.html.

Musashino International Association (MIA) (2024) "End of Life Planning Note in English" https://mia.gr.jp/en/foreigner/retirement.

Niigata University General Hospital (2022) "Guidelines in End-of-Life Care" [in Japanese] https://www.nuh.niigata-u.ac.jp/wp-content/uploads/2022/03/tmc_guideline.pdf.

NPO Ra-Shi-Sa (2021) "Nationwide Survey on End-of-Life Awareness" [in Japanese] https://www.ra-shi-sa.jp/_rashisa/wp-content/themes/rashisa/pdf/20210903_shukatsu-ishiki-survey.pdf.

Ogata, Ayumi (2022) "The Right to Self-Determination and Legal System Design regarding Medical Care at the Final Stage of Life: From a Criminal Legal Perspective" [in Japanese] *Chukyo Lawyer* Volume 36, 1–22.

Ogata, Ayumi (2024) "The Right to Live Life to the Fullest and the Right to End It: Focusing on the Kyoto ALS Contract Murder Case" [in Japanese] *Chukyo Lawyer* Volume 40, 25–46.

Tsuchiya, Tomohiro, N. Mine, T. Matsumoto, et al. (2024) "Introduction and Operation Report of the Nagasaki City Medical Association's Advance Directive "My Wishes" ' [in Japanese] *Journal of Japanese Association for Home Care Medicine* Volume 5 Issue 3, 29–39. https://doi.org/10.34458/jahcm.5.3_29.

Tsukamoto, Yasushi (2022) *Medicine and Law II* [in Japanese]. Tokyo: Shoga-kusha 166–173.

Tsunagari (2024) "List of Municipalities Distributing Ending-Notes [Free Distribution]" [in Japanese] https://sougi-lab.com/shukatsu/endingnote-municipalities/.

4.5 ACP Studies in Japan

Aida, Kaoruko (ed) (2024) *ACP Thinking and Practice: Clinical Ethics of End-of-Life Care* [in Japanese]. Tokyo: University of Tokyo Press.

Japan, MHLW (2021) "Research Survey for Enhancement of End-of-Life Care for Dementia Patients according to Different Treatment Venues: In Light of the Impact of the COVID-19 Epidemic" [in Japanese] https://mhlw-grants.niph.go.jp/project/157717.

Miyashita, Jun, S. Shimizu, R. Shiraishi, et al. (2022) "Culturally Adapted Consensus Definition and Action Guideline: Japan's Advance Care Planning" *Journal of Pain and Symptom Management* Volume 64 Issue 6, 602–613. https://doi.org/10.1016/j.jpainsymman.2022.09.005.

National Cancer Center, Explanatory Oncology Research and Clinical Trial Center (2020) "A Guide to Decision-Making Support for Cancer Treatment for Older Adults" [in Japanese] https://www.ncc.go.jp/jp/epoc/division/psycho_oncology/kashiwa/research_summary/050/020/index.html.

Ogawa, Asao (2019) "End-of-Life Care for Dementia" [in Japanese] *Journal of Psychiatry* Volume 121, 289–297.

Shimizu, Tetsuro (2015) "Supporting Patients and Their Families to Make Informed Decisions: Shared Decision-Making and Advance Care Planning" [in Japanese] *Medicine and Society* Volume 25 Issue 1, 35–48.

Yokohama National University, Regional Collaboration Promotion Organization (2023a) "Unit for the Improvement of Legal Services for Kanagawa Residents—Hosted the First Online Seminar" (July 15, 2023) https://www.chiiki.ynu.ac.jp/news/000225.html.

Yokohama National University, Regional Collaboration Promotion Organization (2023b) "Unit for the Improvement of Legal Services for Kanagawa Residents—Hosted the Second Online Seminar" (November 12, 2023) https://www.chiiki.ynu.ac.jp/news/000269.html.

Chapter 5

5.1 Responses of South Korea, Taiwan, and Singapore to ADs and ACP

South Korea

Fuchigami, Kyoko (2023) "End-of-Life Care and Dignified Death in South Korea: Examining Self-Determination in Death and Meaning in Death" [in Japanese] Conference Materials Presented at the Otani University Pure Land Buddhism Research Institute Tokyo Branch Open Symposium: "Religion and Life: Reflecting on 'A Good Death' from the Current State of End-of-Life Care in Japan, South Korea, and Taiwan" on February 12, 2023.

Fujiwara, Natsuto (2016) "Establishment of the 'Dying with Dignity' Law in South Korea: Legal Measures for End-of-Life Care" [in Japanese] *Foreign Legislation, The National Diet Library* 2016.04. https://dl.ndl.go.jp/view/download/digidepo_9929060_po_02670108.pdf?contentNo=1.

Japan, Cabinet Office (2023) "Annual Report on the Ageing Society FY2023" [in Japanese] https://www8.cao.go.jp/kourei/whitepaper/w-2023/zenbun/05pdf_index.html.

Kim, B., J. Choi, and I. Lee (2022) "Factors Associated with Advance Directives Documentation: A Nationwide Cross-Sectional Survey of Older Adults in Korea" *The International Journal of Environmental Research and Public Health* Volume 19, 3771. https://doi.org/10.3390/ijerph19073771.

Kim, Do Kyong (2017) "Hospice-Palliative Care and Law" *The Korean Journal of Internal Medicine* Volume 92 Issue 6, 489–493. https://doi.org/10.3904/kjm.2017.92.6.489.

Kim, Jeong-A, K. Do-kyung, M. S. Kyung, et al. (2023) "Current Status of Implementation of the Decision to Forgo Life-Sustaining Treatment through Big Data of the National Health Insurance Service" [in Korean] *Biomedical Ethics and Public Policy* Volume 7 Issue 1, 1–24. https://www.riss.kr/link?id=vA108578270.

Lee, Ye Jin, S. Ahn, J. Y. Cho, et al. (2022) "Change in Perception of the Quality of Death in the Intensive Care Unit by Healthcare Workers Associated with the Implementation of the 'Well-Dying Law' " *Intensive Care Medicine* Volume 48, 281–289. https://doi.org/10.1007/s00134-021-06597-7.

Park, H. Y., M. S. Kim, S. H. Yoo et al. (2024) "For the Universal Right to Access Quality End-of-Life Care in Korea: Broadening Our Perspective after the 2018 Life-Sustaining Treatment Decisions Act" *Journal of Korean Medical Science* Volume 39 Issue 12, e123. https://doi.org/10.3346/jkms.2024.39.e123.

Park, S. Y., B. Lee, J. Yeon, et al. (2021) "A National Study of Life-Sustaining Treatments in South Korea: What Factors Affect Decision-Making?" *Cancer Research and Treatment* Volume 53 Issue 2, 593–600. https://doi.org/10.4143/crt.2020.803.

Shimizu, Katsuhiko (2016) "Hospice Life-Sustaining Medical Care Law Legalized in South Korea" [in Japanese] *Living Will* 2016.07. 11–13 http://www.drnagao.com/img/media/related_article2/livwill201607.pdf.

South Korea, National Life-Sustaining Medical Management Institute [in Korean] https://www.lst.go.kr/main/main.do.

South Korea, Statistics Korea (2023) "2023 Statistics the Aged" https://kostat.go.kr/board.es?mid=a20111030000&bid=11759.

Tsuji, Tokiko (2023) "South Korea's Life-Sustaining Treatment Decision Act, 290,000 Deaths Aiming for Direct Reflection of Individual Wishes at 50 %" [in Japanese] *Asahi Shimbun Digital*, October 8, 2023. https://www.asahi.com/articles/ASRB4563ZR9HUTFL015.html.

Wu, Hong Min (2021) "Consideration of the Death with Dignity Act in South Korea" [in Japanese] *Weekly Social Security* Volume 75 (3117), 48–53.

Yong, H. J., and D. Kim (2024) "End-of-Life Care in the Intensive Care Unit: The Optimal Process of Decision to Withdrawing Life-Sustaining Treatment Based on the Korean Medical Environment and Culture" *Acute and Critical Care* Volume 39 Issue 2, 321–322. https://doi.org/10.4266/acc.2024.00675.

Taiwan

Chu, Dachen, Y.-F. Yen, H.-Y. Hu, et al. (2018) "Factors Associated with Advance Directives Completion among Patients with Advance Care Planning Communication in Taipei, Taiwan" *PLoS ONE* Volume 13 Issue 7, e0197552. https://doi.org/10.1371/journal.pone.0197552.

Chung, Yicheng (2015) "The Law and Ethics of End-of-Life Care in Taiwan: On the Practice of Terminal Discharge and a Criminal Court Case Concerning the Hospice and Palliative Care Act" [in Japanese] *Core Ethics* Volume 11, 123–134.

He, Yi-Jhen, M.-H. Lin, J.-L. Hsu, et al. (2021) "Overview of the Motivation of Advance Care Planning: A Study from a Medical Center in Taiwan" *International Journal of Environmental Research and Public Health* Volume 18 Issue 2, 417. https://doi.org/10.3390/ijerph18020417.

Hospice Foundation in Taiwan (2024) "Prof. Co-Shi Chantal Chao Taiwan" https://www.hospice.org.tw/content/3480.

Huang, Sieh-Chuen (2012) "Social Changes and Testamentary Law in Taiwan" [in Japanese] *Ryukei Law Journal* Volume 12 Issue 1, 71–104.

Huang, Sieh-Chuen (2024) "Discussion and Progress on Adult Guardianship System and Decision-Making Support in Taiwan" *Adult Guardianship Law Research* No. 21, 82–92.

Huang, Sieh-Chuen, and Tzu-Chiang Chen (2019) (eds), *New Challenges in Legal Issues in an Aging Society: Focusing on Property Management.* 2nd ed. Taipei: Shingakurin. 448–449.

Kouy, BunRong (2019) "On Taiwan Patient Right to Autonomy Act: How Family Stimulates Autonomy" *Applied Ethics Review* Volume 67, 187–212.

Taiwan, Ministry of Health and Welfare (2024) "Patient Autonomy Law to Take Effect Next Year—Ministry of Health and Welfare Announces Supporting Measures—Regulations Governing the Management of Healthcare Institutions Providing Advanced Care Planning Consultation" [in Chinese] https://www.mohw.gov.tw/cp-3801-44221-1.html.

Taiwan, Ministry of Health and Welfare (2024) "Patient Autonomy Law to Take Effect Next Year: Ministry of Health and Welfare Announces Supporting Measures—Enforcement Rules of the Patient Autonomy Law" [in Chinese] https://www.mohw.gov.tw/cp-3801-44221-1.html.

The Economist Intelligence Unit (2015) *The 2015 Quality of Death Index Ranking.* chrome-extension://efaidnbmnnnibpcajpcglclefindmkaj/https://impact.economist.com/perspectives/sites/default/files/2015%20EIU%20Quality%20of%20Death%20Index%20Oct%2029%20FINAL.pdf.

Tsai, D. F.-C. (2023) "The Law and Practice of Advance Directives in Taiwan" in D. Cheung and M. Dunn (eds), *Advance Directives across Asia: A Comparative Socio-Legal Analysis.* Cambridge: Cambridge University Press. 75–89. DOI: 10.1017/9781009152631.006

Wang, Shu-Chen, C.-J. Chang, S.-Y. Fan, et al. (2015) "Development of an Advance Care Planning Booklet in Taiwan" *Tzu Chi Medical Journal* Volume 27, 170–174. https://doi.org/10.1016/j.tcmj.2015.07.003.

Zhong, Yicheng (2016) "Transformation and Practice of the Concept of 'Good End' in Taiwan—Focusing on the Legalization of End-of-Life Care" [in Japanese] Doctoral Dissertation, Ritsumeikan University. 80.

Singapore

Chan, Tracey (2019a) "Advance Care Planning: A Communitarian Approach?" *Forthcoming in the Journal of Law and Medicine,* NUS Centre for Asian Legal Studies Working Paper 2019.06.

Chan, Tracey (2019b) "Advance Care Planning: A Communitarian Approach?" NUS Centre for Asian Legal Studies Working Paper 2019.06.C.

Chan, Tracey (2023) "Advance Medical Directives in Singapore: A Faltering Policy for End-of-Life Care" in Daisy Cheung and Michael Dunn (eds), *Advance Directives across Asia: A Comparative Socio-Legal Analysis.* Cambridge: Cambridge University Press. 40.

Chan, Tracey, Nicola S. Peart, and Jacqueline Chin (2014) "Evolving Legal Responses to Dependence on Families in New Zealand and Singapore Healthcare" *Journal of Medical Ethics* Volume 40 Issue 12, 861–865. https://doi.org/10.1136/medethics-2012-101225.

Clement, Irwin, Alphonsus Wai, and Hoong Chung (2017) "Advance Care Planning in an Asian Country" in Keri Thomas, Ben Lobo, and Karen Detering (eds), *Advance Care Planning in End of Life Care.* 2nd ed. online ed. Oxford: Oxford Academic. January 18, 2018. https://doi.org/10.1093/oso/9780198802136.003.0023.

Menon, Sundaresh (2013) "Euthanasia: A Matter of Life or Death?" *Singapore Medical Journal* Volume 54 Issue 3, 116–128. PMID: 23546022. https://doi.org/10.11622/smedj.2013043.

Sakurai, Yukio (2018) "Ageing in Singapore and Mental Capacity Act" [in Japanese] *Quarterly Comparative Guardianship Law* Volume 8, 53–67.

Singapore, Ministry of Health (2023) "Number of Sign-Ups for Advanced Medical Directive and Advanced Care Plan" May 8. https://www.moh.gov.sg/news-highlights/details/number-of-sign-ups-for-advanced-medical-directive-and-advanced-care-plan.

Singapore, Ministry of Health (2024) "Advance Medical Directives" https://www.moh.gov.sg/policies-and-legislation/advance-medical-directive.

Singapore, My Legacy (2024) "Live for Today, Plan for Tomorrow" https://mylegacy.life.gov.sg/.

Singapore, Singapore Statute Online (2024) "Advance Medical Directive Act 1996" https://sso.agc.gov.sg/Act/AMDA1996.

Singapore, Statistics Singapore (2024) "Population and Population Structure" https://www.singstat.gov.sg/find-data/search-by-theme/population/population-and-population-structure/latest-data.

Tang, Hang Wu (2022) "Singapore's Adult Guardianship Law and the Role of the Family in Medical Decision-Making" *International Journal of Law, Policy and the Family* Volume 36 Issue 1–12, ebac002. https://doi.org/10.1093/lawfam/ebac002.

Tang, Hang Wu, Yukio Sakurai, and Yue-En Chong (2023) "Aging and the Law in Singapore and Japan: Adult Guardianship and Other Alternatives" *Journal of Ageing and Social Policy* Volume 37, 1–20. https://doi.org/10.1080/08959420.2023.2255484.

5.2 A Comparative Analysis of ADs and ACP between East Asian Countries and Area

Blank, R. H. (2011) "End-of-Life Decision Making across Cultures" *Journal of Law, Medicine & Ethics* Volume 39 Issue 2, 201–214. https://doi.org/10.1111/j.1748-720X.2011.00589.x.

Boerner, K., D. Carr, and S. Moorman (2013) "Family Relationships and Advance Care Planning: Do Supportive and Critical Relations Encourage or Hinder Planning?" *Journals of Gerontology, Series B: Psychological Sciences and Social Sciences* Volume 68 Issue 2, 246–256. https://doi.org/10.1093/geronb/gbs161. Advance Access publication January 3, 2013.

Bullock, K. (2011) "The Influence of Culture on End-of-Life Decision Making" *Journal of Social Work in End-of-Life & Palliative Care* Volume 7 Issue 1, 83–98. PMID: 21391079. https://doi.org/10.1080/15524256.2011.548048.

Chen, Chih-Hsiung (2019) "Legislating the Right-to-Die with Dignity in a Confucian Society—Taiwan's Patient Right to Autonomy Act" *Hastings International and Comparative Law Review* Volume 42 Issue 2, 485–508. https://repository.uchastings.edu/hastings_international_comparative_law_review/vol42/iss2/4.

Cheng, S. Y., C.-P. Lin, H. Y.-L. Chan, et al. (2020) "Advance Care Planning in Asian Culture" *Japanese Journal of Clinical Oncology* Volume 50 Issue 9, 976–989.

Choi, Kyungsuk (2016) "Legal and Ethical Issues regarding End-of-Life Care in Korea." *Development and Society* Volume 45 Issue 1, 151–164. https://doi.org/10.21588/dns.2016.45.1.006.

Dutta, O., P. Lall, P. V. Patinadan, et al. (2020) "Patient Autonomy and Partic-
ipation in End-of-Life Decision-Making: An Interpretive-Systemic Focus Group
Study on Perspectives of Asian Healthcare Professionals" *Palliative Support
Care* Volume 18 Issue 4, 425–430. https://doi.org/10.1017/S1478951519000865.

Dzeng, E., T. Bein, and J. R. Curtis (2022) "The Role of Policy and Law in
Shaping the Ethics and Quality of End-of-Life Care in Intensive Care" *Intensive
Care Medicine* Volume 48, 352–354. https://doi.org/10.1007/s00134-022-06623-2.

Fan, R. (1997) "Self-Determination vs. Family-Determination: Two Incommensurable Principles of Autonomy: A Report from East Asia" *Bioethics* Volume 11
Issue 3–4, 309–322. https://doi.org/10.1111/1467-8519.00070.

Ho, Zheng Jie Marc, L. K. Radha Krishnan, C. P. A. Yee, et al. (2010) "Chinese
Familial Tradition and Western Influence: A Case Study in Singapore on Decision
Making at the End of Life" *Journal of Pain and Symptom Management* Volume 40
Issue 6, 932–937. https://doi.org/10.1016/j.jpainsymman.2010.06.010.

Hsieh, Tian-Huai (2024) "An Empirical Legal Study on the Function of Family
Council in Modern Society" Master Thesis at Taiwan National University. http://
tdr.lib.ntu.edu.tw/jspui/handle/123456789/91629.

Hu, W. Y., T. Y. Chiu, R. B. Chuang, and C. Y. Chen (2002) "Solving Family-Related Barriers to Truthfulness in Cases of Terminal Cancer in Taiwan: A
Professional Perspective" *Cancer Nursing* Volume 25 Issue 6, 486–492. PMID:
12464841. https://doi.org/10.1097/00002820-200212000-00014.

Kang, E. K., B. Keam, N.-R. Lee, et al. (2021) "Impact of Family Caregivers'
Awareness of the Prognosis on Their Quality of Life/Depression and Those of
Patients with Advanced Cancer: A Prospective Cohort Study" *Supportive Care in
Cancer* Volume 29 Issue 1, 397–407. https://doi.org/10.1007/s00520-020-05489-8.

Kawashima, Takeyoshi (1967) *Legal Consciousness in Law in Japan* [in
Japanese]. Tokyo: Iwanami Shoten, Publishers.

Li, W. W., S. Singh, and C. Keerthigha (2021) "A Cross-Cultural Study of
Filial Piety and Palliative Care Knowledge: Moderating Effect of Culture and
Universality of Filial Piety" *Frontiers in Psychology* Volume 12, 787724. PMID:
34925189; PMCID: PMC8678124. https://doi.org/10.3389/fpsyg.2021.787724.

Liang, Y. W., Y.-H. Lin, S.-T. Chen, et al. (2021) "Differential Acceptance
of Advance Directives between Millennials and Baby Boomer Generations:
A Cross-Sectional Survey Study among College Students and Their Relatives" *Journal of Palliative Care* Volume 37 Issue 3, 280–288. https://doi.
org/10.1177/08258597211062757.

Lin, Cheng-Pei, Shao-Yi Cheng, and Ping-Jen Chen (2018) "Advance Care Planning for Older People with Cancer and Its Implications in Asia: Highlighting the Mental Capacity and Relational Autonomy" *Geriatrics* Volume 3 Number 3, 43. https://doi.org/10.3390/geriatrics3030043.

Mori, Masanori, and Morita Tatsuya (2020) "End-of-Life Decision-Making in Asia: A Need for In-Depth Cultural Consideration" *Palliative Medicine* Volume 34 Issue 2, NP4–NP5. https://doi.org/10.1177/0269216319896932.

Seki, Hiroshi (2024) *Legal Consciousness of Modern Japanese People* [in Japanese]. Tokyo: Kodansha.

Singapore, Singapore Statutes Online (2024) "Advance Medical Directive Act 1996" https://sso.agc.gov.sg/Act/AMDA1996.

South Korea, Korean Law Information Center (2024) https://www.law.go.kr/LSW/eng/engLsSc.do?menuId=2&section=lawNm&query=Act+on+Decisions+on+Life-Sustaining+Treatment+for+Patients+in+Hospice+and+Palliative+Care.

Taiwan, Laws & Regulations Database of the Republic of China (2024a) https://law.moj.gov.tw/ENG/LawClass/LawAll.aspx?pcode=L0020189.

Taiwan, Laws & Regulations Database of the Republic of China (2024b) https://law.moj.gov.tw/ENG/LawClass/LawAll.aspx?pcode=L0020066.

Tang, S. T. T.-W. Liu, M.-S. Lai, et al. (2005) "Concordance of Preferences for End-of-Life Care between Terminally Ill Cancer Patients and Their Family Caregivers in Taiwan" *Journal of Pain and Symptom Management* Volume 30 Issue 6, 510–518. https://doi.org/10.1016/j.jpainsymman.2005.05.019.

Trees, A. R., J. E. Ohs, and M. C. Murray (2017) "Family Communication about End-of-Life Decisions and the Enactment of the Decision-Maker Role" *Behavioral Sciences (Basel)* Volume 7 Issue 2, 36. PMID: 28590407; PMCID: PMC5485466. https://doi.org/10.3390/bs7020036.

Zhong, Yicheng. 2016. "Transformation and Practice of the Concept of 'Good End' in Taiwan—Focusing on the Legalization of End-of-Life Care" [in Japanese]. Doctoral Dissertation, Ritsumeikan University, 80.

Zhong Yicheng (2022) "Consideration of End-of-Life Medical Decision-Making Based on 'Filial Piety' and the Role of the Family: Using the Analysis of the

'Double Filial Piety Model' as a Clue" [in Japanese] *Otani University Shinshu Research Institute Research Bulletin* Volume 39, 163–180.

5.3 Discussion on ADs and ACP in the East Asian Model

Chen, Y. C., H. P. Huang, T. H. Tung, et al. (2022) "The Decisional Balance, Attitudes, and Practice Behaviors, Its Predicting Factors, and Related Experiences of Advance Care Planning in Taiwanese Patients with Advanced Cancer" *BMC Palliative Care* Volume 21, 189. https://doi.org/10.1186/s12904-022-01073-5.

Council of Europe, Commissioner for Human Rights (2012) *The Right of People with Disabilities to Live Independently and Be Included in the Community.* https:// book.coe.int/en/commissioner-for-human-rights/7329-pdf-the-right-of-people-with-disabilities-to-live-independently-and-be-included-in-the-community.html.

Fan, Ruiping (1997) "Self-Determination vs. Family-Determination: Two Incommensurable Principles of Autonomy" *Bioethics* Volume 11 Issue 3/4, 309–322.

Fuji, Kazuhiko (2019) "A Proposal for Industrial Promotion in a Multi-Death Society" [in Japanese] Research in Statute of Economy, Trade & Industry (RIETI) Policy Discussion Paper Series 19-P-036.

Haley, William E., R. S. Allen, S. Reynolds, et al. (2002) "Family Issues in End-of-Life Decision Making and End-of-Life Care" *American Behavioral Scientist* Volume 46 Issue 2, 284–298. https://doi.org/10.1177/000276402236680.

Hara, Kazuya (2001) "The Word 'Is' the Thing: The 'Kotodama' Belief in Japanese Communication" *ETC: A Review of General Semantics* Volume 58 Issue 3, 279–291.

Johnston, J. M., and Robert A. Sherman (1993) "Applying the Least Restrictive Alternative Principle to Treatment Decisions: A Legal and Behavioral Analysis" *The Behavior Analyst* Volume 16 Issue 1, 103–115.

Kizawa, Yoshiyuki (2020) "Advance Care Planning (ACP): To Practice Medical Care at the Final Stage of Life in accordance with the Individual's Wishes" [in Japanese] *Pharmacia* Volume 56 Issue 2, 105–109.

Leung, P. P., A. H.-Y. Wan, C. L.-W. Chan, et al. (2015) "The Effects of a Positive Death Education Group on Psycho-Spiritual Outcomes for Chinese with Chronic Illness: A Quasi-Experimental Study" *Illness, Crisis and Loss* Volume 23 Issue 1, 5–19. https://doi.org/10.2190/IL.23.1.b.

Menon, Sumytra, and Shumin Eunice Chua (2024) "Ethics & Law on Advance Care Planning: A Perspective from Singapore" in Raymond Han Lip Ng, D. Marina, C. Lin, et al. (eds), *Advance Care Planning in the Asia Pacific*. Singapore: World Scientific Publishing. 97–103.

Mizuno, Noriko (2011) "Medical Decision-Making and the Role of the Family: A Civil Law Perspective on the Guardianship System for the Mentally Disabled" [in Japanese] *The Journal of Law and Political Science* Volume 74 Issue 6, 880–912.

Ochiai, Emiko (2015) "Why Does the 'Japanese-Style Welfare Regime' Remain Familial? 4: Comments on the Report" [in Japanese] *Japanese Journal of Family Sociology* Volume 27 Issue 1, 61–68.

Sakurai, Yukio (2023) "Value of Legislation Providing Support and Protection to Vulnerable Adults: Consideration for a Core Agency and Supported Decision-Making" *Journal of Aging Law and Policy (Stetson Law School)* Volume 14, 43–96. https://www.stetson.edu/law/agingjournal/media/JALP%20Vol.%20 14%20Final.pdf or, http://hdl.handle.net/10131/0002000039.

Shimizu, Yukihiro (2021) "Practice and Challenges of POLST (Physician Orders for Life-Sustaining Treatment) and Advance Care Planning at Nanto Municipal Hospital" [in Japanese] *The Journal of the Japan Medical Association* Volume 149 Issue 11, 2007–2011.

Suen, M. H. P., A. Y. M. Chow, R. K. W. Woo, et al. (2024) "What Makes Advance Care Planning Discussion so Difficult? A Systematic Review of the Factors of Advance Care Planning in Healthcare Settings" *Palliative and Supportive Care* Volume 22, 1–14. https://doi.org/10.1017/S1478951524000464.

Chapter 6

6.1 A Comparative Analysis of Models between the U.S., Europe, and East Asia

Alzheimer Europe (2005) "Advance Directives" https://www.alzheimer-europe. org/policy/positions/advance-directives#:~:text=Alzheimer%20Europe%20 is%20of%20the,are%20applicable%20to%20the%20current.

American Bar Association (2018) "Advance Directives: Counseling Guide for Lawyers" https://www.americanbar.org/groups/law_aging/resources/ health_care_decision_making/ad-counseling-guide/.

Del Villar, Katrine, and Christopher J. Ryan (2020) "Self-Binding Directives for Mental Health Treatment: When Advance Consent Is Not Effective Consent" *The Medical Journal of Australia* Volume 212 Issue 5, 208–211. https://doi.org/10.5694/mja2.50505.

Jones, K, G. Birchley, R. Huxtable, et al. (2019) "End of Life Care: A Scoping Review of Experiences of Advance Care Planning for People with Dementia" *Dementia: The International Journal of Social Research and Practice* Volume 18 Issue 3, 825–845. https://doi.org/10.1177/1471301216676121.

Kai, Katsunori (2018) "Trends and Issues in Legislating and Establishing Rules for End-of-Life Care from a Comparative Law Perspective" [in Japanese] *Hanrei Jiho* Volume 2379, 130–139.

Kohn, Nina A., and David M. Levy (2023) "The New Uniform Health Care Decisions Act: An Overview" *Bifocal* Volume 45 Issue 1, 6–7. https://www.americanbar.org/groups/law_aging/publications/bifocal/vol45/vol45issue1/new-health-care-decisions-act/.

Kotera, Shoichi (2021) "End-of-Life Care in the UK: Recent Policy Developments" [in Japanese] *The Reference, The National Diet Library* No. 843, 27–56.

Maylea, C. Victoria (2022) "Australia, Is Getting a New Mental Health and Wellbeing Bill" *Bioethical Inquiry* Volume 19, 527–532. https://doi.org/10.1007/s11673-022-10212-9.

NHS (2023) "Advance Decision to Refuse Treatment (Living Will)" September 19. https://www.nhs.uk/conditions/end-of-life-care/planning-ahead/advance-decision-to-refuse-treatment/.

Tanaka, Miho (2024) "Awareness of 'Becoming a Burden to Others' among Older Adults in the End of Life: An Overview of Data from Japan and Other Countries" [in Japanese] Research Report of the Japan Medical Research Institute No. 137.

Uniform Law Commission (ULC) (2023) "Health-Care Decisions Act: Final Act" https://www.uniformlaws.org/committees/community-home/librarydocuments?communitykey=3df274d6-776b-4780-8e4e-018a850ef44e&LibraryFolderKey=&DefaultView=.

Ward, Adrian D. (2018) *Enabling Citizens to Plan for Incapacity.* Council of Europe. chrome-extension://efaidnbmnnnibpcajpcglclefindmkaj/https://rm.coe.int/cdcj-2017-2e-final-rapport-vs-21-06-2018/16808b64ae.

Ward, Adrian D. (2022) "Enhancing Autonomy: Advance Choices as the Key to the Future" Keynote Speech Delivered at the World Congress on Adult Capacity 2022 on June 7–9, 2022 in Edinburgh, Scotland.

6.2 Legal Relationship between Doctors, Patients, and Family Members

Arai, Makoto (2019) "Japan Adult Guardianship Laws: Development and Reform Initiatives" in Lusina Ho and Rebecca Lee (eds), *Special Needs Financial Planning: A Comparative Perspective.* English Edition. Cambridge University Press. 61–86.

Asagumo, Anri (2022) "Relational Autonomy, the Right to Reject Treatment, and Advance Directives in Japan" *Asian Bioethics Review* Volume 14, 57–69. https://doi.org/10.1007/s41649-021-00191-1.

Asai, Atsushi, Taketoshi Okita, and Seiji Bito (2022) "Discussions on Present Japanese Psychocultural-Social Tendencies as Obstacles to Clinical Shared Decision-Making in Japan" *Asian Bioethics Review* Volume 14 Issue 2, 133–150. https://doi.org/10.1007/s41649-021-00201-2.

Beauchamp, Tom, and James Childress (2019) *"Principles of Biomedical Ethics*: Marking Its Fortieth Anniversary" *The American Journal of Bioethics* Volume 19 Issue 11, 9–12. https://doi.org/10.1080/15265161.2019.1665402.

ELI (2022) "European Commission's Public Consultation on the Initiative on the Cross-Border Protection of Vulnerable Adults: C. Inclusion of a Conflicts Rule on Ex Lege Powers of Representation" chrome-extension://efaidnbmnnnibpcajp-cglclefindmkaj/https://www.europeanlawinstitute.eu/fileadmin/user_upload/p_eli/Publications/ELI_Response_Protection_of_Adults.pdf.

Elwyn, Glyn, D. Frosch, R. Thomson, et al. (2012) "Shared Decision Making: A Model for Clinical Practice" *Journal of General Internal Medicine* Volume 27 Issue 10, 1361–1367. https://doi.org/10.1007/s11606-012-2077-6.

FL-EUR (n.d.) "Questionnaire: Legal Protection and Empowerment of Vulnerable Adults" https://fl-eur.eu/working_field_1__empowerment_and_protection/country-reports.

Johnston, Carolyn, and Jane Liddle (2007) "The Mental Capacity Act 2005: A New Framework for Healthcare Decision Making" *Journal of Medical Ethics* Volume 33 Issue 2, 94–97. https://doi.org/10.1136/jme.2006.016972.

JUSTIA, US Law (n.d.) "Canterbury v. Spence, No. 22099 (D.C. Cir. 1972)" https://law.justia.com/cases/federal/appellate-courts/cadc/22099/22099.html.

Kolva, Elissa, Barry Rosenfeld, and Rebecca Saracino (2018) "Assessing the Decision-Making Capacity of Terminally Ill Patients with Cancer" *The American Journal of Geriatric Psychiatry* Volume 26 Issue 5, 523–531. https://doi.org/10.1016/j.jagp.2017.11.012.

Koyama, Teruchika, Nobutoshi Nawa, Yasuhiro Itsui, et al. (2022) "Facilitators and Barriers to Implementing Shared Decision Making: A Cross-Sectional Study of Physicians in Japan" *Patient Education and Counseling* Volume 105 Issue 7, 2546–2556. https://doi.org/10.1016/j.pec.2022.01.016.

Masaki, Sakiko, Hiroko Ishimoto, and Atsushi Asai (2014) "Contemporary Issues Concerning Informed Consent in Japan Based on a Review of Court Decisions and Characteristics of Japanese Culture" *BMC Medical Ethics* Volume 15, Article number 8. https://doi.org/10.1186/1472-6939-15-8.

Nakayama, Shigeki (2024) "Consent and Intimate Relationships in Medical Care: From the Constitutional Perspective of 'Respect for the Individual' (1)" [in Japanese] *Sandai Law Review* Volume 58 Issue 3, 269–296. http://hdl.handle.net/10965/0002000266.

Sobode, Oluwaseun Rebecca, R. Jegan, J. Toelen, et al. (2024) "Shared Decision-Making in Adolescent Healthcare: A Literature Review of Ethical Considerations" *European Journal of Pediatrics* Volume 183, 4195–4203. https://doi.org/10.1007/s00431-024-05687-0.

Then, Shih-Ning, and C. Bigby (2024) "Supported Decision-Making and the Disability Royal Commission" *Research and Practice in Intellectual and Developmental Disabilities* Volume 11 Issue 1, 86–106. https://doi.org/10.1080/23297018.2024.2330961.

UNESCO (2005) "Universal Declaration on Bioethics and Human Rights of 2005" https://www.unesco.org/en/legal-affairs/universal-declaration-bioethics-and-human-rights.

Yang, Yuexi, T. Qu, J. Yang, et al. (2022) "Confucian Familism and Shared Decision Making in End-of-Life Care for Patients with Advanced Cancers" *International Journal of Environmental Research and Public Health* Volume 19, 10071. https://doi.org/10.3390/ijerph191610071.

Zeilstra, Rebecca (2024) "Nudging and the Safeguards of the Rule of Law" *German Law Journal* Volume 25 Issue 5, 750–771. https://doi.org/10.1017/glj.2024.30.

6.3 Proposals for Advance Decision-Making
for Future Disability in East Asia

Australia, Victorian Legislation (2024) "Medical Treatment Planning and Decisions Act 2016, Act Number 69/2016" https://www.legislation.vic.gov.au/in-force/acts/medical-treatment-planning-and-decisions-act-2016/011.

Center for Applied Philosophy and Ethics, Kyoto University (2018) "Respecting Patients' Will in End-of-Life Care Tentative Version 3" [in Japanese] http://www.cape.bun.kyoto-u.ac.jp/project/project02/eol/.

Gutmann, Jerg, and Stefan Voigt (2022) "Testing Todd: Family Types and Development" *Journal of Institutional Economics* Volume 18, 101–118. https://doi.org/10.1017/S1744137421000175.

Power of Attorney Act 1998 (Queensland), Australia https://www.legislation.qld.gov.au/view/html/inforce/current/act-1998-022#sec.103.

Schiff, David N. (1976) "Socio-Legal Theory: Social Structure and Law" *The Modern Law Review* Volume 39 Issue 3, 287–310. https://doi.org/10.1111/j.1468-2230.1976.tb01458.x.

Todd, Emmanuel (1985) *The Explanation of Ideology: Family Structures and Social Systems.* Translated by David Garrioch. Oxford [Oxfordshire]: B. Blackwell.

LEGISLATION

Australia

Criminal Code

Medical Treatment Planning and Decisions Act of 2016 (Victoria)
    https://www.legislation.vic.gov.au/in-force/acts/medical-treatment-planning-
    and-decisions-act-2016/011

Voluntary Assisted Dying Act of 2017 (Victoria)

England

Care Act 2014

Mental Capacity Act 2005

Japan

Act on the Prevention of Infectious Diseases and Medical Care for Patients with
    Infectious Diseases of 1998

Act on the Treatment of Persons Who Have Contracted Disease or Died on a
    Journey of 1899

Act on Organ Transplantation of 1997

The Autopsy Law of 1949

Basic Act on Dementia to Promote an Inclusive Society of 2023

Civil Code of 1898

Constitution of Japan of 1947

Family Register Act of 1947

Medical Practitioners' Act of 1948

South Korea

Act on Decisions on Life-Sustaining Treatment for Patients in Hospice and Palliative Care or at the End of Life (ELDA) of 2016 https://www.law.go.kr/ LSW/eng/engLsSc.do?menuId=2&section=lawNm&query=Act+on+Deci- sions+on+Life-Sustaining+Treatment+for+Patients+in+Hospice+and+Pallia- tive+Care

Dementia Management Act of 2011

Singapore

Advance Medical Directive Act (AMDA) of 1996<https://sso.agc.gov.sg/Act/ AMDA1996>

Maintenance of Parents Act of 1955

Mental Capacity Act of 2008

Scotland

Adult Support and Protection (Scotland) Act of 2007

Adults with Incapacity (Scotland) Act of 2000

Mental Health (Care and Treatment) (Scotland) Act of 2003

Taiwan

Patient Right to Autonomy Act (PRAA) of 2015 https://law.moj.gov.tw/ENG/ LawClass/LawAll.aspx?pcode=L0020189 or, Taiwan, Hospice Foundation of Taiwan. https://www.hospice.org.tw/content/2470

Hospice Palliative Care Act (HPCA) of 2000 https://law.moj.gov.tw/ENG/ LawClass/LawAll.aspx?pcode=L0020066 or, Taiwan, Hospice Foundation of Taiwan. https://www.hospice.org.tw/content/2468

United States

Health Care Decisions Act of 1993 (ULC)

Health-Care Decisions Act of 2023 (ULC)

Model Health-Care Consent Act of 1982 (ULC)

Natural Death Act of 1976 (California)

Patient Self-Determination Act of 1990 (Federal Law)

Uniform Rights of the Terminally Ill Act of 1985 (ULC)

COURT CASE

Australia

Carr v Attorney-General (Cth) [2023] FCA 1500 ("Carr")

Japan

Tokai University Hospital, Kanagawa (April 1991)

Kawasaki Kyodo Hospital, Kanagawa (November 1998)

South Korea

Borame Hospital in Seoul on December 4, 1997, Seoul District Court, Decision 97Gahap11306

Kim Hal-Mon-Ni in Seoul on February 18, 2008, Seoul Western District Court, Decision 2007Gahap3959/ on May 21, 2009, Supreme Court Decision 2009Da17417

The United States

CRUZAN by *Cruzan v. Harmon*, 760 S.W. 2d 408 (MO. Banc 1988), the Supreme Court of Missouri

Canterbury v. Spence, No. 22099 (D.C. Cir. 1972)

JUSTIA US LAW, In Re Quinlan 70 NJ 10 (1976) 355 A.2d 647 N the Matter of Karen Quinlan, an Alleged Incompetent. The Supreme Court of New Jersey. Decided March 31, 1976

Shelton v. Tucker, in which the U.S. Supreme Court ruled on December 12, 1960 (5–4)

APPENDICES

APPENDIX 1

Questionnaire on Advance Directives and ACP in South Korea/Taiwan/
Singapore

Empirical Data

(1) Please provide the website access for statistics on the number of registra-
    tions of ADs on health insurance cards in Taiwan based on the "Patient
    Autonomy Act Enforcement Rules."
(2) If there are statistics or papers indicating the implementation status of
    ACP in Taiwan, please share that information.
(3) If there have been surveys on the opinions of healthcare professionals
    and/or citizens regarding ADs/ACP in Taiwan, please provide access to
    website/papers to the survey results.

Advance Directives (ADs)

(1) The Taiwanese government and legislature have promoted the spread
    of ADs by enacting the Palliative Care Act, Patient Autonomy Act, and
    Patient Autonomy Act Enforcement Rules. What are the driving forces
    and values specifically behind this promotion? How does this align or
    conflict with traditional values in Taiwan?
(2) There is a report that the utilization rate of ADs among the Taiwanese
    population is around 3%.[1] What are the main reasons for the slow progress
    in the spread of ADs? If there are articles expressing views on this, please
    provide representative ones.
(3) Based on item "(2)" in this list, please provide opinions on specific mea-
    sures to improve the slow progress.

---

[1] Tsai, Hsiao Ying (2022) "The Influence of Familism on Taiwan's Advance Care Planning (ACP) for End-of-life" *Journal of the Japanese Society of Nursing Ethics* Volume 14 Issue 1, 48–51.

(4) Could you share your opinion on whether ADs are beneficial to the individuals and stakeholders?

(5) Taiwanese ADs are designed by taking into account relationships with family and other stakeholders. Do you think that this is appropriate, or do you assume that there should be a stronger emphasis on relationships?

(6) Do you consider legal binding essential for ADs, or do you think that legal binding is not necessarily required, or is it better to differentiate the legal binding status by category?

Advance Care Planning (ACP)

(1) It seems that medical institutions and healthcare professionals are promoting ACP, but what is necessary to popularize ACP among the Taiwanese population?

(2) Could you express your opinion on whether ACP is beneficial to individuals and stakeholders?

(3) Please provide your opinions on challenges related to ACP. If there are articles expressing views on this, please provide representative ones.

Matters Related to ADs/ACP

(1) Are there evident generational differences in thinking about end-of-life care? If so, please specify what the generational differences are.

(2) Do legal scholars, legal/medical administrators, and healthcare professionals have opportunities to exchange opinions or deliberate on ADs/ACP? If so, please specify the specific platforms.

(3) Please advise the revisions if draft Table 5.2 in the text (provisions of legislation, omitted here) has any misunderstandings.

(4) Other comments (if any).

APPENDIX 2

Optional Form for Advance Directives (Sec. 11, Healthcare Decisions Act (2023))

Section 11. Optional Form

The following form may be used to create an advance healthcare directive:[1]

ADVANCE HEALTHCARE DIRECTIVE

HOW YOU CAN USE THIS FORM

You can use this form if you wish to name someone to make healthcare decisions for you in case you cannot make decisions for yourself. This is called giving the person a power of attorney for health care. This person is called your Agent.

You can also use this form to state your wishes, preferences, and goals for health care, and to say if you want to be an organ donor after you die.

YOUR NAME AND DATE OF BIRTH

Name:

Date of birth:

PART A: NAMING AN AGENT

This part lets you name someone else to make healthcare decisions for you. You may leave any item blank.

[1.] Uniform Law Commission (ULC) (2023) 'Health-Care Decisions Act' https://www.uniformlaws. org/committees/community-home/librarydocuments?communitykey=3df274d6-776b-4780-8e4e-0 18a850ef44e&LibraryFolderKey=&DefaultView=.

1. NAMING AN AGENT

I want the following person to make healthcare decisions for me if I cannot make decisions for myself:

Name:

Optional contact information (it is helpful to include information such as address, phone, and email):

2. NAMING AN ALTERNATE AGENT

I want the following person to make healthcare decisions for me if I cannot and my Agent is not able or available to make them for me:

Name:

Optional contact information (it is helpful to include information such as address, phone, and email):

3. LIMITING YOUR AGENT'S AUTHORITY

I give my Agent the power to make all healthcare decisions for me if I cannot make those decisions for myself, except the following:

(If you do not add a limitation here, your Agent will be able make all healthcare decisions that an Agent is permitted to make under state law.)

PART B: HEALTHCARE INSTRUCTIONS

This part lets you state your priorities for health care and to state types of health care you do and do not want.

1. INSTRUCTIONS ABOUT LIFE-SUSTAINING TREATMENT

This section gives you the opportunity to say how you want your Agent to act while making decisions for you. You may mark or initial each choice. You also may leave any choice blank.

Treatment. Medical treatment needed to keep me alive but not needed for comfort or any other purpose should (mark or initial all that apply):

(_____) Always be given to me. (If you mark or initial this choice, you should not mark or initial other choices in this "treatment" section.).

(____) Not be given to me if It have a condition that is not curable and is expected to cause my death soon, even if treated.

(____) Not be given to me if I am unconscious and I am not expected to be conscious again.

(____) Not be given to me if I have a medical condition from which I am not expected to recover that prevents me from communicating with people I care about, caring for myself, and recognizing family and friends.

(____) Other (write what you want or do not want):

Food and liquids. If I can't swallow and staying alive requires me to get food or liquids through a tube or other means for the rest of my life, then food or liquids should (mark or initial all that apply):

(____) Always be given to me. (If you mark or initial this choice, you should not mark or initial other choices in this "food and liquids" section).

(____) Not be given to me if I have a condition that is not curable and is expected to cause me to die soon, even if treated.

(____) Not be given to me if I am unconscious and am not expected to be conscious again.

(____) Not be given to me if I have a medical condition from which I am not expected to recover that prevents me from communicating with people I care about, caring for myself, and recognizing family and friends.

(____) Other (write what you want or do not want):

Pain relief. If I am in significant pain, care that will keep me comfortable but is likely to shorten my life should (mark or initial all that apply):

(____) Always be given to me. (If you mark or initial this choice, you should not mark or initial other choices in this "pain relief" section.)

(____) Never be given to me. (If you mark or initial this choice, you should not mark or initial other choices in this "pain relief" section.)

(____) Be given to me if I have a condition that is not curable and is expected to cause me to die soon, even if treated.

(____) Be given to me if I am unconscious and am not expected to be conscious again.

(____) Be given to me if I have a medical condition from which I am not expected to recover that prevents me from communicating with people I care about, caring for myself, and recognizing family and friends.

(____) Other (write what you want or do not want):

2. MY PRIORITIES

You can use this section to indicate what is important to you, and what is not important to you. This information can help your Agent make decisions for you if you cannot. It also helps others understand your preferences.

You may mark or initial each choice. You also may leave any choice blank. Staying alive as long as possible even if I have substantial physical limitations is:

(____) Very important

(____) Somewhat important

(____) Not important

Staying alive as long as possible even if I have substantial mental limitations is:

(____) Very important

(____) Somewhat important

(____) Not important

Being free from significant pain is:

(____) Very important

(____) Somewhat important

(____) Not important

Being independent is:

(_____) Very important

(_____) Somewhat important

(_____) Not important

Having my Agent talk with my family before making decisions about my care is:

(_____) Very important

(_____) Somewhat important

(_____) Not important

Having my Agent talk with my friends before making decisions about my care is:

(_____) Very important

(_____) Somewhat important

(_____) Not important

3. OTHER INSTRUCTIONS

You can write in this section more information about your goals, values, and preferences for treatment, including care you want or do not want. You can also use this section to name anyone whom you do not want to make decisions for you under any conditions.

PART C: OPTIONAL SPECIAL POWERS AND GUIDANCE

This part lets you give your Agent additional powers, and to provide more guidance about your wishes. You may mark or initial each choice. You also may leave any choice blank.

1. OPTIONAL SPECIAL POWERS

My Agent can do the following things ONLY if I have marked or initialed them below:

(_____) Admit me as a voluntary patient to a facility for mental health treatment for up to _____ days (write in the number of days you want like 7, 14, 30, or another number).

(If I do not mark or initial this choice, my Agent MAY NOT admit me as a voluntary patient to this type of facility.)

(____) Place me in a nursing home for more than [100] days even if my
needs can be met somewhere else, I am not terminally ill, and I object.

(If I do not mark or initial this choice, my Agent MAY NOT do this.)

2. ACCESS TO MY HEALTH INFORMATION

My Agent may obtain, examine, and share information about my health needs
and health care if I am not able to make decisions for myself. If I mark or initial
below, my Agent may also do that at any time my Agent thinks it will help me.

(____) I give my Agent permission to obtain, examine, and share information
about my health needs and health care whenever my Agent thinks it
will help me.

3. FLEXIBILITY FOR MY AGENT

Mark or initial below if you want to give your Agent flexibility in following
instructions you provide in this form. If you do not, your Agent must follow the
instructions even if your Agent thinks something else would be better for you.

(____) I give my Agent permission to be flexible in applying these instructions
if my Agent thinks it would be in my best interest based on what my
Agent knows about me.

4. NOMINATION OF GUARDIAN

You can say who you would want as your guardian if you needed one.
A guardian is a person appointed by a court to make decisions for someone
who cannot make decisions. Filling this out does NOT mean you want or
need a guardian.

If a court appoints a guardian to make personal decisions for me, I want the
court to choose:

(____) My Agent named in this form. If my Agent cannot be a guardian,
I want the Alternate Agent named in this form.

(____) Other (write who you would want and their contact information):

PART D: ORGAN DONATION

This part lets you donate your organs after you die. You may leave any item blank.

1. DONATION

You may mark or initial only one choice.

(_____) I donate my organs, tissues, and other body parts after I die, even if it requires maintaining treatments that conflict with other instructions I have put in this form, EXCEPT for those I list below (list any body parts you do NOT want to donate):

(_____) I do not want my organs, tissues, or body parts donated to anybody for any reason. (If you mark or initial this choice, you should skip the "purpose of donation" section.)

2. PURPOSE OF DONATION

You may mark or initial all that apply. (If you do not mark or initial any of the purposes below, your donation can be used for all of them.)

Organs, tissues, or body parts that I donate may be used for:

(_____) Transplant

(_____) Therapy

(_____) Research

(_____) Education

(_____) All of the above

PART E: SIGNATURES

YOUR SIGNATURE

Sign your name:

Today's date:

City/Town/Village and State (optional):

SIGNATURE OF A WITNESS

You need a witness if you are using this form to name an Agent. The witness must be an adult and cannot be the person you are naming as Agent or the Agent's spouse [, domestic partner,] or someone the Agent lives with as a couple. If you live or are receiving care in a nursing home, the witness cannot be an employee or contractor of the home or someone who owns or runs the home.

Name of Witness:

Signature of Witness:

(Only sign as a witness if you think the person signing above is doing it voluntarily.)

Date witness signed:

PART F: INFORMATION FOR AGENTS

1. If this form names you as an Agent, you can make decisions about health care for the person who named you when the person cannot make their own.
2. If you make a decision for the person, follow any instructions the person gave, including any in this form.
3. If you do not know what the person would want, make the decision that you think is in the person's best interest. To figure out what is in the person's best interest, consider the person's values, preferences, and goals if you know them or can learn them. Some of these preferences may be in this form. You should also consider any behavior or communication from the person that indicates what the person currently wants.
4. If this form names you as an Agent, you can also get and share the person's health information. But unless the person has said so in this form, you can get or share this information only when the person cannot make decisions about the person's health care.

INDEX

Note: Page numbers in *italics* denote figures and **bold** denote tables.

A

abuse, 19

Act on Decisions on Life-Sustaining Treatment for Patients in Hospice and Palliative Care at End of Life of 2016 (ELDA), 89
  Article 5, 89
  Article 8, 89
  Article 9, 89
  Article 10, 89
  Article 11, 89
  Article 12(8), 92
  Article 33, 89
  commentary, 94
  criteria for discontinuation of life-sustaining treatment for patients in dying process (Article 17 to Article 18), **90**
  provisions of, 89–91
  significance and challenge of, 91–94
  termination of medical acts, 89
  withdrawal of treatment, 90

advance care planning (ACP), 3, 129, 138, 139, 147, 149, 151–153
  decision-making support program, for older cancer patients, 80–81
  defined, 45, 79
  in Japan, 78–85
  MHLW's commissioned research, 79–80
  online seminar by Yokohama National University, 81–85
  in Taiwan, 97–100

advance choices, 8

advance decision-making, 131
  challenges for establishing, 150–152
  draft main provisions for, 155–160
  guiding principles for, 154–155
  possible avenue for, 160–162
  principal concepts of, 152–154

advance decision-making legislation draft
  appointed decision-maker, powers of, 159
  appointment of support person, 159
  clinical ethics committee, 160
  decision-maker, appointment of, 159
  decision-making capacity, 157
  eligibility, 159
  end of life, 157
  healthcare professionals cannot be compelled, 159
  principles, 158–159
  purposes of, 156–157
  role of support person, 160
  types of directives, 157–158

advance decisions of patients, 148–149

advance directives (ADs), 3
  advancement of, 44–45
  comparison and evaluation of, 46–48
  comparison between South Korea, Taiwan, and Singapore, **108–112**
  historical background, 39–40
  in Japan, **69**, 143, 148, 151
  Karen Ann Quinlan case, 40–42
  Law Society of Scotland, 132
  limitations and criticisms, 43–45
  relational autonomy-based approach, 70–78
  SUPPORT study, 43–44
  types of, **46**
  in U.S., 129–138

Advance Medical Directive Act (AMDA) of 1996, 42, 102–105

advance statements, 152

advocacy, defined, 31

advocacy dimension, 31–33

Alzheimer Europe, 136

American civil rights movement, 39

asset management *versus* healthcare, 119–121

assistance, defined, 31
assistance dimension, 33
Australia, training healthcare providers decision-making, 147

B
best interests of doctors, 148–149
bioethics, in healthcare, 35–36
Buddhism, 32, 115, 138, 150

C
California's Natural Death Act of 1976, 41
Canterbury v. Spence, 142
Carr v Attorney-General, 52
Chan, Evans, 103–104
Civil Code, 27–28, 77
Commercial Code, 77
Confucianism, 32, 115, 138, 150
consumer choices *versus* one-size-fits-all, 121–123
COVID-19 pandemic, 59, 80
Criminal Code, 77
Cruzan v. Harmon, 42

D
decision-making support program, for older cancer patients, 80–81
dementia, 6–7
national strategies and legislation against, 59–61
Dignified Death Bill, 73
Dignitas, 50
DNAR (Do Not Attempt Resuscitate), 44
Do Not Attempt Resuscitate (DNAR), 44
doctors–patients relationship
justification of clinical actions, 142–143
justification of clinical actions in end-of-life medical care, 143–144

E
East Asia
autonomy in, 27–29
comparison of ADs and ACP in, 105–119
policy orientation in, 32–34
proactive measures, social factors, 5–7
rate of aging, 6
societal challenge, 10
traditional beliefs, 115–118
virtue approach, 32

East Asian project, 138–140
doctors, patients/family members, legal relationship between, 140–149
importance of, 5–10
methodology, 13–16
objective and research, 10–13
proposals for, 149–162
U.S., Europe/East Asia, comparative analysis of models between, 129–140
value model for, 29–34
East Asian Project of Advance Decision-Making, 9–10
elder abuse, 19
Enabling Citizens to Plan for Incapacity, 137
end-of-life medical care, 130, 143–144
categories, 15
England
asset management and healthcare, LPA for, 131
comparison between, 133–135
hospice services in, 131
ethical principles, 35–36
Europe
end-of-life medical care in, 136
human rights, 136
legal systems of, 144
European Convention on Human Rights and the European Court of Human Rights, 136
European Law Institute (ELI), 135, 137
European model, 135–138
European Project of Advance Choices, 8–9
ex lege representation, 145

F
family involvement *versus* proactive preparation, 1–3
Fineman, Martha Albertson, 22

G
gastrostomy procedure, 2
Go Gentle Australia, 50

H
Health Care Decisions Act, 130, 137
health insurance, 2, 55–57
healthcare, 148
versus asset management, 119–121
laws, hierarchy, 35

family involvement in end-of-life
      medical care, 113–115
Hospice Palliative Care Act (HPCA),
      96–100
legal systems, 153
life-sustaining treatments in, 148
mortality rate, 7
Patient Right to Autonomy Act
      (PRAA), 96–100, 117
PRAA of, 145
Takemi, Keizo, 73
Tanaka, Shigeaki, 161
Tang, Hang Wu, 104
Taoism, 32, 115, 138, 150
Todd, Emmanuel, 150
traditional values, 144

U
ULC (Uniform Law Commission), 130
Uniform Law Commission
      (ULC), 130
Uniform Rights of the Terminally Ill Act
      of 1985, 130
United Nations Convention on the
      Rights for Persons with Disabilities
      (CRPD), 30
Universal Declaration on Bioethics and
      Human Rights of 2005, 143
unselfish assisted suicide, 48
U.S. model, 129–135
      comparison between, 133–135

Health Care Decisions Act of 2023,
      75, 137
legal systems of, 144
medical justification, 142
Patient Self-Determination Act of
      1990, 143

V
The Victorian Medical Treatment Plan-
      ning and Decisions Act 2016, 132
Voluntary Assisted Dying (VAD), 48
      case study in State of Victoria, 50–52
      countries' responses, **49**
      recent development, 48–50
vulnerability approach, 17–18
vulnerability, defined, 17–18
Vulnerable Adults Act, 101

W
Wales
      asset management and healthcare, LPA
      for, 131
Ward, Adrian D., 137, 162
WHO (World Health Organization),
      35, 59
World Health Organization (WHO),
      35, 59

Y
Yokohama National University, online
      seminar, 81–85